THE POETRY AND SHORT STORIES OF DOROTHY PARKER

THE POETRY AND SHORT STORIES OF DOROTHY PARKER

THE MODERN LIBRARY
NEW YORK

1994 Modern Library Edition

 Published in the United States by Random House, Inc., New York, and simultaneously in Canada by Random House of Canada Limited, Toronto.

The poems in this work were originally published in *Enough Rope, Sunset Gun,* and *Death and Taxes and Other Poems*. The short stories in this work were originally published in *Here Lies*.

Reprinted by arrangement with Penguin Books USA Inc.

Jacket photograph courtesy of UPI/Bettmann

Printed on recycled, acid-free paper.

ISBN 0-679-60132-5

Manufactured in the United States of America

2 4 6 8 9 7 5 3 1

DOROTHY PARKER

Dorothy Parker (née Rothschild) was supposed to have been born in New York City; instead she showed up prematurely, in stormy weather, on August 22, 1893, at her family's summer home in the New Jersey beach resort of West End. Her mother, the former Eliza Marston, was a Scottish Presbyterian who died when the child was five; her strict Jewish father, J. Henry Rothschild, was a well-to-do clothier who was no relation to the international banking family of the same name. ("My God, *no*, dear! We'd never *heard* of *those* Rothschilds!" as Dorothy Parker later remarked.) Her even stricter stepmother, who was also a Scottish Presbyterian, enrolled the young girl in the fashionable Blessed Sacrament Academy, a Catholic convent school, not far from the Rothschild's brownstone on Manhattan's Upper West Side. About adolescence spent among the nuns, she remembered only her departure: "I was fired from there, finally, for a lot of things, among them my insistence that the Immaculate Conception was spontaneous combustion." Afterward, she was sent to the prestigious, mostly Episcopalian, yet progressive Miss Dana's School in Morristown, New Jersey, and thrived there briefly under the rigorous curriculum that stressed the classics, creative writing, and elocution.

After the death of her father in 1913, Dorothy Rothschild's fortunes took a turn for the worse: at one point she moved into a Manhattan boardinghouse and supported herself by playing the piano at night in a dancing school. Meanwhile, she fell into writing and regularly submitted light verse to *The Saturday Evening Post* and other magazines; in 1915 *Vogue* editor Frank Crowninshield bought one of her poems and hired the novice twenty-two-year-old to write captions for fashion illustrations. ("Brevity is the Soul of Lingerie" was one of her memorable *Vogue* banners.)

Delighted with her work, Crowninshield promptly offered his protégée a far better position as drama critic for *Vanity Fair*. There she met Robert Benchley and Robert Sherwood, and her career as the wittiest member of the now legendary Algonquin Round Table was soon launched. At about the same time she met Edwin Pond Parker II, a promising stockbroker and scion of an old Connecticut family. They married in June 1917.

"I was just a little Jewish girl trying to be cute," *Mrs.* Parker—as she always preferred to be called thereafter—said of the wisecracks and wicked put-downs that flowed effortlessly from her lips. Having left *Vanity Fair*, she became one of the handful of writers who helped form the character of *The New Yorker*, founded by Harold Ross in 1925. A number of the poems in her three bestselling collections of poetry—*Enough Rope* (1926), *Sunset Gun* (1928), and *Death and Taxes* (1931)—first appeared there. In addition, Mrs. Parker reviewed books for the magazine under the byline "Constant Reader." But it was her short fiction that made such an indelible mark on the publication. According to Brendan Gill, "her short stories in the magazine, at first scarcely more than scraps of lacerating dialogue, led to the development of what was afterward . . . a recognizable genre—*The New Yorker* short story." Over the years she published three volumes of stories: *Laments for the Living* (1930), *After Such Pleasures* (1933), and *Here Lies* (1939).

Like many of the writers in the Algonquin circle, Mrs. Parker lived with hedonistic flair, both long before and after she was divorced in 1928. On a journey with Hemingway in France she met the Fitzgeralds and stayed with the Gerald Murphys in Cap d'Antibes. Back in New York, nightly rounds of fashionable speakeasies and brothels (in the company of Robert Benchley) often left her with hangovers that she insisted "ought to be in the Smithsonian under glass." Yet numerous unhappy love affairs resulted in a string of suicide attempts and, as John Updike has noted, "afforded her a thorough education in the self-wounding perversity of the human heart."

Largely because of her reputation as a mistress of repartee—by many estimates she was the most cleverly amusing woman in America—Mrs. Parker found work in Hollywood in the thirties and forties turning out movie scripts. By then she was married to Alan Campbell, a fellow writer (and rumored homosexual) eleven years her junior, who was likewise of Jewish and Scottish-Presbyterian ancestry. The two endured an unsatisfying but lucrative screenwriting career—sometimes earning more than $5,000 a week. They also bought a farm in Bucks County, Pennsylvania. Much to her delight, she became pregnant at the age of forty-two, but lost the baby in the third month.

Ultimately Mrs. Parker's commitment to left-wing politics jeopardized their fortunes in Hollywood, and the couple divorced in 1947. They remarried in 1950, however, only to separate the following year. (During the fifties another estrangement ensued: Mrs. Parker's thirty-year association with *The New Yorker* ended, and she began writing book reviews for *Esquire*.) Ten years later, in 1961, she and Campbell staged a reconciliation of sorts and remained together until his apparent suicide in 1963. Asked at the time by a meddling acquaintance if there was anything she needed, Mrs. Parker dryly replied: "Get me a new husband." When the woman expressed disgust at what she considered the callousness of the remark, Mrs. Parker, her wit ever intact, sighed and said gently: "So sorry. Then run down to the corner and get me a ham and cheese on rye and tell them to hold the mayo."

Following Campbell's death, Dorothy Parker returned to New York, where she lived in precarious financial circumstances in a residential hotel on Manhattan's Upper East Side with her poodle C'est Tout—not unlike the lonely characters in her unsuccessful 1953 Broadway play *Ladies of the Corridor*. She died there of a heart attack on June 7, 1967. In 1969 Lillian Hellman recalled her friend "Dottie" in *An Unfinished Woman*: "I enjoyed her more than I have ever enjoyed any other woman. She was modest—this wasn't all virtue, she liked to think that she was not worth much—her view of people was original and sharp, her elaborate, overdelicate manners made her a pleasure to live with, she liked books and was generous about writers, and the wit, of course, was so wonderful that neither age nor illness ever dried up the spring from which it came fresh each day. No remembrance of her can exclude it."

CONTENTS

The Poetry
1
The Stories
225

THE POETRY OF DOROTHY PARKER

To

FRANKLIN PIERCE ADAMS

CONTENTS

ENOUGH ROPE

Threnody 13
The Small Hours 14
The False Friends 15
The Trifler 16
A Very Short Song 17
A Well-Worn Story 18
Convalescent 19
The Dark Girl's Rhyme 20
Epitaph 22
Light of Love 23
Wail 24
The Satin Dress 25
Somebody's Song 27
Anecdote 28
Braggart 29
Epitaph for a Darling Lady 30
To a Much Too Unfortunate Lady 31
Paths 32
Hearthside 33
The New Love 34
Rainy Night 35
For a Sad Lady 37
Recurrence 38
Story of Mrs. W— 39

The Dramatists 40
August 41
The White Lady 42
I Know I Have Been Happiest 43
Testament 44
I Shall Come Back 45
Condolence 46
The Immortals 47
A Portrait 48
Portrait of the Artist 49
Chant for Dark Hours 50
Unfortunate Coincidence 52
Inventory 53
Now at Liberty 54
Comment 55
Plea 56
Pattern 57
De Profundis 58
They Part 59
Ballade of a Great Weariness 60
Résumé 62
Renunciation 63
The Veteran 64
Prophetic Soul 65
Verse for a Certain Dog 66
Godspeed 67
Song of Perfect Propriety 68
Social Note 70
One Perfect Rose 71
Ballade at Thirty-Five 72
The Thin Edge 74
Love Song 75
Indian Summer 76
Philosophy 77

For an Unknown Lady 78
The Leal 79
Words of Comfort to Be Scratched on a Mirror 80
Men 81
News Item 82
Song of One of the Girls 83
Lullaby 84
Faute de Mieux 85
Roundel 86
A Certain Lady 87
Observation 88
Symptom Recital 89
Rondeau Redoublé 90
Fighting Words 92
The Choice 93
General Review of the Sex Situation 94
Inscription for the Ceiling of a Bedroom 95
Pictures in the Smoke 96
Nocturne 97
Interview 98
Experience 99
Neither Bloody nor Bowed 100
The Burned Child 101

SUNSET GUN
Godmother 105
Partial Comfort 107
The Red Dress 108
Victoria 109
The Counselor 110
Parable for a Certain Virgin 111
Bric-a-Brac 113
Interior 114
Reuben's Children 115

On Cheating the Fiddler 116
There Was One 117
Incurable 119
Fable 120
The Second Oldest Story 121
A Pig's-Eye View of Literature 122
The Lives and Times of John Keats, Percy Bysshe Shelley, and George Gordon Noel, Lord Byron
Oscar Wilde 122
Harriet Beecher Stowe 122
D. G. Rossetti 123
Thomas Carlyle 123
Charles Dickens 123
Alexandre Dumas and His Son 123
Alfred, Lord Tennyson 124
George Gissing 124
Walter Savage Landor 124
George Sand 124
Mortal Enemy 125
Penelope 126
Bohemia 127
The Searched Soul 128
The Trusting Heart 129
Thought for a Sunshiny Morning 130
The Gentlest Lady 131
The Maid-Servant at the Inn 132
Fulfillment 133
Daylight Saving 134
Surprise 135
On Being a Woman 136
Afternoon 137
A Dream Lies Dead 138
The Homebody 139

Second Love 140
Fair Weather 141
The Whistling Girl 142
Story 143
Frustration 144
Healed 145
Landscape 146
Post-Graduate 147
For a Favorite Granddaughter 148
Liebestod 149
Dilemma 151
Theory 152
A Fairly Sad Tale 153
The Last Question 154
Superfluous Advice 155
But Not Forgotten 156
Two-Volume Novel 157
Pour Prendre Congé 158
For a Lady Who Must Write Verse 159
Rhyme Against Living 160
Wisdom 161
Coda 162

DEATH AND TAXES AND OTHER POEMS
Prayer for a Prayer 165
After a Spanish Proverb 166
The Flaw in Paganism 167
The Danger of Writing Defiant Verse 168
Distance 170
The Evening Primrose 171
Sanctuary 172
Cherry White 173
Salome's Dancing-Lesson 174
My Own 175

Solace 176
Little Words 177
Ornithology for Beginners 178
Garden-Spot 179
Tombstones in the Starlight 180
I. The Minor Poet 180
II. The Pretty Lady 180
III. The Very Rich Man 180
IV. The Fisherwoman 181
V. The Crusader 181
VI. The Actress 181
The Little Old Lady in Lavender Silk 182
Vers Démodé 184
Sonnet for the End of a Sequence 185
The Apple Tree 186
Iseult of Brittany 187
"Star Light, Star Bright—" 188
The Sea 189
Guinevere at Her Fireside 190
Transition 192
Lines on Reading Too Many Poets 193
From a Letter from Lesbia 194
Ballade of Unfortunate Mammals 195
Purposely Ungrammatical Love Song 197
Prayer for a New Mother 198
Midnight 199
Ninon de Lenclos, on Her Last Birthday 200
Ultimatum 201
Of a Woman, Dead Young 202
The Willow 203
Sonnet on an Alpine Night 204
Ballade of a Talked-Off Ear 205
Requiescat 207
Sweet Violets 208

Prologue to a Saga 209
Summary 210
Sight 211
The Lady's Reward 212
Prisoner 213
Temps Perdu 214
Autumn Valentine 215

INDEX OF FIRST LINES 217

ENOUGH ROPE

THRENODY

Lilacs blossom just as sweet
Now my heart is shattered.
If I bowled it down the street,
Who's to say it mattered?
If there's one that rode away
What would I be missing?
Lips that taste of tears, they say,
Are the best for kissing.

Eyes that watch the morning star
Seem a little brighter;
Arms held out to darkness are
Usually whiter.
Shall I bar the strolling guest,
Bind my brow with willow,
When, they say, the empty breast
Is the softer pillow?

That a heart falls tinkling down,
Never think it ceases.
Every likely lad in town
Gathers up the pieces.
If there's one gone whistling by
Would I let it grieve me?
Let him wonder if I lie;
Let him half believe me.

THE SMALL HOURS

No more my little song comes back;
  And now of nights I lay
My head on down, to watch the black
  And wait the unfailing gray.

Oh, sad are winter nights, and slow;
  And sad's a song that's dumb;
And sad it is to lie and know
  Another dawn will come.

THE FALSE FRIENDS

They laid their hands upon my head,
They stroked my cheek and brow;
And time could heal a hurt, they said,
And time could dim a vow.

And they were pitiful and mild
Who whispered to me then,
"The heart that breaks in April, child,
Will mend in May again."

Oh, many a mended heart they knew,
So old they were, and wise.
And little did they have to do
To come to me with lies!

Who flings me silly talk of May
Shall meet a bitter soul;
For June was nearly spent away
Before my heart was whole.

THE TRIFLER

Death's the lover that I'd be taking;
  Wild and fickle and fierce is he.
Small's his care if my heart be breaking—
  Gay young Death would have none of me.

Hear them clack of my haste to greet him!
  No one other my mouth had kissed.
I had dressed me in silk to meet him—
  False young Death would not hold the tryst.

Slow's the blood that was quick and stormy,
  Smooth and cold is the bridal bed;
I must wait till he whistles for me—
  Proud young Death would not turn his head.

I must wait till my breast is wilted,
  I must wait till my back is bowed,
I must rock in the corner, jilted—
  Death went galloping down the road.

Gone's my heart with a trifling rover.
  Fine he was in the game he played—
Kissed, and promised, and threw me over,
  And rode away with a prettier maid.

A VERY SHORT SONG

Once, when I was young and true,
  Someone left me sad—
Broke my brittle heart in two;
  And that is very bad.

Love is for unlucky folk,
  Love is but a curse.
Once there was a heart I broke;
  And that, I think, is worse.

A WELL-WORN STORY

In April, in April,
My one love came along,
And I ran the slope of my high hill
To follow a thread of song.

His eyes were hard as porphyry
With looking on cruel lands;
His voice went slipping over me
Like terrible silver hands.

Together we trod the secret lane
And walked the muttering town.
I wore my heart like a wet, red stain
On the breast of a velvet gown.

In April, in April,
My love went whistling by,
And I stumbled here to my high hill
Along the way of a lie.

Now what should I do in this place
But sit and count the chimes,
And splash cold water on my face
And spoil a page with rhymes?

CONVALESCENT

How shall I wail, that wasn't meant for weeping?
Love has run and left me, oh, what then?
Dream, then, I must, who never can be sleeping;
What if I should meet Love, once again?

What if I met him, walking on the highway?
Let him see how lightly I should care.
He'd travel his way, I would follow my way;
Hum a little song, and pass him there.

What if at night, beneath a sky of ashes,
He should seek my doorstep, pale with need?
There could he lie, and dry would be my lashes;
Let him stop his noise, and let me read.

Oh, but I'm gay, that's better off without him;
Would he'd come and see me, laughing here.
Lord! Don't I know I'd have my arms about him,
Crying to him, "Oh, come in, my dear!"

THE DARK GIRL'S RHYME

Who was there had seen us
    Wouldn't bid him run?
Heavy lay between us
    All our sires had done.

There he was, a-springing
    Of a pious race,
Setting hags a-swinging
    In a market-place;

Sowing turnips over
    Where the poppies lay;
Looking past the clover,
    Adding up the hay;

Shouting through the Spring song,
    Clumping down the sod;
Toadying, in sing-song,
    To a crabbèd god.

There I was, that came of
    Folk of mud and flame—
I that had my name of
    Them without a name.

Up and down a mountain
  Streeled my silly stock;
Passing by a fountain,
  Wringing at a rock;

Devil-gotten sinners,
  Throwing back their heads;
Fiddling for their dinners,
  Kissing for their beds.

Not a one had seen us
  Wouldn't help him flee.
Angry ran between us
  Blood of him and me.

How shall I be mating
  Who have looked above—
Living for a hating,
  Dying of a love?

EPITAPH

The first time I died, I walked my ways;
I followed the file of limping days.

I held me tall, with my head flung up,
But I dared not look on the new moon's cup.

I dared not look on the sweet young rain,
And between my ribs was a gleaming pain.

The next time I died, they laid me deep.
They spoke worn words to hallow my sleep.

They tossed me petals, they wreathed me fern,
They weighted me down with a marble urn.

And I lie here warm, and I lie here dry,
And watch the worms slip by, slip by.

LIGHT OF LOVE

Joy stayed with me a night—
Young and free and fair—
And in the morning light
He left me there.

Then Sorrow came to stay;
And lay upon my breast;
He walked with me in the day,
And knew me best.

I'll never be a bride,
Nor yet celibate,
So I'm living now with Pride—
A cold bedmate.

He must not hear nor see,
Nor could he forgive
That Sorrow still visits me
Each day I live.

WAIL

Love has gone a-rocketing.
 That is not the worst;
I could do without the thing,
 And not be the first.

Joy has gone the way it came.
 That is nothing new;
I could get along the same—
 Many people do.

Dig for me the narrow bed,
 Now I am bereft.
All my pretty hates are dead,
 And what have I left?

THE SATIN DRESS

Needle, needle, dip and dart,
Thrusting up and down,
Where's the man could ease a heart
Like a satin gown?

See the stitches curve and crawl
Round the cunning seams—
Patterns thin and sweet and small
As a lady's dreams.

Wantons go in bright brocades;
Brides in organdie;
Gingham's for the plighted maid;
Satin's for the free!

Wool's to line a miser's chest;
Crape's to calm the old;
Velvet hides an empty breast;
Satin's for the bold!

Lawn is for a bishop's yoke;
Linen's for a nun;
Satin is for wiser folk—
Would the dress were done!

Satin glows in candlelight—
Satin's for the proud!
They will say who watch at night,
"What a fine shroud!"

SOMEBODY'S SONG

This is what I vow:
He shall have my heart to keep;
Sweetly will we stir and sleep,
All the years, as now.
Swift the measured sands may run;
Love like this is never done;
He and I are welded one:
This is what I vow.

This is what I pray:
Keep him by me tenderly;
Keep him sweet in pride of me,
Ever and a day;
Keep me from the old distress;
Let me, for our happiness,
Be the one to love the less:
This is what I pray.

This is what I know:
Lovers' oaths are thin as rain;
Love's a harbinger of pain—
Would it were not so!
Ever is my heart a-thirst,
Ever is my love accurst;
He is neither last nor first:
This is what I know.

ANECDOTE

So silent I when Love was by
  He yawned, and turned away;
But Sorrow clings to my apron-strings,
  I have so much to say.

BRAGGART

The days will rally, wreathing
Their crazy tarantelle;
And you must go on breathing,
But I'll be safe in hell.

Like January weather,
The years will bite and smart,
And pull your bones together
To wrap your chattering heart.

The pretty stuff you're made of
Will crack and crease and dry.
The thing you are afraid of
Will look from every eye.

You will go faltering after
The bright, imperious line,
And split your throat on laughter,
And burn your eyes with brine.

You will be frail and musty
With peering, furtive head,
Whilst I am young and lusty
Among the roaring dead.

EPITAPH FOR A DARLING LADY

All her hours were yellow sands,
Blown in foolish whorls and tassels;
Slipping warmly through her hands;
Patted into little castles.

Shiny day on shiny day
Tumbled in a rainbow clutter,
As she flipped them all away,
Sent them spinning down the gutter.

Leave for her a red young rose,
Go your way, and save your pity;
She is happy, for she knows
That her dust is very pretty.

TO A MUCH TOO UNFORTUNATE LADY

He will love you presently
If you be the way you be.
Send your heart a-skittering,
He will stoop, and lift the thing.
Be your dreams as thread, to tease
Into patterns he shall please.
Let him see your passion is
Ever tenderer than his . . .
Go and bless your star above,
Thus are you, and thus is Love.

He will leave you white with woe,
If you go the way you go.
If your dreams were thread to weave,
He will pluck them from his sleeve.
If your heart had come to rest,
He will flick it from his breast.
Tender though the love he bore,
You had loved a little more . . .
Lady, go and curse your star,
Thus Love is, and thus you are.

PATHS

I shall tread, another year,
  Ways I walked with Grief,
Past the dry, ungarnered ear
  And the brittle leaf.

I shall stand, a year apart,
  Wondering, and shy,
Thinking, "Here she broke her heart;
  Here she pled to die."

I shall hear the pheasants call,
  And the raucous geese;
Down these ways, another Fall,
  I shall walk with Peace.

But the pretty path I trod
  Hand-in-hand with Love—
Underfoot, the nascent sod,
  Brave young boughs above,

And the stripes of ribbon grass
  By the curling way—
I shall never dare to pass
  To my dying day.

HEARTHSIDE

Half across the world from me
Lie the lands I'll never see—
I, whose longing lives and dies
Where a ship has sailed away;
I, that never close my eyes
But to look upon Cathay.

Things I may not know nor tell
Wait, where older waters swell;
Ways that flowered at Sappho's tread,
Winds that sighed in Homer's strings,
Vibrant with the singing dead,
Golden with the dust of wings.

Under deeper skies than mine,
Quiet valleys dip and shine.
Where their tender grasses heal
Ancient scars of trench and tomb
I shall never walk; nor kneel
Where the bones of poets bloom.

If I seek a lovelier part,
Where I travel goes my heart;
Where I stray my thought must go;
With me wanders my desire.
Best to sit and watch the snow,
Turn the lock, and poke the fire.

THE NEW LOVE

If it shine or if it rain,
Little will I care or know.
Days, like drops upon a pane,
Slip, and join, and go.

At my door's another lad;
Here's his flower in my hair
If he see me pale and sad,
Will he see me fair?

I sit looking at the floor.
Little will I think or say
If he seek another door;
Even if he stay.

RAINY NIGHT

Ghosts of all my lovely sins,
  Who attend too well my pillow,
Gay the wanton rain begins;
  Hide the limp and tearful willow,

Turn aside your eyes and ears,
  Trail away your robes of sorrow.
You shall have my further years—
  You shall walk with me tomorrow.

I am sister to the rain;
  Fey and sudden and unholy,
Petulant at the windowpane,
  Quickly lost, remembered slowly.

I have lived with shades, a shade;
  I am hung with graveyard flowers.
Let me be tonight arrayed
  In the silver of the showers.

Every fragile thing shall rust;
  When another April passes
I may be a furry dust,
  Sifting through the brittle grasses.

All sweet sins shall be forgot;
    Who will live to tell their siring?
Hear me now, nor let me rot
    Wistful still, and still aspiring.

Ghosts of dear temptations, heed;
    I am frail, be you forgiving.
See you not that I have need
    To be living with the living?

Sail, tonight, the Styx's breast;
    Glide among the dim processions
Of the exquisite unblest,
    Spirits of my shared transgressions.

Roam with young Persephone,
    Plucking poppies for your slumber . . .
With the morrow, there shall be
    One more wraith among your number.

FOR A SAD LADY

And let her loves, when she is dead,
  Write this above her bones:
"No more she lives to give us bread
  Who asked her only stones."

RECURRENCE

We shall have our little day.
Take my hand and travel still
Round and round the little way,
Up and down the little hill.

It is good to love again;
Scan the renovated skies,
Dip and drive the idling pen,
Sweetly tint the paling lies.

Trace the dripping, piercèd heart,
Speak the fair, insistent verse,
Vow to God, and slip apart,
Little better, little worse.

Would we need not know before
How shall end this prettiness;
One of us must love the more,
One of us shall love the less.

Thus it is, and so it goes;
We shall have our day, my dear
Where, unwilling, dies the rose
Buds the new, another year.

STORY OF MRS. W——

My garden blossoms pink and white,
  A place of decorous murmuring,
Where I am safe from August night
  And cannot feel the knife of Spring.

And I may walk the pretty place
  Before the curtsying hollyhocks
And laundered daisies, round of face—
  Good little girls, in party frocks.

My trees are amiably arrayed
  In pattern on the dappled sky,
And I may sit in filtered shade
  And watch the tidy years go by.

And I may amble pleasantly
  And hear my neighbors list their bones
And click my tongue in sympathy,
  And count the cracks in paving-stones.

My door is grave in oaken strength,
  The cool of linen calms my bed,
And there at night I stretch my length
  And envy no one but the dead.

THE DRAMATISTS

A string of shiny days we had,
  A spotless sky, a yellow sun;
And neither you nor I was sad
  When that was through and done.

But when, one day, a boy comes by
  And pleads me with your happiest vow.
"There was a lad I knew—" I'll sigh;
  "I do not know him now."

And when another girl shall pass
  And speak a little name I said,
Then you will say, "There was a lass—
  I wonder is she dead."

And each of us will sigh, and start
  A-talking of a faded year,
And lay a hand above a heart,
  And dry a pretty tear.

AUGUST

When my eyes are weeds,
And my lips are petals, spinning
Down the wind that has beginning
Where the crumpled beeches start
In a fringe of salty reeds;
When my arms are elder-bushes,
And the rangy lilac pushes
Upward, upward through my heart;

Summer, do your worst!
Light your tinsel moon, and call on
Your performing stars to fall on
Headlong through your paper sky;
Nevermore shall I be cursed
By a flushed and amorous slattern,
With her dusty laces' pattern
Trailing, as she straggles by.

THE WHITE LADY

I cannot rest, I cannot rest
  In strait and shiny wood,
My woven hands upon my breast—
  The dead are all so good!

The earth is cool across their eyes;
  They lie there quietly.
But I am neither old nor wise;
  They do not welcome me.

Where never I walked alone before,
  I wander in the weeds;
And people scream and bar the door,
  And rattle at their beads.

We cannot rest, we never rest
  Within a narrow bed
Who still must love the living best—
  Who hate the drowsy dead!

I KNOW I HAVE BEEN HAPPIEST

I know I have been happiest at your side;
But what is done, is done, and all's to be.
And small the good, to linger dolefully—
Gayly it lived, and gallantly it died.
I will not make you songs of hearts denied,
And you, being man, would have no tears of me,
And should I offer you fidelity,
You'd be, I think, a little terrified.

Yet this the need of woman, this her curse:
To range her little gifts, and give, and give,
Because the throb of giving's sweet to bear.
To you, who never begged me vows or verse,
My gift shall be my absence, while I live;
But after that, my dear, I cannot swear.

TESTAMENT

Oh, let it be a night of lyric rain
And singing breezes, when my bell is tolled.
I have so loved the rain that I would hold
Last in my ears its friendly, dim refrain.
I shall lie cool and quiet, who have lain
Fevered, and watched the book of day unfold.
Death will not see me flinch; the heart is bold
That pain has made incapable of pain.

Kinder the busy worms than ever love;
It will be peace to lie there, empty-eyed,
My bed made secret by the leveling showers,
My breast replenishing the weeds above.
And you will say of me, "Then has she died?
Perhaps I should have sent a spray of flowers."

I SHALL COME BACK

I shall come back without fanfaronade
Of wailing wind and graveyard panoply;
But, trembling, slip from cool Eternity—
A mild and most bewildered little shade.
I shall not make sepulchral midnight raid,
But softly come where I had longed to be
In April twilight's unsung melody,
And I, not you, shall be the one afraid.

Strange, that from lovely dreamings of the dead
I shall come back to you, who hurt me most.
You may not feel my hand upon your head,
I'll be so new and inexpert a ghost.
Perhaps you will not know that I am near—
And that will break my ghostly heart, my dear.

CONDOLENCE

They hurried here, as soon as you had died,
Their faces damp with haste and sympathy,
And pressed my hand in theirs, and smoothed my knee,
And clicked their tongues, and watched me, mournful eyed.
Gently they told me of that Other Side—
How, even then, you waited there for me,
And what ecstatic meeting ours would be.
Moved by the lovely tale, they broke, and cried.

And when I smiled, they told me I was brave,
And they rejoiced that I was comforted,
And left, to tell of all the help they gave.
But I had smiled to think how you, the dead,
So curiously preoccupied and grave,
Would laugh, could you have heard the things they said.

THE IMMORTALS

If you should sail for Trebizond, or die,
Or cry another name in your first sleep,
Or see me board a train, and fail to sigh,
Appropriately, I'd clutch my breast and weep.
And you, if I should wander through the door,
Or sin, or seek a nunnery, or save
My lips and give my cheek, would tread the floor
And aptly mention poison and the grave.

Therefore the mooning world is gratified,
Quoting how prettily we sigh and swear;
And you and I, correctly side by side,
Shall live as lovers when our bones are bare;
And though we lie forever enemies,
Shall rank with Abélard and Héloïse.

A PORTRAIT

Because my love is quick to come and go—
A little here, and then a little there—
What use are any words of mine to swear
My heart is stubborn, and my spirit slow
Of weathering the drip and drive of woe?
What is my oath, when you have but to bare
My little, easy loves; and I can dare
Only to shrug, and answer, "They are so"?

You do not know how heavy a heart it is
That hangs about my neck—a clumsy stone
Cut with a birth, a death, a bridal-day.
Each time I love, I find it still my own,
Who take it, now to that lad, now to this,
Seeking to give the wretched thing away.

PORTRAIT OF THE ARTIST

Oh, lead me to a quiet cell
  Where never footfall rankles,
And bar the window passing well,
  And gyve my wrists and ankles.

Oh, wrap my eyes with linen fair,
  With hempen cord go bind me,
And, of your mercy, leave me there,
  Nor tell them where to find me.

Oh, lock the portal as you go,
  And see its bolts be double. . . .
Come back in half an hour or so,
  And I will be in trouble.

CHANT FOR DARK HOURS

Some men, some men
Cannot pass a
Book shop.
(Lady, make your mind up, and wait your life away.)

Some men, some men
Cannot pass a
Crap game.
(He said he'd come at moonrise, and here's another day!)

Some men, some men
Cannot pass a
Bar-room.
(Wait about, and hang about, and that's the way it goes.)

Some men, some men
Cannot pass a
Woman.
(Heaven never send me another one of those!)

Some men, some men
Cannot pass a
Golf course.
(Read a book, and sew a seam, and slumber if you can.)

Some men, some men
Cannot pass a
Haberdasher's.
(All your life you wait around for some damn man!)

UNFORTUNATE COINCIDENCE

By the time you swear you're his,
  Shivering and sighing,
And he vows his passion is
  Infinite, undying—
Lady, make a note of this:
  One of you is lying.

INVENTORY

Four be the things I am wiser to know:
Idleness, sorrow, a friend, and a foe.

Four be the things I'd been better without:
Love, curiosity, freckles, and doubt.

Three be the things I shall never attain:
Envy, content, and sufficient champagne.

Three be the things I shall have till I die:
Laughter and hope and a sock in the eye.

NOW AT LIBERTY

Little white love, your way you've taken;
  Now I am left alone, alone.
Little white love, my heart's forsaken.
  (Whom shall I get by telephone?)
Well do I know there's no returning;
  Once you go out, it's done, it's done.
All of my days are gray with yearning.
  (Nevertheless, a girl needs fun.)

Little white love, perplexed and weary,
  Sadly your banner fluttered down.
Sullen the days, and dreary, dreary.
  (Which of the boys is still in town?)
Radiant and sure, you came a-flying;
  Puzzled, you left on lagging feet.
Slow in my breast, my heart is dying.
  (Nevertheless, a girl must eat.)

Little white love, I hailed you gladly;
  Now I must wave you out of sight.
Ah, but you used me badly, badly.
  (Who'd like to take me out tonight?)
All of the blundering words I've spoken,
  Little white love, forgive, forgive.
Once you went out, my heart fell, broken.
  (Nevertheless, a girl must live.)

COMMENT

Oh, life is a glorious cycle of song,
A medley of extemporanea;
And love is a thing that can never go wrong;
And I am Marie of Roumania.

PLEA

Secrets, you said, would hold us two apart;
   You'd have me know of you your least transgression,
And so the intimate places of your heart,
   Kneeling, you bared to me, as in confession.
Softly you told of loves that went before—
   Of clinging arms, of kisses gladly given;
Luxuriously clean of heart once more,
   You rose up, then, and stood before me, shriven.

When this, my day of happiness, is through,
   And love, that bloomed so fair, turns brown and brittle,
There is a thing that I shall ask of you—
   I, who have given so much, and asked so little.
Some day, when there's another in my stead,
   Again you'll feel the need of absolution,
And you will go to her, and bow your head,
   And offer her your past, as contribution.

When with your list of loves you overcome her,
For Heaven's sake, keep this one secret from her!

PATTERN

Leave me to my lonely pillow.
  Go, and take your silly posies;
Who has vowed to wear the willow
  Looks a fool, tricked out in roses.

Who are you, my lad, to ease me?
  Leave your pretty words unspoken.
Tinkling echoes little please me,
  Now my heart is freshly broken.

Over young are you to guide me,
  And your blood is slow and sleeping.
If you must, then sit beside me . . .
  Tell me, why have I been weeping?

DE PROFUNDIS

Oh, is it, then, Utopian
To hope that I may meet a man
Who'll not relate, in accents suave,
The tales of girls he used to have?

THEY PART

And if, my friend, you'd have it end,
There's naught to hear or tell.
But need you try to black my eye
In wishing me farewell?

Though I admit an edgéd wit
In woe is warranted,
May I be frank? . . . Such words as "____"
Are better left unsaid.

There's rosemary for you and me;
But is it usual, dear,
To hire a man, and fill a van
By way of *souvenir*?

BALLADE OF A GREAT WEARINESS

There's little to have but the things I had,
  There's little to bear but the things I bore.
There's nothing to carry and naught to add,
  And glory to Heaven, I paid the score.
There's little to do but I did before,
  There's little to learn but the things I know;
And this is the sum of a lasting lore:
  Scratch a lover, and find a foe.

And couldn't it be I was young and mad
  If ever my heart on my sleeve I wore?
There's many to claw at a heart unclad,
  And little the wonder it ripped and tore.
There's one that'll join in their push and roar,
  With stories to jabber, and stones to throw;
He'll fetch you a lesson that costs you sore—
  Scratch a lover, and find a foe.

So little I'll offer to you, my lad;
  It's little in loving I set my store.
There's many a maid would be flushed and glad,
  And better you'll knock at a kindlier door.
I'll dig at my lettuce, and sweep my floor—
  Forever, forever I'm done with woe—
And happen I'll whistle about my chore,
  "Scratch a lover, and find a foe."

L'ENVOI

Oh, beggar or prince, no more, no more!
  Be off and away with your strut and show.
The sweeter the apple, the blacker the core—
  Scratch a lover, and find a foe!

RÉSUMÉ

Razors pain you;
Rivers are damp;
Acids stain you;
And drugs cause cramp.
Guns aren't lawful;
Nooses give;
Gas smells awful;
You might as well live.

RENUNCIATION

Chloe's hair, no doubt, was brighter;
  Lydia's mouth more sweetly sad;
Hebe's arms were rather whiter;
  Languorous-lidded Helen had
Eyes more blue than e'er the sky was;
  Lalage's was subtler stuff;
Still, you used to think that I was
  Fair enough.

Now you're casting yearning glances
  At the pale Penelope;
Cutting in on Claudia's dances;
  Taking Iris out to tea.
Iole you find warm-hearted;
  Zoe's cheek is far from rough—
Don't you think it's time we parted? . . .
  Fair enough!

THE VETERAN

When I was young and bold and strong,
Oh, right was right, and wrong was wrong!
My plume on high, my flag unfurled,
I rode away to right the world.
"Come out, you dogs, and fight!" said I,
And wept there was but once to die.

But I am old; and good and bad
Are woven in a crazy plaid.
I sit and say, "The world is so;
And he is wise who lets it go.
A battle lost, a battle won—
The difference is small, my son."

Inertia rides and riddles me;
The which is called Philosophy.

PROPHETIC SOUL

Because your eyes are slant and slow,
  Because your hair is sweet to touch,
My heart is high again; but oh,
  I doubt if this will get me much.

VERSE FOR A CERTAIN DOG

Such glorious faith as fills your limpid eyes,
   Dear little friend of mine, I never knew.
All-innocent are you, and yet all-wise.
   (For Heaven's sake, stop worrying that shoe!)
You look about, and all you see is fair;
   This mighty globe was made for you alone.
Of all the thunderous ages, you're the heir.
   (Get off the pillow with that dirty bone!)

A skeptic world you face with steady gaze;
   High in young pride you hold your noble head;
Gayly you meet the rush of roaring days.
   (*Must* you eat puppy biscuit on the bed?)
Lancelike your courage, gleaming swift and strong,
   Yours the white rapture of a wingèd soul,
Yours is a spirit like a May-day song.
   (God help you, if you break the goldfish bowl!)

"Whatever is, is good"—your gracious creed.
   You wear your joy of living like a crown.
Love lights your simplest act, your every deed.
   (Drop it, I tell you—put that kitten down!)
You are God's kindliest gift of all—a friend.
   Your shining loyalty unflecked by doubt,
You ask but leave to follow to the end.
   (Couldn't you wait until I took you out?)

GODSPEED

Oh, seek, my love, your newer way;
   I'll not be left in sorrow.
So long as I have yesterday,
   Go take your damned tomorrow!

SONG OF PERFECT PROPRIETY

Oh, I should like to ride the seas,
   A roaring buccaneer;
A cutlass banging at my knees,
   A dirk behind my ear.
And when my captives' chains would clank
   I'd howl with glee and drink,
And then fling out the quivering plank
   And watch the beggars sink.

I'd like to straddle gory decks,
   And dig in laden sands,
And know the feel of throbbing necks
   Between my knotted hands.
Oh, I should like to strut and curse
   Among my blackguard crew . . .
But I am writing little verse,
   As little ladies do.

Oh, I should like to dance and laugh
   And pose and preen and sway,
And rip the hearts of men in half,
   And toss the bits away.
I'd like to view the reeling years
   Through unastonished eyes,
And dip my finger-tips in tears,
   And give my smiles for sighs.

I'd stroll beyond the ancient bounds,
   And tap at fastened gates,
And hear the prettiest of sounds—
   The clink of shattered fates.
My slaves I'd like to bind with thongs
   That cut and burn and chill . . .
But I am writing little songs,
   As little ladies will.

SOCIAL NOTE

Lady, lady, should you meet
One whose ways are all discreet,
One who murmurs that his wife
Is the lodestar of his life,
One who keeps assuring you
That he never was untrue,
Never loved another one . . .
Lady, lady, better run!

ONE PERFECT ROSE

A single flow'r he sent me, since we met.
  All tenderly his messenger he chose;
Deep-hearted, pure, with scented dew still wet—
  One perfect rose.

I knew the language of the floweret;
  "My fragile leaves," it said, "his heart enclose."
Love long has taken for his amulet
  One perfect rose.

Why is it no one ever sent me yet
  One perfect limousine, do you suppose?
Ah no, it's always just my luck to get
  One perfect rose.

BALLADE AT THIRTY-FIVE

This, no song of an ingénue,
  This, no ballad of innocence;
This, the rhyme of a lady who
  Followed ever her natural bents.
  This, a solo of sapience,
This, a chantey of sophistry,
  This, the sum of experiments—
I loved them until they loved me.

Decked in garments of sable hue,
  Daubed with ashes of myriad Lents,
Wearing shower bouquets of rue,
  Walk I ever in penitence.
  Oft I roam, as my heart repents,
Through God's acre of memory,
  Marking stones, in my reverence,
"I loved them until they loved me."

Pictures pass me in long review—
  Marching columns of dead events.
I was tender and, often, true;
  Ever a prey to coincidence.
  Always knew I the consequence;
Always saw what the end would be.
  We're as Nature has made us—hence
I loved them until they loved me.

L'ENVOI

Princes, never I'd give offense,
  Won't you think of me tenderly?
Here's my strength and my weakness, gents—
  I loved them until they loved me.

THE THIN EDGE

With you, my heart is quiet here,
And all my thoughts are cool as rain.
I sit and let the shifting year
Go by before the windowpane,
And reach my hand to yours, my dear . . .
I wonder what it's like in Spain.

LOVE SONG

My own dear love, he is strong and bold
  And he cares not what comes after.
His words ring sweet as a chime of gold,
  And his eyes are lit with laughter.
He is jubilant as a flag unfurled—
  Oh, a girl, she'd not forget him.
My own dear love, he is all my world—
  And I wish I'd never met him.

My love, he's mad, and my love, he's fleet,
  And a wild young wood-thing bore him!
The ways are fair to his roaming feet,
  And the skies are sunlit for him.
As sharply sweet to my heart he seems
  As the fragrance of acacia.
My own dear love, he is all my dreams—
  And I wish he were in Asia.

My love runs by like a day in June,
  And he makes no friends of sorrows.
He'll tread his galloping rigadoon
  In the pathway of the morrows.
He'll live his days where the sunbeams start
  Nor could storm or wind uproot him.
My own dear love, he is all my heart—
  And I wish somebody'd shoot him.

INDIAN SUMMER

In youth, it was a way I had
  To do my best to please,
And change, with every passing lad,
  To suit his theories.

But now I know the things I know,
  And do the things I do;
And if you do not like me so,
  To hell, my love, with you!

PHILOSOPHY

If I should labor through daylight and dark,
   Consecrate, valorous, serious, true,
Then on the world I may blazon my mark;
   And what if I don't, and what if I do?

FOR AN UNKNOWN LADY

Lady, if you'd slumber sound,
Keep your eyes upon the ground.
If you'd toss and turn at night,
Slip your glances left and right.
Would the mornings find you gay,
Never give your heart away.
Would they find you pale and sad
Fling it to a whistling lad.
Ah, but when his pleadings burn,
Will you let my words return?
Will you lock your pretty lips,
And deny your finger-tips,
Veil away your tender eyes,
Just because some words were wise?
If he whistles low and clear
When the insistent moon is near
And the secret stars are known—
Will your heart be still your own
Just because some words were true? . . .
Lady, I was told them, too!

THE LEAL

The friends I made have slipped and strayed.
    And who's the one that cares?
A trifling lot and best forgot—
    And that's my tale, and theirs.

Then if my friendships break and bend,
    There's little need to cry
The while I know that every foe
    Is faithful till I die.

WORDS OF COMFORT TO BE SCRATCHED ON A MIRROR

Helen of Troy had a wandering glance;
Sappho's restriction was only the sky;
Ninon was ever the chatter of France;
But oh, what a good girl am I!

MEN

They hail you as their morning star
Because you are the way you are.
If you return the sentiment,
They'll try to make you different;
And once they have you, safe and sound,
They want to change you all around.
Your moods and ways they put a curse on;
They'd make of you another person.
They cannot let you go your gait;
They influence and educate.
They'd alter all that they admired.
They make me sick, they make me tired.

NEWS ITEM

Men seldom make passes
At girls who wear glasses.

SONG OF ONE OF THE GIRLS

Here in my heart I am Helen;
   I'm Aspasia and Hero, at least.
I'm Judith, and Jael, and Madame de Staël;
   I'm Salome, moon of the East.

Here in my soul I am Sappho;
   Lady Hamilton am I, as well.
In me Récamier vies with Kitty O'Shea,
   With Dido, and Eve, and poor Nell.

I'm of the glamorous ladies
   At whose beckoning history shook.
But you are a man, and see only my pan,
   So I stay at home with a book.

LULLABY

Sleep, pretty lady, the night is enfolding you;
  Drift, and so lightly, on crystalline streams.
Wrapped in its perfumes, the darkness is holding you;
  Starlight bespangles the way of your dreams.
Chorus the nightingales, wistfully amorous;
  Blessedly quiet, the blare of the day.
All the sweet hours may your visions be glamorous—
  Sleep, pretty lady, as long as you may.

Sleep, pretty lady, the night shall be still for you;
  Silvered and silent, it watches your rest.
Each little breeze, in its eagerness, will for you
  Murmur the melodies ancient and blest.
So in the midnight does happiness capture us;
  Morning is dim with another day's tears.
Give yourself sweetly to images rapturous—
  Sleep, pretty lady, a couple of years.

Sleep, pretty lady, the world awaits day with you;
  Girlish and golden, the slender young moon.
Grant the fond darkness its mystical way with you;
  Morning returns to us ever too soon.
Roses unfold, in their loveliness, all for you;
  Blossom the lilies for hope of your glance.
When you're awake, all the men go and fall for you—
  Sleep, pretty lady, and give me a chance.

FAUTE DE MIEUX

Travel, trouble, music, art,
 A kiss, a frock, a rhyme—
I never said they feed my heart,
 But still they pass my time.

ROUNDEL

She's passing fair; but so demure is she,
So quiet is her gown, so smooth her hair,
That few there are who note her and agree
    She's passing fair.

Yet when was ever beauty held more rare
Than simple heart and maiden modesty?
What fostered charms with virtue could compare?

Alas, no lover ever stops to see;
The best that she is offered is the air.
Yet–if the passing mark is minus D–
    She's passing fair.

A CERTAIN LADY

Oh, I can smile for you, and tilt my head,
  And drink your rushing words with eager lips,
And paint my mouth for you a fragrant red,
  And trace your brows with tutored finger-tips.
When you rehearse your list of loves to me,
  Oh, I can laugh and marvel, rapturous-eyed.
And you laugh back, nor can you ever see
  The thousand little deaths my heart has died.
And you believe, so well I know my part,
  That I am gay as morning, light as snow,
And all the straining things within my heart
  You'll never know.

Oh, I can laugh and listen, when we meet,
  And you bring tales of fresh adventurings—
Of ladies delicately indiscreet,
  Of lingering hands, and gently whispered things.
And you are pleased with me, and strive anew
  To sing me sagas of your late delights.
Thus do you want me—marveling, gay, and true—
  Nor do you see my staring eyes of nights.
And when, in search of novelty, you stray,
  Oh, I can kiss you blithely as you go . . .
And what goes on, my love, while you're away,
  You'll never know.

OBSERVATION

If I don't drive around the park,
I'm pretty sure to make my mark.
If I'm in bed each night by ten,
I may get back my looks again.
If I abstain from fun and such,
I'll probably amount to much;
But I shall stay the way I am,
Because I do not give a damn.

SYMPTOM RECITAL

I do not like my state of mind;
I'm bitter, querulous, unkind.
I hate my legs, I hate my hands,
I do not yearn for lovelier lands.
I dread the dawn's recurrent light;
I hate to go to bed at night.
I snoot at simple, earnest folk.
I cannot take the gentlest joke.
I find no peace in paint or type.
My world is but a lot of tripe.
I'm disillusioned, empty-breasted.
For what I think, I'd be arrested.
I am not sick, I am not well.
My quondam dreams are shot to hell.
My soul is crushed, my spirit sore;
I do not like me any more.
I cavil, quarrel, grumble, grouse.
I ponder on the narrow house.
I shudder at the thought of men . . .
I'm due to fall in love again.

RONDEAU REDOUBLÉ (AND SCARCELY WORTH THE TROUBLE, AT THAT)

The same to me are somber days and gay.
  Though joyous dawns the rosy morn, and bright,
Because my dearest love is gone away
  Within my heart is melancholy night.

My heart beats low in loneliness, despite
  That riotous Summer holds the earth in sway.
In cerements my spirit is bedight;
  The same to me are somber days and gay.

Though breezes in the rippling grasses play,
  And waves dash high and far in glorious might,
I thrill no longer to the sparkling day,
  Though joyous dawns the rosy morn, and bright.

Ungraceful seems to me the swallow's flight;
  As well might heaven's blue be sullen gray;
My soul discerns no beauty in their sight
  Because my dearest love is gone away.

Let roses fling afar their crimson spray,
    And virgin daisies splash the fields with white,
Let bloom the poppy hotly as it may,
    Within my heart is melancholy night.

And this, O love, my pitiable plight
    Whenever from my circling arms you stray;
This little world of mine has lost its light . . .
    I hope to God, my dear, that you can say
                                        The same to me.

FIGHTING WORDS

Say my love is easy had,
   Say I'm bitten raw with pride,
Say I am too often sad—
   Still behold me at your side.

Say I'm neither brave nor young,
   Say I woo and coddle care,
Say the devil touched my tongue—
   Still you have my heart to wear.

But say my verses do not scan,
   And I get me another man!

THE CHOICE

He'd have given me rolling lands,
   Houses of marble, and billowing farms,
Pearls, to trickle between my hands,
   Smoldering rubies, to circle my arms.
You—you'd only a lilting song,
   Only a melody, happy and high,
You were sudden and swift and strong—
   Never a thought for another had I.

He'd have given me laces rare,
   Dresses that glimmered with frosty sheen,
Shining ribbons to wrap my hair,
   Horses to draw me, as fine as a queen.
You—you'd only to whistle low,
   Gayly I followed wherever you led.
I took you, and I let him go—
   Somebody ought to examine my head!

GENERAL REVIEW OF THE SEX SITUATION

Woman wants monogamy;
Man delights in novelty.
Love is woman's moon and sun;
Man has other forms of fun.
Woman lives but in her lord;
Count to ten, and man is bored.
With this the gist and sum of it,
What earthly good can come of it?

INSCRIPTION FOR THE CEILING OF A BEDROOM

Daily dawns another day;
I must up, to make my way.
Though I dress and drink and eat,
Move my fingers and my feet,
Learn a little, here and there,
Weep and laugh and sweat and swear,
Hear a song, or watch a stage,
Leave some words upon a page,
Claim a foe, or hail a friend—
Bed awaits me at the end.

Though I go in pride and strength,
I'll come back to bed at length.
Though I walk in blinded woe,
Back to bed I'm bound to go.
High my heart, or bowed my head,
All my days but lead to bed.
Up, and out, and on; and then
Ever back to bed again,
Summer, Winter, Spring, and Fall—
I'm a fool to rise at all!

PICTURES IN THE SMOKE

Oh, gallant was the first love, and glittering and fine;
The second love was water, in a clear white cup;
The third love was his, and the fourth was mine;
And after that, I always get them all mixed up.

NOCTURNE

Always I knew that it could not last
  (Gathering clouds, and the snowflakes flying),
Now it is part of the golden past
  (Darkening skies, and the night-wind sighing);
It is but cowardice to pretend.
  Cover with ashes our love's cold crater—
Always I've known that it had to end
  Sooner or later.

Always I knew it would come like this
  (Pattering rain, and the grasses springing),
Sweeter to you is a new love's kiss
  (Flickering sunshine, and young birds singing).
Gone are the raptures that once we knew,
  Now you are finding a new joy greater—
Well, I'll be doing the same thing, too,
  Sooner or later.

INTERVIEW

The ladies men admire, I've heard,
Would shudder at a wicked word.
Their candle gives a single light;
They'd rather stay at home at night.
They do not keep awake till three,
Nor read erotic poetry.
They never sanction the impure,
Nor recognize an overture.
They shrink from powders and from paints . . .
So far, I've had no complaints.

EXPERIENCE

Some men break your heart in two,
  Some men fawn and flatter,
Some men never look at you;
  And that cleans up the matter.

NEITHER BLOODY NOR BOWED

They say of me, and so they should,
It's doubtful if I come to good.
I see acquaintances and friends
Accumulating dividends,
And making enviable names
In science, art, and parlor games.
But I, despite expert advice,
Keep doing things I think are nice,
And though to good I never come—
Inseparable my nose and thumb!

THE BURNED CHILD

Love has had his way with me.
   This my heart is torn and maimed
Since he took his play with me.
   Cruel well the bow-boy aimed,

Shot, and saw the feathered shaft
   Dripping bright and bitter red.
He that shrugged his wings and laughed—
   Better had he left me dead.

Sweet, why do you plead me, then,
   Who have bled so sore of that?
Could I bear it once again? . . .
   Drop a hat, dear, drop a hat!

SUNSET GUN

GODMOTHER

The day that I was christened—
It's a hundred years, and more!—
A hag came and listened
At the white church door,
A-hearing her that bore me
And all my kith and kin
Considerately, for me,
Renouncing sin.
While some gave me corals,
And some gave me gold,
And porringers, with morals
Agreeably scrolled,
The hag stood, buckled
In a dim gray cloak;
Stood there and chuckled,
Spat, and spoke:
"There's few enough in life'll
Be needing my help,
But I've got a trifle
For your fine young whelp.
I give her sadness,
And the gift of pain,
The new-moon madness,
And the love of rain."

And little good to lave me
　　In their holy silver bowl
After what she gave me—
　　Rest her soul!

PARTIAL COMFORT

Whose love is given over-well
Shall look on Helen's face in hell,
Whilst they whose love is thin and wise
May view John Knox in paradise.

THE RED DRESS

I always saw, I always said
  If I were grown and free,
I'd have a gown of reddest red
  As fine as you could see,

To wear out walking, sleek and slow,
  Upon a Summer day,
And there'd be one to see me so,
  And flip the world away.

And he would be a gallant one,
  With stars behind his eyes,
And hair like metal in the sun,
  And lips too warm for lies.

I always saw us, gay and good,
  High honored in the town.
Now I am grown to womanhood. . . .
  I have the silly gown.

VICTORIA

Dear dead Victoria
   Rotted cosily;
In excelsis gloria,
   And R. I. P.

And her shroud was buttoned neat,
   And her bones were clean and round,
And her soul was at her feet
   Like a bishop's marble hound.

Albert lay a-drying,
   Lavishly arrayed,
With his soul out flying
   Where his heart had stayed.

And there's some could tell you what land
   His spirit walks serene
(But I've heard them say in Scotland
   It's never been seen).

THE COUNSELOR

I met a man the other day—
  A kindly man, and serious—
Who viewed me in a thoughtful way,
  And spoke me so, and spoke me thus:

"Oh, dallying's a sad mistake;
  'Tis craven to survey the morrow!
Go give your heart, and if it break—
  A wise companion is Sorrow.

"Oh, live, my child, nor keep your soul
  To crowd your coffin when you're dead. . . ."
I asked his work; he dealt in coal,
  And shipped it up the Tyne, he said.

PARABLE FOR A CERTAIN VIRGIN

Oh, ponder, friend, the porcupine;
  Refresh your recollection,
And sit a moment, to define
  His means of self-protection.

How truly fortified is he!
  Where is the beast his double
In forethought of emergency
  And readiness for trouble?

Recall his figure, and his shade—
  How deftly planned and clearly
For slithering through the dappled glade
  Unseen, or pretty nearly.

Yet should an alien eye discern
  His presence in the woodland,
How little has he left to learn
  Of self-defense! My good land!

For he can run, as swift as sound,
  To where his goose may hang high;
Or thrust his head against the ground
  And tunnel half to Shanghai;

Or he can climb the dizziest bough—
   Unhesitant, mechanic—
And, resting, dash from off his brow
   The bitter beads of panic;

Or should pursuers press him hot,
   One scarcely needs to mention
His quick and cruel barbs, that got
   Shakespearean attention;

Or driven to his final ditch,
   To his extremest thicket,
He'll fight with claws and molars (which
   Is not considered cricket).

How amply armored, he, to fend
   The fear of chase that haunts him!
How well prepared our little friend!—
   And who the devil wants him?

BRIC-A-BRAC

Little things that no one needs—
  Little things to joke about—
Little landscapes, done in beads.
  Little morals, woven out,
Little wreaths of gilded grass,
  Little brigs of whittled oak
Bottled painfully in glass;
  These are made by lonely folk.

Lonely folk have lines of days
  Long and faltering and thin;
Therefore—little wax bouquets,
  Prayers cut upon a pin,
Little maps of pinkish lands,
  Little charts of curly seas,
Little plats of linen strands,
  Little verses, such as these.

INTERIOR

Her mind lives in a quiet room,
  A narrow room, and tall,
With pretty lamps to quench the gloom
  And mottoes on the wall.

There all the things are waxen neat
  And set in decorous lines;
And there are posies, round and sweet,
  And little, straightened vines.

Her mind lives tidily, apart
  From cold and noise and pain,
And bolts the door against her heart,
  Out wailing in the rain.

REUBEN'S CHILDREN

Accursed from their birth they be
Who seek to find monogamy,
Pursuing it from bed to bed—
I think they would be better dead.

ON CHEATING THE FIDDLER

"Then we will have tonight!" we said.
"Tomorrow—may we not be dead?"
The morrow touched our eyes, and found
Us walking firm above the ground,
Our pulses quick, our blood alight.
Tomorrow's gone—we'll have tonight!

THERE WAS ONE

There was one a-riding grand
On a tall brown mare.
And a fine gold band
He brought me there.

A little, gold band
He held to me
That would shine on a hand
For the world to see.

There was one a-walking swift
To a little, new song,
And a rose was the gift
He carried along,

First of all the posies,
Dewy and red.
They that have roses
Never need bread.

There was one with a swagger
And a soft, slow tongue,
And a bright, cold dagger
Where his left hand swung—

Carven and gilt,
  Old and bad–
And his stroking of the hilt
  Set a girl mad.

There was one a-riding grand
  As he rode from me.
And he raised his golden band
  And he threw it in the sea.

There was one a-walking slow
  To a sad, long sigh.
And his rose drooped low,
  And he flung it down to die.

There was one with a swagger
  And a little, sharp pride,
And a bright, cold dagger
  Ever at his side.

At his side it stayed
  When he ran to part.
What is this blade
  Struck through my heart?

INCURABLE

And if my heart be scarred and burned,
The safer, I, for all I learned;
The calmer, I, to see it true
That ways of love are never new—
The love that sets you daft and dazed
Is every love that ever blazed;
The happier, I, to fathom this:
A kiss is every other kiss.
The reckless vow, the lovely name,
When Helen walked, were spoke the same;
The weighted breast, the grinding woe,
When Phaon fled, were ever so.
Oh, it is sure as it is sad
That any lad is every lad,
And what's a girl, to dare implore
Her dear be hers forevermore?
Though he be tried and he be bold,
And swearing death should he be cold,
He'll run the path the others went. . . .
But you, my sweet, are different.

FABLE

Oh, there once was a lady, and so I've been told,
Whose lover grew weary, whose lover grew cold.
"My child," he remarked, "though our episode ends,
In the manner of men, I suggest we be friends."
And the truest of friends ever after they were—
Oh, they lied in their teeth when they told me of her!

THE SECOND OLDEST STORY

Go I must along my ways
  Though my heart be ragged,
Dripping bitter through the days,
  Festering, and jagged.
Smile I must at every twinge,
  Kiss, to time its throbbing;
He that tears a heart to fringe
  Hates the noise of sobbing.

. . . .

Weep, my love, till Heaven hears;
  Curse and moan and languish.
While I wash your wound with tears,
  Ease aloud your anguish.
Bellow of the pit in Hell
  Where you're made to linger.
There and there and well and well—
  Did he prick his finger!

A PIG'S-EYE VIEW OF LITERATURE

THE LIVES AND TIMES OF JOHN KEATS, PERCY BYSSHE SHELLEY, AND GEORGE GORDON NOEL, LORD BYRON

Byron and Shelley and Keats
Were a trio of lyrical treats.
The forehead of Shelley was cluttered with curls,
And Keats never was a descendant of earls,
And Byron walked out with a number of girls,
    But it didn't impair the poetical feats
        Of Byron and Shelley,
        Of Byron and Shelley,
    Of Byron and Shelley and Keats.

OSCAR WILDE

If, with the literate, I am
Impelled to try an epigram,
I never seek to take the credit;
We all assume that Oscar said it.

HARRIET BEECHER STOWE

The pure and worthy Mrs. Stowe
Is one we all are proud to know
As mother, wife, and authoress—
Thank God, I am content with less!

D. G. ROSSETTI

Dante Gabriel Rossetti
Buried all of his *libretti*,
Thought the matter over—then
Went and dug them up again.

THOMAS CARLYLE

Carlyle combined the lit'ry life
With throwing teacups at his wife,
Remarking, rather testily,
"Oh, stop your dodging, Mrs. C.!"

CHARLES DICKENS

Who call him spurious and shoddy
Shall do it o'er my lifeless body.
I heartily invite such birds
To come outside and say those words!

ALEXANDRE DUMAS AND HIS SON

Although I work, and seldom cease,
At Dumas *père* and Dumas *fils*,
Alas, I cannot make me care
For Dumas *fils* and Dumas *père*.

ALFRED, LORD TENNYSON

Should Heaven send me any son,
I hope he's not like Tennyson.
I'd rather have him play a fiddle
Than rise and bow and speak an idyll.

GEORGE GISSING

When I admit neglect of Gissing,
They say I don't know what I'm missing.
Until their arguments are subtler,
I think I'll stick to Samuel Butler.

WALTER SAVAGE LANDOR

Upon the work of Walter Landor
I am unfit to write with candor.
If you can read it, well and good;
But as for me, I never could.

GEORGE SAND

What time the gifted lady took
Away from paper, pen, and book,
She spent in amorous dalliance
(They do those things so well in France).

MORTAL ENEMY

Let another cross his way—
    She's the one will do the weeping!
Little need I fear he'll stray
    Since I have his heart in keeping.

Let another hail him dear—
    Little chance that he'll forget me!
Only need I curse and fear
    Her he loved before he met me.

PENELOPE

In the pathway of the sun,
    In the footsteps of the breeze,
Where the world and sky are one,
    He shall ride the silver seas,
        He shall cut the glittering wave.
I shall sit at home, and rock;
Rise, to heed a neighbor's knock;
Brew my tea, and snip my thread;
Bleach the linen for my bed.
        They will call him brave.

BOHEMIA

Authors and actors and artists and such
Never know nothing, and never know much.
Sculptors and singers and those of their kidney
Tell their affairs from Seattle to Sydney.
Playwrights and poets and such horses' necks
Start off from anywhere, end up at sex.
Diarists, critics, and similar roe
Never say nothing, and never say no.
People Who Do Things exceed my endurance;
God, for a man that solicits insurance!

THE SEARCHED SOUL

When I consider, pro and con,
What things my love is built upon—
A curly mouth; a sinewed wrist;
A questioning brow; a pretty twist
Of words as old and tried as sin;
A pointed ear; a cloven chin;
Long, tapered limbs; and slanted eyes
Not cold nor kind nor darkly wise—
When so I ponder, here apart,
What shallow boons suffice my heart,
What dust-bound trivia capture me,
I marvel at my normalcy.

THE TRUSTING HEART

Oh, I'd been better dying,
  Oh, I was slow and sad;
A fool I was, a-crying
  About a cruel lad!

But there was one that found me,
  That wept to see me weep,
And had his arm around me,
  And gave me words to keep.

And I'd be better dying,
  And I am slow and sad;
A fool I am, a-crying
  About a tender lad!

THOUGHT FOR A SUNSHINY MORNING

It costs me never a stab nor squirm
To tread by chance upon a worm.
"Aha, my little dear," I say,
"Your clan will pay me back one day."

THE GENTLEST LADY

They say He was a serious child,
  And quiet in His ways;
They say the gentlest lady smiled
  To hear the neighbors' praise.

The coffers of her heart would close
  Upon their smallest word.
Yet did they say, "How tall He grows!"
  They thought she had not heard.

They say upon His birthday eve
  She'd rock Him to His rest
As if she could not have Him leave
  The shelter of her breast.

The poor must go in bitter thrift,
  The poor must give in pain,
But ever did she set a gift
  To greet His day again.

They say she'd kiss the Boy awake,
  And hail Him gay and clear,
But oh, her heart was like to break
  To count another year.

THE MAID-SERVANT AT THE INN

"It's queer," she said; "I see the light
   As plain as I beheld it then,
All silver-like and calm and bright—
   We've not had stars like that again!

"And she was such a gentle thing
   To birth a baby in the cold.
The barn was dark and frightening—
   This new one's better than the old.

"I mind my eyes were full of tears,
   For I was young, and quick distressed,
But she was less than me in years
   That held a son against her breast.

"I never saw a sweeter child—
   The little one, the darling one! —
I mind I told her, when he smiled
   You'd know he was his mother's son.

"It's queer that I should see them so—
   The time they came to Bethlehem
Was more than thirty years ago;
   I've prayed that all is well with them."

FULFILLMENT

For this my mother wrapped me warm,
And called me home against the storm,
And coaxed my infant nights to quiet,
And gave me roughage in my diet,
And tucked me in my bed at eight,
And clipped my hair, and marked my weight,
And watched me as I sat and stood:
That I might grow to womanhood
To hear a whistle and drop my wits
And break my heart to clattering bits.

DAYLIGHT SAVING

My answers are inadequate
To those demanding day and date.
And ever set a tiny shock
Through strangers asking what's o'clock;
Whose days are spent in whittling rhyme—
What's time to her, or she to Time?

SURPRISE

My heart went fluttering with fear
Lest you should go, and leave me here
To beat my breast and rock my head
And stretch me sleepless on my bed.
Ah, clear they see and true they say
That one shall weep, and one shall stray
For such is Love's unvarying law. . . .
I never thought, I never saw
That I should be the first to go;
How pleasant that it happened so!

ON BEING A WOMAN

Why is it, when I am in Rome,
I'd give an eye to be at home,
But when on native earth I be,
My soul is sick for Italy?

And why with you, my love, my lord,
Am I spectacularly bored,
Yet do you up and leave me—then
I scream to have you back again?

AFTERNOON

When I am old, and comforted,
  And done with this desire,
With Memory to share my bed
  And Peace to share my fire,

I'll comb my hair in scalloped bands
  Beneath my laundered cap,
And watch my cool and fragile hands
  Lie light upon my lap.

And I will have a spriggèd gown
  With lace to kiss my throat;
I'll draw my curtain to the town,
  And hum a purring note.

And I'll forget the way of tears,
  And rock, and stir my tea.
But oh, I wish those blessed years
  Were further than they be!

A DREAM LIES DEAD

A dream lies dead here. May you softly go
Before this place, and turn away your eyes,
Nor seek to know the look of that which dies
Importuning Life for life. Walk not in woe,
But, for a little, let your step be slow.
And, of your mercy, be not sweetly wise
With words of hope and Spring and tenderer skies.
A dream lies dead; and this all mourners know:

Whenever one drifted petal leaves the tree—
Though white of bloom as it had been before
And proudly waitful of fecundity—
One little loveliness can be no more;
And so must Beauty bow her imperfect head
Because a dream has joined the wistful dead!

THE HOMEBODY

There still are kindly things for me to know,
Who am afraid to dream, afraid to feel—
This little chair of scrubbed and sturdy deal,
This easy book, this fire, sedate and slow.
And I shall stay with them, nor cry the woe
Of wounds across my breast that do not heal;
Nor wish that Beauty drew a duller steel,
Since I am sworn to meet her as a foe.

It may be, when the devil's own time is done,
That I shall hear the dropping of the rain
At midnight, and lie quiet in my bed;
Or stretch and straighten to the yellow sun;
Or face the turning tree, and have no pain;
So shall I learn at last my heart is dead.

SECOND LOVE

"So surely is she mine," you say, and turn
Your quick and steady mind to harder things—
To bills and bonds and talk of what men earn—
And whistle up the stair, of evenings.
And do you see a dream behind my eyes,
Or ask a simple question twice of me—
"Thus women are," you say; for men are wise
And tolerant, in their security.

How shall I count the midnights I have known
When calm you turn to me, nor feel me start,
To find my easy lips upon your own
And know my breast beneath your rhythmic heart.
Your god defer the day I tell you this:
My lad, my lad, it is not you I kiss!

FAIR WEATHER

This level reach of blue is not my sea;
Here are sweet waters, pretty in the sun,
Whose quiet ripples meet obediently
A marked and measured line, one after one.
This is no sea of mine, that humbly laves
Untroubled sands, spread glittering and warm.
I have a need of wilder, crueler waves;
They sicken of the calm, who knew the storm.

So let a love beat over me again,
Loosing its million desperate breakers wide;
Sudden and terrible to rise and wane;
Roaring the heavens apart; a reckless tide
That casts upon the heart, as it recedes,
Splinters and spars and dripping, salty weeds.

THE WHISTLING GIRL

Back of my back, they talk of me,
  Gabble and honk and hiss;
Let them batten, and let them be—
  Me, I can sing them this:

"Better to shiver beneath the stars,
  Head on a faithless breast,
Than peer at the night through rusted bars,
  And share an irksome rest.

"Better to see the dawn come up,
  Along of a trifling one,
Than set a steady man's cloth and cup
  And pray the day be done.

"Better be left by twenty dears
  Than lie in a loveless bed;
Better a loaf that's wet with tears
  Than cold, unsalted bread."

Back of my back, they wag their chins,
  Whinny and bleat and sigh;
But better a heart a-bloom with sins
  Than hearts gone yellow and dry!

STORY

"And if he's gone away," said she,
"Good riddance, if you're asking me.
I'm not a one to lie awake
And weep for anybody's sake.
There's better lads than him about!
I'll wear my buckled slippers out
A-dancing till the break of day.
I'm better off with him away!
And if he never come," said she,
"Now what on earth is that to me?
I wouldn't have him back!"
                                        I hope
Her mother washed her mouth with soap.

FRUSTRATION

If I had a shiny gun,
I could have a world of fun
Speeding bullets through the brains
Of the folk who give me pains;

Or had I some poison gas,
I could make the moments pass
Bumping off a number of
People whom I do not love.

But I have no lethal weapon—
Thus does Fate our pleasure step on!
So they still are quick and well
Who should be, by rights, in hell.

HEALED

Oh, when I flung my heart away,
  The year was at its fall.
I saw my dear, the other day,
  Beside a flowering wall;
And this was all I had to say:
  "I thought that he was tall!"

LANDSCAPE

Now this must be the sweetest place
   From here to heaven's end;
The field is white with flowering lace,
   The birches leap and bend,

The hills, beneath the roving sun,
   From green to purple pass,
And little, trifling breezes run
   Their fingers through the grass.

So good it is, so gay it is,
   So calm it is, and pure,
A one whose eyes may look on this
   Must be the happier, sure.

But me—I see it flat and gray
   And blurred with misery,
Because a lad a mile away
   Has little need of me.

POST-GRADUATE

Hope it was that tutored me,
And Love that taught me more;
And now I learn at Sorrow's knee
The self-same lore.

FOR A FAVORITE GRANDDAUGHTER

Never love a simple lad,
  Guard against a wise,
Shun a timid youth and sad,
  Hide from haunted eyes.

Never hold your heart in pain
  For an evil-doer;
Never flip it down the lane
  To a gifted wooer.

Never love a loving son,
  Nor a sheep astray;
Gather up your skirts and run
  From a tender way.

Never give away a tear,
  Never toss and pine;
Should you heed my words, my dear,
  You're no blood of mine!

LIEBESTOD

When I was bold, when I was bold–
  And that's a hundred years! –
Oh, never I thought my breast could hold
  The terrible weight of tears.

I said: "Now some be dolorous;
  I hear them wail and sigh,
And if it be Love that play them thus,
  Then never a love will I."

I said: "I see them rack and rue,
  I see them wring and ache,
And little I'll crack my heart in two
  With little the heart can break."

When I was gay, when I was gay–
  It's ninety years and nine! –
Oh, never I thought that Death could lay
  His terrible hand in mine.

I said: "He plies his trade among
  The musty and infirm;
A body so hard and bright and young
  Could never be meat for worm."

"I see him dull their eyes," I said,
"And still their rattling breath.
And how under God could I be dead
That never was meant for Death?"

But Love came by, to quench my sleep,
And here's my sundered heart;
And bitter's my woe, and black, and deep,
And little I guessed a part.

Yet this there is to cool my breast,
And this to ease my spell;
Now if I were Love's, like all the rest,
Then can I be Death's, as well.

And he shall have me, sworn and bound,
And I'll be done with Love.
And better I'll be below the ground
Than ever I'll be above.

DILEMMA

If I were mild, and I were sweet,
And laid my heart before your feet,
And took my dearest thoughts to you,
And hailed your easy lies as true;
Were I to murmur "Yes," and then
"How true, my dear," and "Yes," again,
And wear my eyes discreetly down,
And tremble whitely at your frown,
And keep my words unquestioning—
My love, you'd run like anything!

Should I be frail, and I be mad,
And share my heart with every lad,
But beat my head against the floor
What times you wandered past my door;
Were I to doubt, and I to sneer,
And shriek "Farewell!" and still be here,
And break your joy, and quench your trust—
I should not see you for the dust!

THEORY

Into love and out again,
  Thus I went, and thus I go.
Spare your voice, and hold your pen—
  Well and bitterly I know
All the songs were ever sung,
  All the words were ever said;
Could it be, when I was young,
  Some one dropped me on my head?

A FAIRLY SAD TALE

I think that I shall never know
Why I am thus, and I am so.
Around me, other girls inspire
In men the rush and roar of fire,
The sweet transparency of glass,
The tenderness of April grass,
The durability of granite;
But me—I don't know how to plan it.
The lads I've met in Cupid's deadlock
Were—shall we say?—born out of wedlock.
They broke my heart, they stilled my song,
And said they had to run along,
Explaining, so to sop my tears,
First came their parents or careers.
But ever does experience
Deny me wisdom, calm, and sense!
Though she's a fool who seeks to capture
The twenty-first fine, careless rapture,
I must go on, till ends my rope,
Who from my birth was cursed with hope.
A heart in half is chaste, archaic;
But mine resembles a mosaic—
The thing's become ridiculous!
Why am I so? Why am I thus?

THE LAST QUESTION

New love, new love, where are you to lead me?
  All along a narrow way that marks a crooked line.
How are you to slake me, and how are you to feed me?
  With bitter yellow berries, and a sharp new wine.

New love, new love, shall I be forsaken?
  One shall go a-wandering, and one of us must sigh.
Sweet it is to slumber, but how shall we awaken—
  Whose will be the broken heart, when dawn comes by?

SUPERFLUOUS ADVICE

Should they whisper false of you,
  Never trouble to deny;
Should the words they say be true,
  Weep and storm and swear they lie.

BUT NOT FORGOTTEN

I think, no matter where you stray,
That I shall go with you a way.
Though you may wander sweeter lands,
You will not soon forget my hands,
Nor yet the way I held my head,
Nor all the tremulous things I said.
You still will see me, small and white
And smiling, in the secret night,
And feel my arms about you when
The day comes fluttering back again.
I think, no matter where you be,
You'll hold me in your memory
And keep my image, there without me,
By telling later loves about me.

TWO-VOLUME NOVEL

The sun's gone dim, and
 The moon's turned black;
For I loved him, and
 He didn't love back.

POUR PRENDRE CONGÉ

I'm sick of embarking in dories
    Upon an emotional sea.
I'm wearied of playing Dolores
    (A role never written for me).

I'll never again like a cub lick
    My wounds while I squeal at the hurt.
No more I'll go walking in public,
    My heart hanging out of my shirt.

I'm tired of entwining me garlands
    Of weather-worn hemlock and bay.
I'm over my longing for far lands—
    I wouldn't give that for Cathay.

I'm through with performing the ballet
    Of love unrequited and told.
Euterpe, I tender you *vale*;
    Good-by, and take care of that cold.

I'm done with this burning and giving
    And reeling the rhymes of my woes.
And how I'll be making my living,
    The Lord in His mystery knows.

FOR A LADY WHO MUST WRITE VERSE

Unto seventy years and seven,
   Hide your double birthright well—
You, that are the brat of Heaven
   And the pampered heir to Hell.

Let your rhymes be tinsel treasures,
   Strung and seen and thrown aside.
Drill your apt and docile measures
   Sternly as you drill your pride.

Show your quick, alarming skill in
   Tidy mockeries of art;
Never, never dip your quill in
   Ink that rushes from your heart.

When your pain must come to paper,
   See it dust, before the day;
Let your night light curl and caper,
   Let it lick the words away.

Never print, poor child, a lay on
   Love and tears and anguishing,
Lest a cooled, benignant Phaon
   Murmur, "Silly little thing!"

RHYME AGAINST LIVING

If wild my breast and sore my pride,
I bask in dreams of suicide;
If cool my heart and high my head,
I think, "How lucky are the dead!"

WISDOM

This I say, and this I know:
  Love has seen the last of me.
Love's a trodden lane to woe,
  Love's a path to misery.

This I know, and knew before,
  This I tell you, of my years:
Hide your heart, and lock your door.
  Hell's afloat in lovers' tears.

Give your heart, and toss and moan;
  What a pretty fool you look!
I am sage, who sit alone;
  Here's my wool, and here's my book.

Look! A lad's a-waiting there,
  Tall he is and bold, and gay.
What the devil do I care
  What I know, and what I say?

CODA

There's little in taking or giving,
  There's little in water or wine;
This living, this living, this living
  Was never a project of mine.
Oh, hard is the struggle, and sparse is
  The gain of the one at the top,
For art is a form of catharsis,
  And love is a permanent flop,
And work is the province of cattle,
  And rest's for a clam in a shell,
So I'm thinking of throwing the battle—
  Would you kindly direct me to hell?

DEATH AND TAXES AND OTHER POEMS

PRAYER FOR A PRAYER

Dearest one, when I am dead
   Never seek to follow me.
      Never mount the quiet hill
      Where the copper leaves are still,
   As my heart is, on the tree
Standing at my narrow bed.

Only, of your tenderness,
   Pray a little prayer at night.
      Say: "I have forgiven now—
      I, so weak and sad; O Thou,
   Wreathed in thunder, robed in light,
Surely Thou wilt do no less."

AFTER A SPANISH PROVERB

Oh, mercifullest one of all,
   Oh, generous as dear,
None lived so lowly, none so small,
   Thou couldst withhold thy tear:

How swift, in pure compassion,
   How meek in charity,
To offer friendship to the one
   Who begged but love of thee!

Oh, gentle word, and sweetest said!
   Oh, tender hand, and first
To hold the warm, delicious bread
   To lips burned black of thirst.

THE FLAW IN PAGANISM

Drink and dance and laugh and lie,
   Love, the reeling midnight through.
For tomorrow we shall die!
   (But, alas, we never do.)

THE DANGER OF WRITING DEFIANT VERSE

And now I have another lad!
  No longer need you tell
How all my nights are slow and sad
  For loving you too well.

His ways are not your wicked ways,
  He's not the like of you.
He treads his path of reckoned days,
  A sober man, and true.

They'll never see him in the town,
  Another on his knee.
He'd cut his laden orchards down,
  If that would pleasure me.

He'd give his blood to paint my lips
  If I should wish them red.
He prays to touch my finger-tips
  Or stroke my prideful head.

He never weaves a glinting lie,
  Or brags the hearts he'll keep.
I have forgotten how to sigh—
  Remembered how to sleep.

He's none to kiss away my mind—
A slower way is his.
Oh, Lord! On reading this, I find
A silly lot he is.

DISTANCE

Were you to cross the world, my dear,
  To work or love or fight,
I could be calm and wistful here,
  And close my eyes at night.

It were a sweet and gallant pain
  To be a sea apart;
But, oh, to have you down the lane
  Is bitter to my heart.

THE EVENING PRIMROSE

You know the bloom, unearthly white,
That none has seen by morning light—
The tender moon, alone, may bare
Its beauty to the secret air.
Who'd venture past its dark retreat
Must kneel, for holy things and sweet.
That blossom, mystically blown,
No man may gather for his own
Nor touch it, lest it droop and fall. . . .
Oh, I am not like that at all!

SANCTUARY

My land is bare of chattering folk;
  The clouds are low along the ridges,
And sweet's the air with curly smoke
  From all my burning bridges.

CHERRY WHITE

I never see that prettiest thing—
A cherry bough gone white with Spring—
But what I think, "How gay 'twould be
To hang me from a flowering tree."

SALOME'S DANCING-LESSON

She that begs a little boon
  (*Heel and toe! Heel and toe!*)
Little gets—and nothing, soon.
  (*No, no, no! No, no, no!*)
She that calls for costly things
Priceless finds her offerings—
What's impossible to kings?
  (*Heel and toe! Heel and toe!*)

Kings are shaped as other men.
  (*Step and turn! Step and turn!*)
Ask what none may ask again.
  (*Will you learn? Will you learn?*)
Lovers whine, and kisses pall,
Jewels tarnish, kingdoms fall—
Death's the rarest prize of all!
  (*Step and turn! Step and turn!*)

Veils are woven to be dropped.
  (*One, two, three! One, two, three!*)
Aging eyes are slowest stopped.
  (*Quietly! Quietly!*)
She whose body's young and cool
Has no need of dancing-school—
Scratch a king and find a fool!
  (*One, two, three! One, two, three!*)

MY OWN

Then let them point my every tear,
　And let them mock and moan;
Another week, another year,
　And I'll be with my own

Who slumber now by night and day
　In fields of level brown;
Whose hearts within their breasts were clay
　Before they laid them down.

SOLACE

There was a rose that faded young;
I saw its shattered beauty hung
   Upon a broken stem.
I heard them say, "What need to care
With roses budding everywhere?"
   I did not answer them.

There was a bird, brought down to die;
They said, "A hundred fill the sky—
   What reason to be sad?"
There was a girl, whose lover fled;
I did not wait, the while they said,
   "There's many another lad."

LITTLE WORDS

When you are gone, there is nor bloom nor leaf,
  Nor singing sea at night, nor silver birds;
And I can only stare, and shape my grief
  In little words.

I cannot conjure loveliness, to drown
  The bitter woe that racks my cords apart.
The weary pen that sets my sorrow down
  Feeds at my heart.

There is no mercy in the shifting year,
  No beauty wraps me tenderly about.
I turn to little words—so you, my dear,
  Can spell them out.

ORNITHOLOGY FOR BEGINNERS

The bird that feeds from off my palm
Is sleek, affectionate, and calm,
But double, to me, is worth the thrush
A-flickering in the elder-bush.

GARDEN-SPOT

God's acre was her garden-spot, she said;
She sat there often, of the Summer days,
Little and slim and sweet, among the dead,
Her hair a fable in the leveled rays.

She turned the fading wreath, the rusted cross,
And knelt to coax about the wiry stem.
I see her gentle fingers on the moss
Now it is anguish to remember them.

And once I saw her weeping when she rose
And walked a way and turned to look around
The quick and envious tears of one that knows
She shall not lie in consecrated ground.

TOMBSTONES IN THE STARLIGHT

I. THE MINOR POET

His little trills and chirpings were his best.
No music like the nightingale's was born
Within his throat; but he, too, laid his breast
Upon a thorn.

II. THE PRETTY LADY

She hated bleak and wintry things alone.
All that was warm and quick, she loved too well—
A light, a flame, a heart against her own;
It is forever bitter cold, in Hell.

III. THE VERY RICH MAN

He'd have the best, and that was none too good;
No barrier could hold, before his terms.
He lies below, correct in cypress wood,
And entertains the most exclusive worms.

IV. THE FISHERWOMAN

The man she had was kind and clean
  And well enough for every day,
But, oh, dear friends, you should have seen
  The one that got away!

V. THE CRUSADER

Arrived in Heaven, when his sands were run,
  He seized a quill, and sat him down to tell
The local press that something should be done
  About that noisy nuisance, Gabriel.

VI. THE ACTRESS

Her name, cut clear upon this marble cross,
  Shines, as it shone when she was still on earth;
While tenderly the mild, agreeable moss
  Obscures the figures of her date of birth.

THE LITTLE OLD LADY IN LAVENDER SILK

I was seventy-seven, come August,
    I shall shortly be losing my bloom;
I've experienced zephyr and raw gust
    And (symbolical) flood and simoom.

When you come to this time of abatement,
    To this passing from Summer to Fall,
It is manners to issue a statement
    As to what you got out of it all.

So I'll say, though reflection unnerves me
    And pronouncements I dodge as I can,
That I think (if my memory serves me)
    There was nothing more fun than a man!

In my youth, when the crescent was too wan
    To embarrass with beams from above,
By the aid of some local Don Juan
    I fell into the habit of love.

And I learned how to kiss and be merry—an
    Education left better unsung.
My neglect of the waters Pierian
    Was a scandal, when Grandma was young.

Though the shabby unbalanced the splendid,
  And the bitter outmeasured the sweet,
I should certainly do as I then did,
  Were I given the chance to repeat.

For contrition is hollow and wraithful,
  And regret is no part of my plan,
And I think (if my memory's faithful)
  There was nothing more fun than a man!

VERS DÉMODÉ

For one, the amaryllis and the rose;
  The poppy, sweet as never lilies are;
The ripen'd vine, that beckons as it blows;
  The dancing star.

For one, the trodden rosemary and rue;
  The bowl, dipt ever in the purple stream.
And, for the other one, a fairer due—
  Sleep, and no dream.

SONNET FOR THE END OF A SEQUENCE

So take my vows and scatter them to sea;
Who swears the sweetest is no more than human.
And say no kinder words than these of me:
"Ever she longed for peace, but was a woman!
And thus they are, whose silly female dust
Needs little enough to clutter it and bind it,
Who meet a slanted gaze, and ever must
Go build themselves a soul to dwell behind it."

For now I am my own again, my friend!
This scar but points the whiteness of my breast;
This frenzy, like its betters, spins an end,
And now I am my own. And that is best.
Therefore, I am immeasurably grateful
To you, for proving shallow, false, and hateful.

THE APPLE TREE

When first we saw the apple tree
  The boughs were dark and straight,
But never grief to give had we,
  Though Spring delayed so late.

When last I came away from there
  The boughs were heavy hung,
But little grief had I to spare
  For Summer, perished young.

ISEULT OF BRITTANY

So delicate my hands, and long,
They might have been my pride.
And there were those to make them song
Who for their touch had died.

Too frail to cup a heart within,
Too soft to hold the free—
How long these lovely hands have been
A bitterness to me!

"STAR LIGHT, STAR BRIGHT—"

Star, that gives a gracious dole,
  What am I to choose?
Oh, will it be a shriven soul,
  Or little buckled shoes?

Shall I wish a wedding-ring,
  Bright and thin and round,
Or plead you send me covering—
  A newly spaded mound?

Gentle beam, shall I implore
  Gold, or sailing-ships,
Or beg I hate forevermore
  A pair of lying lips?

Swing you low or high away,
  Burn you hot or dim;
My only wish I dare not say—
  Lest you should grant me him.

THE SEA

Who lay against the sea, and fled,
  Who lightly loved the wave,
Shall never know, when he is dead,
  A cool and murmurous grave.

But in a shallow pit shall rest
  For all eternity,
And bear the earth upon the breast
  That once had worn the sea.

GUINEVERE AT HER FIRESIDE

A nobler king had never breath—
  I say it now, and said it then.
Who weds with such is wed till death
  And wedded stays in Heaven. Amen.

(And oh, the shirts of linen-lawn,
  And all the armor, tagged and tied,
And church on Sundays, dusk and dawn,
  And bed a thing to kneel beside!)

The bravest one stood tall above
  The rest, and watched me as a light.
I heard and heard them talk of love;
  I'd naught to do but think, at night.

The bravest man has littlest brains;
  That chalky fool from Astolat
With all her dying and her pains!—
  Thank God, I helped him over that.

I found him not unfair to see—
  I like a man with peppered hair!
And thus it came about. Ah, me,
  Tristram was busied otherwhere. . . .

A nobler king had never breath—
I say it now, and said it then.
Who weds with such is wed till death
And wedded stays in Heaven. Amen.

TRANSITION

Too long and quickly have I lived to vow
   The woe that stretches me shall never wane,
   Too often seen the end of endless pain
To swear that peace no more shall cool my brow.
I know, I know—again the shriveled bough
   Will burgeon sweetly in the gentle rain,
   And these hard lands be quivering with grain—
I tell you only: it is Winter now.

What if I know, before the Summer goes
Where dwelt this bitter frenzy shall be rest?
What is it now, that June shall surely bring
New promise, with the swallow and the rose?
My heart is water, that I first must breast
The terrible, slow loveliness of Spring.

LINES ON READING TOO MANY POETS

Roses, rooted warm in earth,
  Bud in rhyme, another age;
Lilies know a ghostly birth
  Strewn along a patterned page;
Golden lad and chimbley sweep
Die; and so their song shall keep.

Wind that in Arcadia starts
  In and out a couplet plays;
And the drums of bitter hearts
  Beat the measure of a phrase.
Sweets and woes but come to print
Quae cum ita sint.

FROM A LETTER FROM LESBIA

. . . So, praise the gods, at last he's away!
And let me tend you this advice, my dear:
Take any lover that you will, or may,
Except a poet. All of them are queer.

It's just the same—a quarrel or a kiss
Is but a tune to play upon his pipe.
He's always hymning that or wailing this;
Myself, I much prefer the business type.

That thing he wrote, the time the sparrow died—
(Oh, most unpleasant—gloomy, tedious words!)
I called it sweet, and made believe I cried;
The stupid fool! I've always hated birds. . . .

BALLADE OF UNFORTUNATE MAMMALS

Love is sharper than stones or sticks;
   Lone as the sea, and deeper blue;
Loud in the night as a clock that ticks;
   Longer-lived than the Wandering Jew.
Show me a love was done and through,
   Tell me a kiss escaped its debt!
Son, to your death you'll pay your due—
   Women and elephants never forget.

Ever a man, alas, would mix,
   Ever a man, heigh-ho, must woo;
So he's left in the world-old fix,
   Thus is furthered the sale of rue.
Son, your chances are thin and few—
   Won't you ponder, before you're set?
Shoot if you must, but hold in view
   Women and elephants never forget.

Down from Cæsar past Joynson-Hicks
   Echoes the warning, ever new:
Though they're trained to amusing tricks,
   Gentler, they, than the pigeon's coo,
Careful, son, of the cursèd two—
   Either one is a dangerous pet;
Natural history proves it true—
   Women and elephants never forget.

L'ENVOI

Prince, a precept I'd leave for you,
    Coined in Eden, existing yet:
Skirt the parlor, and shun the zoo—
    Women and elephants never forget.

PURPOSELY UNGRAMMATICAL LOVE SONG

There's many and many, and not so far,
   Is willing to dry my tears away;
There's many to tell me what you are,
   And never a lie to all they say.

It's little the good to hide my head,
   It's never the use to bar my door;
There's many as counts the tears I shed,
   There's mourning hearts for my heart is sore.

There's honester eyes than your blue eyes,
   There's better a mile than such as you.
But when did I say that I was wise,
   And when did I hope that you were true?

PRAYER FOR A NEW MOTHER

The things she knew, let her forget again—
  The voices in the sky, the fear, the cold,
The gaping shepherds, and the queer old men
  Piling their clumsy gifts of foreign gold.

Let her have laughter with her little one;
  Teach her the endless, tuneless songs to sing;
Grant her her right to whisper to her son
  The foolish names one dare not call a king.

Keep from her dreams the rumble of a crowd,
  The smell of rough-cut wood, the trail of red,
The thick and chilly whiteness of the shroud
  That wraps the strange new body of the dead.

Ah, let her go, kind Lord, where mothers go
  And boast his pretty words and ways, and plan
The proud and happy years that they shall know
  Together, when her son is grown a man.

MIDNIGHT

The stars are soft as flowers, and as near;
    The hills are webs of shadow, slowly spun;
No separate leaf or single blade is here—
    All blend to one.

No moonbeam cuts the air; a sapphire light
    Rolls lazily, and slips again to rest.
There is no edgèd thing in all this night,
    Save in my breast.

NINON DE LENCLOS, ON HER LAST BIRTHDAY

So let me have the rouge again,
   And comb my hair the curly way.
The poor young men, the dear young men—
   They'll all be here by noon today.

And I shall wear the blue, I think—
   They beg to touch its rippled lace;
Or do they love me best in pink,
   So sweetly flattering the face?

And are you sure my eyes are bright,
   And is it true my cheek is clear?
Young what's-his-name stayed half the night;
   He vows to cut his throat, poor dear!

So bring my scarlet slippers, then,
   And fetch the powder-puff to me.
The dear young men, the poor young men—
   They think I'm only seventy!

ULTIMATUM

I'm wearied of wearying love, my friend,
  Of worry and strain and doubt;
Before we begin, let us view the end,
  And maybe I'll do without.
There's never the pang that was worth the tear,
  And toss in the night I won't—
So either you do or you don't, my dear,
  Either you do or you don't!

The table is ready, so lay your cards
  And if they should augur pain,
I'll tender you ever my kind regards
  And run for the fastest train.
I haven't the will to be spent and sad;
  My heart's to be gay and true—
Then either you don't or you do, my lad,
  Either you don't or you do!

OF A WOMAN, DEAD YOUNG

(J. H., 1905–1930)

If she had been beautiful, even,
Or wiser than women about her,
Or had moved with a certain defiance;
If she had had sons at her sides,
And she with her hands on their shoulders,
Sons, to make troubled the Gods—
But where was there wonder in her?
What had she, better or eviler,
Whose days were a pattering of peas
From the pod to the bowl in her lap?

That the pine tree is blasted by lightning,
And the bowlder split raw from the mountain,
And the river dried short in its rushing—
That I can know, and be humble.
But that They who have trodden the stars
Should turn from Their echoing highway
To trample a daisy, unnoticed
In a field full of small, open flowers—
Where is Their triumph in that?
Where is Their pride, and Their vengeance?

THE WILLOW

On sweet young earth where the myrtle presses,
    Long we lay, when the May was new;
The willow was winding the moon in her tresses,
    The bud of the rose was told with dew.

And now on the brittle ground I'm lying,
    Screaming to die with the dead year's dead;
The stem of the rose is black and drying,
    The willow is tossing the wind from her head.

SONNET ON AN ALPINE NIGHT

My hand, a little raised, might press a star;
Where I may look, the frosted peaks are spun,
So shaped before Olympus was begun,
Spanned each to each, now, by a silver bar.
Thus to face Beauty have I traveled far,
But now, as if around my heart were run
Hard, lacing fingers, so I stand undone.
Of all my tears, the bitterest these are.

Who humbly followed Beauty all her ways,
Begging the brambles that her robe had passed,
Crying her name in corridors of stone,
That day shall know his weariedest of days—
When Beauty, still and suppliant at last,
Does not suffice him, once they are alone.

BALLADE OF A TALKED-OFF EAR

Daily I listen to wonder and woe,
Nightly I hearken to knave or to ace,
Telling me stories of lava and snow,
Delicate fables of ribbon and lace,
Tales of the quarry, the kill, the chase,
Longer than heaven and duller than hell—
Never you blame me, who cry my case:
"Poets alone should kiss and tell!"

Dumbly I hear what I never should know,
Gently I counsel of pride and of grace;
Into minutiæ gayly they go,
Telling the name and the time and the place.
Cede them your silence and grant them space—
Who tenders an inch shall be raped of an ell!
Sympathy's ever the boaster's brace;
Poets alone should kiss and tell.

Why am I tithed what I never did owe?
Choked with vicarious saffron and mace?
Weary my lids, and my fingers are slow—
Gentlemen, damn you, you've halted my pace.
Only the lads of the cursèd race,
Only the knights of the desolate spell,
May point me the lines the blood-drops trace—
Poets alone should kiss and tell.

L'ENVOI

Prince or commoner, tenor or bass,
Painter or plumber or never-do-well,
Do me a favor and shut your face—
Poets alone should kiss and tell.

REQUIESCAT

Tonight my love is sleeping cold
  Where none may see and none shall pass.
The daisies quicken in the mold,
  And richer fares the meadow grass.

The warding cypress pleads the skies,
  The mound goes level in the rain.
My love all cold and silent lies—
  Pray God it will not rise again!

SWEET VIOLETS

You are brief and frail and blue—
Little sisters, I am, too.
You are Heaven's masterpieces—
Little loves, the likeness ceases.

PROLOGUE TO A SAGA

Maidens, gather not the yew,
　　Leave the glossy myrtle sleeping;
Any lad was born untrue,
　　Never a one is fit your weeping.

Pretty dears, your tumult cease;
　　Love's a fardel, burthening double.
Clear your hearts, and have you peace—
　　Gangway, girls: I'll show you trouble.

SUMMARY

Every love's the love before
  In a duller dress.
That's the measure of my lore—
  Here's my bitterness:
Would I knew a little more,
  Or very much less!

SIGHT

Unseemly are the open eyes
   That watch the midnight sheep,
That look upon the secret skies
   Nor close, abashed, in sleep;

That see the dawn drag in, unbidden,
   To birth another day—
Oh, better far their gaze were hidden
   Below the decent clay.

THE LADY'S REWARD

Lady, lady, never start
Conversation toward your heart;
Keep your pretty words serene;
Never murmur what you mean.
Show yourself, by word and look,
Swift and shallow as a brook.
Be as cool and quick to go
As a drop of April snow;
Be as delicate and gay
As a cherry flower in May.
Lady, lady, never speak
Of the tears that burn your cheek—
She will never win him, whose
Words had shown she feared to lose.
Be you wise and never sad,
You will get your lovely lad.
Never serious be, nor true,
And your wish will come to you—
And if that makes you happy, kid,
You'll be the first it ever did.

PRISONER

Long I fought the driving lists,
  Plume a-stream and armor clanging;
Link on link, between my wrists,
  Now my heavy freedom's hanging.

TEMPS PERDU

I never may turn the loop of a road
   Where sudden, ahead, the sea is lying,
But my heart drags down with an ancient load—
   My heart, that a second before was flying.

I never behold the quivering rain—
   And sweeter the rain than a lover to me—
But my heart is wild in my breast with pain;
   My heart, that was tapping contentedly.

There's never a rose spreads new at my door
   Nor a strange bird crosses the moon at night
But I know I have known its beauty before,
   And a terrible sorrow along with the sight.

The look of a laurel tree birthed for May
   Or a sycamore bared for a new November
Is as old and as sad as my furtherest day—
   What is it, what is it, I almost remember?

AUTUMN VALENTINE

In May my heart was breaking—
   Oh, wide the wound, and deep!
And bitter it beat at waking,
   And sore it split in sleep.

And when it came November,
   I sought my heart, and sighed,
"Poor thing, do you remember?"
   "What heart was that?" it cried.

INDEX OF FIRST LINES

PAGE

Accursed from their birth they be 115
All her hours were yellow sands 30
Although I work, and seldom cease 123
Always I knew that it could not last 97
"And if he's gone away," said she 143
And if, my friend, you'd have it end 59
And if my heart be scarred and burned 119
And let her loves, when she is dead 37
And now I have another lad! 168
Arrived in Heaven, when his sands were run 181
Authors and actors and artists and such 127

Back of my back, they talk of me 142
Because my love is quick to come and go 48
Because your eyes are slant and slow 65
Bird that feeds from off my palm, The 178
By the time you swear you're his 52
Byron and Shelley and Keats 122

Carlyle combined the lit'ry life 123
Chloe's hair, no doubt, was brighter 63

Daily dawns another day 95
Daily I listen to wonder and woe 205
Dante Gabriel Rossetti 123

Day that I was christened, The 105
Days will rally, wreathing, The 29
Dear dead Victoria 109
Dearest one, when I am dead 165
Death's the lover that I'd be taking 16
Dream lies dead here. May you softly go, A 138
Drink and dance and laugh and lie 167

Every love's the love before 210

First time I died, I walked my ways, The 22
For one, the amaryllis and the rose 184
For this my mother wrapped me warm 133
Four be the things I am wiser to know 53
Friends I made have slipped and strayed, The 79

Ghosts of all my lovely sins 35
Go I must along my ways 121
God's acre was her garden-spot, she said 179

Half across the world from me 33
He will love you presently 31
He'd have given me rolling lands 93
He'd have the best, and that was none too good 180
Helen of Troy had a wandering glance 80
Her mind lives in a quiet room 114
Her name, cut clear upon this marble cross 181
Here in my heart I am Helen 83
His little trills and chirpings were his best 180
Hope it was that tutored me 147
How shall I wail, that wasn't meant for weeping? 19

I always saw, I always said 108
I cannot rest, I cannot rest 42

I do not like my state of mind 89
I know I have been happiest at your side 43
I met a man the other day 110
I never may turn the loop of a road 214
I never see that prettiest thing 173
I shall come back without fanfaronade 45
I shall tread, another year 32
I think, no matter where you stray 156
I think that I shall never know 153
I was seventy-seven, come August 182
If I don't drive around the park 88
If I had a shiny gun 144
If I should labor through daylight and dark 77
If I were mild, and I were sweet 151
If it shine or if it rain 34
If she had been beautiful, even 202
If wild my breast and sore my pride 160
If, with the literate, I am 122
If you should sail for Trebizond, or die 47
I'm sick of embarking in dories 158
I'm wearied of wearying love, my friend 201
In April, in April 18
In May my heart was breaking 215
In the pathway of the sun 126
In youth, it was a way I had 76
Into love and out again 152
It costs me never a stab nor squirm 130
"It's queer," she said; "I see the light 132

Joy stayed with me a night 23

Ladies men admire, I've heard, The 98
Lady, if you'd slumber sound 78
Lady, lady, never start 212

Lady, lady, should you meet 70
Leave me to my lonely pillow 57
Let another cross his way 125
Lilacs blossom just as sweet 13
Little things that no one needs 113
Little white love, your way you've taken 54
Long I fought the driving lists 213
Love has gone a-rocketing 24
Love has had his way with me 101
Love is sharper than stones or sticks 195

Maidens, gather not the yew 209
Man she had was kind and clean, The 180
Men seldom make passes 82
My answers are inadequate 134
My garden blossoms pink and white 39
My hand, a little raised, might press a star 204
My heart went fluttering with fear 135
My land is bare of chattering folk 172
My own dear love, he is strong and bold 75

Needle, needle, dip and dart 25
Never love a simple lad 148
New love, new love, where are you to lead me? 154
No more my little song comes back 14
Nobler king had never breath, A 190
Now this must be the sweetest place 146

Oh, gallant was the first love, and glittering and fine 96
Oh, I can smile for you, and tilt my head 87
Oh, I should like to ride the seas 68
Oh, I'd been better dying 129
Oh, is it, then, Utopian 58
Oh, lead me to a quiet cell 49

Oh, let it be a night of lyric rain 44
Oh, life is a glorious cycle of song 55
Oh, mercifullest one of all 166
Oh, ponder, friend, the porcupine 111
Oh, seek, my love, your newer way 67
Oh, there once was a lady, and so I've been told 120
Oh, when I flung my heart away 145
On sweet young earth where the myrtle presses 203
Once, when I was young and true 17

Pure and worthy Mrs. Stowe, The 122

Razors pain you 62
Roses, rooted warm in earth 193

Same to me are somber days and gay, The 90
Say my love is easy had 92
Secrets, you said, would hold us two apart 56
She hated bleak and wintry things alone 180
She that begs a little boon 174
She's passing fair; but so demure is she 86
Should Heaven send me any son 124
Should they whisper false of you 155
Single flow'r he sent me, since we met, A 71
Sleep, pretty lady, the night is enfolding you 84
So delicate my hands, and long 187
So let me have the rouge again 200
So, praise the gods, at last he's away! 194
So silent I when Love was by 28
"So surely is she mine," you say, and turn 140
So take my vows and scatter them to sea 185
Some men break your heart in two 99
Some men, some men 50
Star, that gives a gracious dole 188

Stars are soft as flowers, and as near, The 199
String of shiny days we had, A 40
Such glorious faith as fills your limpid eyes 66
Sun's gone dim, and, The 157

Then let them point my every tear 175
"Then we will have tonight!" we said 116
There still are kindly things for me to know 139
There was a rose that faded young 176
There was one a-riding grand 117
There's little in taking or giving 162
There's little to have but the things I had 60
There's many and many, and not so far 197
They hail you as their morning star 81
They hurried here, as soon as you had died 46
They laid their hands upon my head 15
They say He was a serious child 131
They say of me, and so they should 100
Things she knew, let her forget again, The 198
This I say, and this I know 161
This is what I vow 27
This level reach of blue is not my sea 141
This, no song of an ingénue 72
Tonight my love is sleeping cold 207
Too long and quickly have I lived to vow 192
Travel, trouble, music, art 85

Unseemly are the open eyes 211
Unto seventy years and seven 159
Upon the work of Walter Landor 124

We shall have our little day 38
Were you to cross the world, my dear 170
What time the gifted lady took 124

When first we saw the apple tree 186
When I admit neglect of Gissing 124
When I am old, and comforted 137
When I consider, pro and con 128
When I was bold, when I was bold 149
When I was young and bold and strong 64
When my eyes are weeds 41
When you are gone, there is nor bloom nor leaf 177
Who call him spurious and shoddy 123
Who lay against the sea, and fled 189
Who was there had seen us 20
Whose love is given over-well 107
Why is it, when I am in Rome 136
With you, my heart is quiet here 74
Woman wants monogamy 94

You are brief and frail and blue 208
You know the bloom, unearthly white 171

THE SHORT STORIES OF DOROTHY PARKER

To

Lillian Hellman

FOREWORD
by Franklin P. Adams

Poets often write good prose; but never a writer of excellent prose who is not, or has not been, a poet. That goes from Dryden to Parker. Conversely, the verbose, turgid, pretentious, confused poets write prose that is thus qualified.

Dorothy Parker's stories are as tightly and compactly written as her verse—the gay and the dismal-yew-garlanded. More lasting than brass is the monument she has builded with her verse. My fame will rest, and rest safe, because in The Conning Tower of *The World* and the *New York Herald Tribune* I printed the best as well as the most quoted of her poems.

I wish I had published some—even one—of these stories. Short stories they are, but only technically. Each is a novel, and in the unbridled hands of some of the wordier novelists—and I could name you plenty—would have become a novel of at least 500,000 words. And a book of that length gets, if not always great and widespread praise, at least many long and respectful reviews.

It seems foolish of me to write a foreword to the stories, the satires, the concentrated hatreds of stupidity, pretentiousness, and hypocrisy contained in this volume. Nobody can write such ironic things unless he has a deep sense of injustice—injustice to those members of the human race who are the victims of the stupid, the pretentious, and the hypocritical. These victims, my mathematics assures me, are in the majority. Therefore Dorothy Parker likes more people than she hates . . . It occurs to me, for the first time, that one who hated the same things, and would have hated the same persons, was Abraham Lincoln.

I never was one to rank poets in one of those What-Is-Your-Favorite-Poem symposia. Nor could I tell which is my favorite story in a collection like this. (Not that there is a collection like it.) But picking one is like choosing a favorite season of the year; my favorite time is now, regardless. My favorite Dorothy Parker story is the one I am reading at the time, though I have reread them all often. I can't reread a novel. The first of these stories I remember to have read was "Big Blonde," back in the days of *The Bookman*. And "Soldiers of the Republic" is the recentest. There are no second-raters. Dorothy Parker is one of that tiny group I once described as the Dudless Authors.

I don't know you, beloved reader, but if you don't like these stories, you are some of those things that the author of these stories wouldn't care much for.

If you like *The Collected Stories of Dorothy Parker*, and this Modern Library book is your first introduction to these stories, tell her so. If you don't, tell me, whose fault, among others, this republication is.

CONTENTS

Arrangement in Black and White 231

The Sexes 236

The Wonderful Old Gentleman 241

A Telephone Call 254

Here We Are 260

Lady with a Lamp 270

Too Bad 278

Mr. Durant 290

Just a Little One 303

Horsie 308

Clothe the Naked 325

The Waltz 335

Little Curtis 340

The Little Hours 356

Big Blonde 362

From the Diary of a New York Lady 387

Soldiers of the Republic 392

Dusk Before Fireworks	397
New York to Detroit	414
Glory in the Daytime	418
The Last Tea	434
Sentiment	439
You Were Perfectly Fine	445
The Custard Heart	449

ARRANGEMENT IN BLACK AND WHITE

THE woman with the pink velvet poppies twined round the assisted gold of her hair traversed the crowded room at an interesting gait combining a skip with a sidle, and clutched the lean arm of her host.

"Now I got you!" she said. "Now you can't get away!"

"Why, hello," said her host. "Well. How are you?"

"Oh, I'm finely," she said. "Just simply finely. Listen, I want you to do me the most terrible favor. Will you? Will you please? Pretty please?"

"What is it?" said her host.

"Listen," she said. "I want to meet Walter Williams. Honestly, I'm just simply crazy about that man. Oh, when he sings! When he sings those spirituals! Well, I said to Burton, 'It's a good thing for you Walter Williams is colored,' I said, 'or you'd have lots of reason to be jealous.' I'd really love to meet him. I'd like to tell him I've heard him sing. Will you be an angel and introduce me to him?"

"Why, certainly," said her host. "I thought you'd met him. The party's for him. Where is he, anyway?"

"He's over there by the bookcase," she said. "Let's wait till those people get through talking to him. Well, I think you're simply marvelous, giving this perfectly marvelous party for him, and having him meet all these white people, and all. Isn't he terribly grateful?"

"I hope not," said her host.

"I think it's really terribly nice," she said. "I do. I don't see why on earth it isn't perfectly all right to meet colored people. I haven't any feeling at all about it—not one single bit. Burton—oh, he's just the other way. Well, you know, he comes from Virginia, and you know how they are."

"Did he come tonight?" said her host.

"No, he couldn't," she said. "I'm a regular grass widow tonight. I told him when I left, 'There's no telling what I'll do,' I said. He was just so tired out, he couldn't move. Isn't it a shame?"

"Ah," said her host.

"Wait till I tell him I met Walter Williams!" she said. "He'll just about die. Oh, we have more arguments about colored people. I talk to him like I don't know what, I get so excited. 'Oh, don't be so silly,' I say. But I must say for Burton, he's heaps broader-minded than lots of these Southerners. He's really awfully fond of colored people. Well, he says himself, he wouldn't have white servants. And you know, he had this old colored nurse, this regular old nigger mammy, and he just simply loves her. Why, every time he goes home, he goes out in the kitchen to see her. He does, really, to this day. All he says is, he says he hasn't got a word to say against colored people as long as they keep their place. He's always doing things for them—giving them clothes and I don't know what all. The only thing he says, he says he wouldn't sit down at the table with one for a million dollars. 'Oh,' I say to him, 'you make me sick, talking like that.' I'm just terrible to him. Aren't I terrible?"

"Oh, no, no, no," said her host. "No, no."

"I am," she said. "I know I am. Poor Burton! Now, me, I don't feel that way at all. I haven't the slightest feeling about colored people. Why, I'm just crazy about some of them. They're just like children—just as easy-going, and always singing and laughing and everything. Aren't they the happiest things you ever saw in your life? Honestly, it makes me laugh just to hear them. Oh, I like them. I really do. Well, now, listen, I have this colored laundress, I've had her for years, and I'm devoted to her. She's a real character. And I want to tell you, I think of her as my friend. That's the way I think of her. As I say to Burton, 'Well, for Heaven's sakes, we're all human beings!' Aren't we?"

"Yes," said her host. "Yes, indeed."

"Now this Walter Williams," she said. "I think a man like that's a real artist. I do. I think he deserves an awful lot of credit. Goodness, I'm so crazy about music or anything, I don't care *what* color he is. I honestly think if a person's an artist, nobody ought to have any feeling at all about meeting them. That's absolutely what I say to Burton. Don't you think I'm right?"

"Yes," said her host. "Oh, yes."

"That's the way I feel," she said. "I just can't understand people being narrow-minded. Why, I absolutely think it's a privilege to meet a man like Walter Williams. Yes, I do. I haven't any feeling at all. Well, my goodness, the good Lord made him, just the same as He did any of us. Didn't He?"

"Surely," said her host. "Yes, indeed."

"That's what I say," she said. "Oh, I get so furious when people are narrow-minded about colored people. It's just all I can do not to say something. Of course, I do admit when you get a bad colored man, they're simply terrible. But as I say to Burton, there are some bad white people, too, in this world. Aren't there?"

"I guess there are," said her host.

"Why, I'd really be glad to have a man like Walter Williams come to my house and sing for us, some time," she said. "Of course, I couldn't ask him on account of Burton, but I wouldn't have any feeling about it at all. Oh, can't he sing! Isn't it marvelous, the way they all have music in them? It just seems to be right *in* them. Come on, let's us go on over and talk to him. Listen, what shall I do when I'm introduced? Ought I to shake hands? Or what?"

"Why, do whatever you want," said her host.

"I guess maybe I'd better," she said. "I wouldn't for the world have him think I had any feeling. I think I'd better shake hands, just the way I would with anybody else. That's just exactly what I'll do."

They reached the tall young Negro, standing by the bookcase. The host performed introductions; the Negro bowed.

"How do you do?" he said.

The woman with the pink velvet poppies extended her hand at the length of her arm and held it so for all the world to see, until the Negro took it, shook it, and gave it back to her.

"Oh, how do you do, Mr. Williams," she said. "Well, how do you do. I've just been saying, I've enjoyed your singing so awfully much. I've been to your concerts, and we have you on the phonograph and everything. Oh, I just enjoy it!"

She spoke with great distinctness, moving her lips meticulously, as if in parlance with the deaf.

"I'm so glad," he said.

"I'm just simply crazy about that 'Water Boy' thing you sing," she said. "Honestly, I can't get it out of my head. I have my husband nearly crazy, the way I go around humming it all the time. Oh, he looks just as black as the ace of—Well. Tell me, where on earth do you ever get all those songs of yours? How do you ever get hold of them?"

"Why," he said, "there are so many different——"

"I should think you'd love singing them," she said. "It must be more fun. All those darling old spirituals—oh, I just love them! Well, what are you doing, now? Are you still keeping up your singing? Why don't you have another concert, some time?"

"I'm having one the sixteenth of this month," he said.

"Well, I'll be there," she said. "I'll be there, if I possibly can. You can count on me. Goodness, here comes a whole raft of people to talk to you. You're just a regular guest of honor! Oh, who's that girl in white? I've seen her some place."

"That's Katherine Burke," said her host.

"Good Heavens," she said, "is that Katherine Burke? Why, she looks entirely different off the stage. I thought she was much better-looking. I had no idea she was so terribly dark. Why, she looks almost like—Oh, I think she's a wonderful actress! Don't you think she's a wonderful actress, Mr. Williams? Oh, I think she's marvelous. Don't you?"

"Yes, I do," he said.

"Oh, I do, too," she said. "Just wonderful. Well, goodness, we must give someone else a chance to talk to the guest of honor. Now, don't forget, Mr. Williams, I'm going to be at that concert if I possibly can. I'll be there applauding like everything. And if I can't come, I'm going to tell everybody I know to go, anyway. Don't you forget!"

"I won't," he said. "Thank you so much."

The host took her arm and piloted her into the next room.

"Oh, my dear," she said. "I nearly died! Honestly, I give you my word, I nearly passed away. Did you hear that terrible break I made? I was just going to say Katherine Burke looked almost like a nigger. I just caught myself in time. Oh, do you think he noticed?"

"I don't believe so," said her host.

"Well, thank goodness," she said, "because I wouldn't have embarrassed him for anything. Why, he's awfully nice. Just as nice as he can be. Nice manners, and everything. You know, so many colored people, you give them an inch, and they walk all over you. But he doesn't try any of that. Well, he's got more sense, I suppose. He's really nice. Don't you think so?"

"Yes," said her host.

"I liked him," she said. "I haven't any feeling at all because he's a colored man. I felt just as natural as I would with anybody. Talked to him just as naturally, and everything. But honestly, I could hardly keep a straight face. I kept thinking of Burton. Oh, wait till I tell Burton I called him 'Mister'!"

THE SEXES

THE young man with the scenic cravat glanced nervously down the sofa at the girl in the fringed dress. She was examining her handkerchief; it might have been the first one of its kind she had seen, so deep was her interest in its material, form, and possibilities. The young man cleared his throat, without necessity or success, producing a small, syncopated noise.

"Want a cigarette?" he said.

"No, thank you," she said. "Thank you ever so much just the same."

"Sorry I've only got these kind," he said. "You got any of your own?"

"I really don't know," she said. "I probably have, thank you."

"Because if you haven't," he said, "it wouldn't take me a minute to go up to the corner and get you some."

"Oh, thank you, but I wouldn't have you go to all that trouble for anything," she said. "It's awfully sweet of you to think of it. Thank you ever so much."

"Will you for God's sakes stop thanking me?" he said.

"Really," she said, "I didn't know I was saying anything out of the way. I'm awfully sorry if I hurt your feelings. I know what it feels like to get your feelings hurt. I'm sure I didn't realize it was an insult to say 'thank you' to a person. I'm not exactly in the habit of having people swear at me because I say 'thank you' to them."

"I did not swear at you!" he said.

"Oh, you didn't?" she said. "I see."

"My God," he said, "all I said, I simply asked you if I couldn't go out and get you some cigarettes. Is there anything in that to get up in the air about?"

"Who's up in the air?" she said. "I'm sure I didn't know it was a criminal offense to say I wouldn't dream of giving you all that trouble. I'm afraid I must be awfully stupid, or something."

"Do you want me to go out and get you some cigarettes; or don't you?" he said.

"Goodness," she said, "if you want to go so much, please don't feel you have to stay here. I wouldn't have you feel you had to stay for anything."

"Ah, don't be that way, will you?" he said.

"Be what way?" she said. "I'm not being any way."

"What's the matter?" he said.

"Why, nothing," she said. "Why?"

"You've been funny all evening," he said. "Hardly said a word to me, ever since I came in."

"I'm terribly sorry you haven't been having a good time," she said. "For goodness' sakes, don't feel you have to stay here and be bored. I'm sure there are millions of places you could be having a lot more fun. The only thing, I'm a little bit sorry I didn't know before, that's all. When you said you were coming over tonight, I broke a lot of dates to go to the theater and everything. But it doesn't make a bit of difference. I'd much rather have you go and have a good time. It isn't very pleasant to sit here and feel you're boring a person to death."

"I'm not bored!" he said. "I don't want to go any place! Ah, honey, won't you tell me what's the matter? Ah, please."

"I haven't the faintest idea what you're talking about," she said. "There isn't a thing on earth the matter. I don't know what you mean."

"Yes, you do," he said. "There's something the trouble. Is it anything I've done, or anything?"

"Goodness," she said, "I'm sure it isn't any of my business, anything you do. I certainly wouldn't feel I had any right to criticize."

"Will you stop talking like that?" he said. "Will you, please?"

"Talking like what?" she said.

"You know," he said. "That's the way you were talking over the telephone today, too. You were so snotty when I called you up, I was afraid to talk to you."

"I beg your pardon," she said. "What did you say I was?"

"Well, I'm sorry," he said. "I didn't mean to say that. You get me so balled up."

"You see," she said, "I'm really not in the habit of hearing language like that. I've never had a thing like that said to me in my life."

"I told you I was sorry, didn't I?" he said. "Honest, honey, I didn't mean it. I don't know how I came to say a thing like that. Will you excuse me? Please?"

"Oh, certainly," she said. "Goodness, don't feel you have to apologize to me. It doesn't make any difference at all. It just seems a little bit funny to have somebody you were in the habit of thinking was a gentleman come to your home and use language like that to you, that's all. But it doesn't make the slightest bit of difference."

"I guess nothing I say makes any difference to you," he said. "You seem to be sore at me."

"I'm sore at you?" she said. "I can't understand what put that idea in your head. Why should I be sore at you?"

"That's what I'm asking you," he said. "Won't you tell me what I've done? Have I done something to hurt your feelings, honey? The way you were, over the phone, you had me worried all day. I couldn't do a lick of work."

"I certainly wouldn't like to feel," she said, "that I was interfering with your work. I know there are lots of girls that don't think anything of doing things like that, but I think it's terrible. It certainly isn't very nice to sit here and have someone tell you you interfere with his business."

"I didn't say that!" he said. "I didn't say it!"

"Oh, didn't you?" she said. "Well, that was the impression I got. It must be my stupidity."

"I guess maybe I better go," he said. "I can't get right. Everything I say seems to make you sorer and sorer. Would you rather I'd go?"

"Please do just exactly whatever you like," she said. "I'm sure the last thing I want to do is have you stay here when you'd rather be some place else. Why don't you go some place where you won't be bored? Why don't you go up to Florence Leaming's? I know she'd love to have you."

"I don't want to go up to Florence Leaming's!" he said. "What would I want to go up to Florence Leaming's for? She gives me a pain."

"Oh, really?" she said. "She didn't seem to be giving you so much of a pain at Elsie's party last night, I notice. I notice you couldn't even talk to anybody else, that's how much of a pain she gave you."

"Yeah, and you know why I was talking to her?" he said.

"Why, I suppose you think she's attractive," she said. "I suppose some people do. It's perfectly natural. Some people think she's quite pretty."

"I don't know whether she's pretty or not," he said. "I wouldn't know her if I saw her again. Why I was talking to her was you wouldn't even give me a tumble, last night. I came up and tried to talk to you, and you just said, 'Oh, how do you do'—just like that, 'Oh, how do you do'—and you turned right away and wouldn't look at me."

"I wouldn't look at you?" she said. "Oh, that's awfully funny. Oh, that's marvelous. You don't mind if I laugh, do you?"

"Go ahead and laugh your head off," he said. "But you wouldn't."

"Well, the minute you came in the room," she said, "you started making such a fuss over Florence Leaming, I thought you never wanted to see anybody else. You two seemed to be having such a wonderful time together, goodness knows I wouldn't have butted in for anything."

"My God," he said, "this what's-her-name girl came up and began talking to me before I even saw anybody else, and what could I do? I couldn't sock her in the nose, could I?"

"I certainly didn't see you try," she said.

"You saw me try to talk to you, didn't you?" he said. "And what did you do? 'Oh, how do you do.' Then this what's-her-name came up again, and there I was, stuck. Florence Leaming! I think she's terrible. Know what I think of her? I think she's a damn little fool. That's what I think of her."

"Well, of course," she said, "that's the impression she always gave me, but I don't know. I've heard people say she's pretty. Honestly I have."

"Why, she can't be pretty in the same room with you," he said.

"She has got an awfully funny nose," she said. "I really feel sorry for a girl with a nose like that."

"She's got a terrible nose," he said. "You've got a beautiful nose. Gee, you've got a pretty nose."

"Oh, I have not," she said. "You're crazy."

"And beautiful eyes," he said, "and beautiful hair and a beautiful mouth. And beautiful hands. Let me have one of the little hands. Ah, look atta little hand! Who's got the prettiest hands in the world? Who's the sweetest girl in the world?"

"I don't know," she said. "Who?"

"You don't know!" he said. "You do so, too, know."

"I do not," she said. "Who? Florence Leaming?"

"Oh, Florence Leaming, my eye!" he said. "Getting sore about Florence Leaming! And me not sleeping all last night and not doing a stroke of work all day because you wouldn't speak to me! A girl like you getting sore about a girl like Florence Leaming!"

"I think you're just perfectly crazy," she said. "I was not sore! What on earth ever made you think I was? You're simply crazy. Ow, my new pearl beads! Wait a second till I take them off. There!"

THE WONDERFUL OLD GENTLEMAN

IF THE Bains had striven for years, they could have been no more successful in making their living-room into a small but admirably complete museum of objects suggesting strain, discomfort, or the tomb. Yet they had never even tried for the effect. Some of the articles that the room contained were wedding-presents; some had been put in from time to time as substitutes as their predecessors succumbed to age and wear; a few had been brought along by the Old Gentleman when he had come to make his home with the Bains some five years before.

It was curious how perfectly they all fitted into the general scheme. It was as if they had all been selected by a single enthusiast to whom time was but little object, so long as he could achieve the eventual result of transforming the Bain living-room into a home chamber of horrors, modified a bit for family use.

It was a high-ceilinged room, with heavy, dark old woodwork, that brought long and unavoidable thoughts of silver handles and weaving worms. The paper was the color of stale mustard. Its design, once a dashing affair of a darker tone splashed with twinkling gold, had faded into lines and smears that resolved themselves, before the eyes of the sensitive, into hordes of battered heads and tortured profiles, some eyeless, some with clotted gashes for mouths.

The furniture was dark and cumbersome and subject to painful creakings—sudden, sharp creaks that seemed to be wrung from its brave silence only when it could bear no more. A close, earthy smell came from its dulled tapestry cushions, and try as Mrs. Bain might, furry gray dust accumulated in the crevices.

The center-table was upheld by the perpetually strained arms of three carved figures, insistently female to the waist, then trailing discreetly off into a confusion of scrolls and scales. Upon it rested a row of blameless books, kept in place at the ends by the straining shoulder-muscles of two bronze-colored plaster elephants, forever pushing at their tedious toil.

On the heavily carved mantel was a gayly colored figure of a curly-headed peasant boy, ingeniously made so that he sat on the shelf and dangled one leg over. He was in the eternal act of removing a thorn from his chubby foot, his round face realistically wrinkled with the cruel pain. Just above him hung a steel-engraving of a chariot-race, the dust flying, the chariots careening wildly, the drivers ferociously lashing their maddened horses, the horses themselves caught by the artist the moment before their hearts burst, and they dropped in their traces.

The opposite wall was devoted to the religious in art; a steel-engraving of the Crucifixion, lavish of ghastly detail; a sepia-print of the martyrdom of Saint Sebastian, the cords cutting deep into the arms writhing from the stake, arrows bristling in the thick, soft-looking body; a water-color copy of a "Mother of Sorrows," the agonized eyes raised to a cold heaven, great, bitter tears forever on the wan cheeks, paler for the grave-like draperies that wrapped the head.

Beneath the windows hung a painting in oil of two lost sheep, huddled hopelessly together in the midst of a wild blizzard. This was one of the Old Gentleman's contributions to the room. Mrs. Bain was wont to observe of it that the frame was worth she didn't know how much.

The wall-space beside the door was reserved for a bit of modern art that had once caught Mr. Bain's eye in a stationer's window—a colored print, showing a railroad-crossing, with a train flying relentlessly toward it, and a low, red automobile trying to dash across the track before the iron terror shattered it into eternity. Nervous visitors who were given chairs facing this scene usually made opportunity to change their seats before they could give their whole minds to the conversation.

The ornaments, placed with careful casualness on the table and the upright piano, included a small gilt lion of Lucerne, a little, chipped, plaster Laocoön, and a savage china kitten eternally about to pounce upon a plump and helpless china mouse. This last had been one of the Old Gentleman's own wedding-gifts. Mrs. Bain explained, in tones low with awe, that it was very old.

The ash-receivers, of Oriental manufacture, were in the form of grotesque heads, tufted with bits of gray human hair, and given bulging, dead, glassy eyes and mouths stretched into great gapes, into which those who had the heart for it might flick their ashes. Thus the smallest details of the room kept loyally to the spirit of the thing, and carried on the effect.

But the three people now sitting in the Bains' living-room were not in the least oppressed by the decorative scheme. Two of them, Mr. and Mrs. Bain, not only had had twenty-eight years of the room to accustom themselves to it, but had been stanch admirers of it from the first. And no surroundings, however morbid, could close in on the aristocratic calm of Mrs. Bain's sister, Mrs. Whittaker.

She graciously patronized the very chair she now sat in, smiled kindly on the glass of cider she held in her hand. The Bains were poor, and Mrs. Whittaker had, as it is ingenuously called, married well, and none of them ever lost sight of these facts.

But Mrs. Whittaker's attitude of kindly tolerance was not confined to her less fortunate relatives. It extended to friends of her youth, working people, the arts, politics, the United States in general, and God, Who had always supplied her with the best of service. She could have given Him an excellent reference at any time.

The three people sat with a comfortable look of spending the evening. There was an air of expectancy about them, a not unpleasant little nervousness, as of those who wait for a curtain to rise. Mrs. Bain had brought in cider in the best tumblers, and had served some of her nut cookies in the plate painted by hand with clusters of cherries—the plate she had used for sandwiches when, several years ago, her card club had met at her house.

She had thought it over a little tonight, before she lifted out the cherry plate, then quickly decided and resolutely heaped it with cookies. After all, it was an occasion—informal, perhaps, but still an occasion. The Old Gentleman was dying upstairs. At five o'clock that afternoon the doctor had said that it would be a surprise to him if the Old Gentleman lasted till the middle of the night—a big surprise, he had augmented.

There was no need for them to gather at the Old Gentleman's bedside. He would not have known any of them. In fact, he had not known them for almost a year, addressing them by wrong names and asking them grave, courteous questions about the health of husbands or wives or children who belonged to other branches of the family. And he was quite unconscious now.

Miss Chester, the nurse who had been with him since 'this last stroke,' as Mrs. Bain importantly called it, was entirely competent to attend and watch him. She had promised to call them if, in her tactful words, she saw any signs.

So the Old Gentleman's daughters and son-in-law waited in the warm living-room, and sipped their cider, and conversed in low, polite tones.

Mrs. Bain cried a little in pauses in the conversation. She had always cried easily and often. Yet, in spite of her years of practice, she did not do it well. Her eyelids grew pink and sticky, and her nose gave her no little trouble, necessitating almost constant sniffling. She sniffled loudly and conscientiously, and frequently removed her pince-nez to wipe her eyes with a crumpled handkerchief, gray with damp.

Mrs. Whittaker, too, bore a handkerchief, but she appeared to be holding it in waiting. She was dressed, in compliment to the occasion, in her black crepe de Chine, and she had left her lapis-lazuli pin, her olivine bracelet, and her topaz and amethyst rings at home in her bureau drawer, retaining only her lorgnette on its gold chain, in case there should be any reading to be done.

Mrs. Whittaker's dress was always studiously suited to its occasion; thus, her bearing had always that calm that only the correctly attired may enjoy. She was an authority on where to place monograms on linen, how to instruct working folk, and what to say in letters of condolence. The word "lady" figured largely in her conversation. Blood, she often predicted, would tell.

Mrs. Bain wore a rumpled white shirt-waist and the old blue skirt she saved for "around the kitchen." There had been time to change, after she had telephoned the doctor's verdict to her sister, but she had not been quite sure whether it was the thing to do. She had thought that Mrs. Whittaker might expect her to display a little distraught untidiness at a time like this; might even go in for it in a mild way herself.

Now Mrs. Bain looked at her sister's elaborately curled, painstakingly brown coiffure, and nervously patted her own straggling hair, gray at the front, with strands of almost lime-color in the little twist at the back. Her eyelids grew wet and sticky again, and she hung her glasses over one forefinger while she applied the damp handkerchief. After all, she reminded herself and the others, it was her poor father.

Oh, but it was really the best thing, Mrs. Whittaker explained in her gentle, patient voice.

"You wouldn't want to see Father go on like this," she pointed out. Mr. Bain echoed her, as if struck with the idea. Mrs. Bain had nothing to reply to them. No, she wouldn't want to see the Old Gentleman go on like this.

Five years before, Mrs. Whittaker had decided that the Old Gentleman was getting too old to live alone with only old Annie to cook for him and look after him. It was only a question of a little time before it "wouldn't have looked right," his living alone, when he had his children to take care of him. Mrs. Whittaker always stopped things before they got to the stage where they didn't look right. So he had come to live with the Bains.

Some of his furniture had been sold; a few things, such as his silver, his tall clock, and the Persian rug he had bought at the Exposition, Mrs. Whittaker had found room for in her own house; and some he brought with him to the Bains'.

Mrs. Whittaker's house was much larger than her sister's, and she had three servants and no children. But, as she told her friends, she had held back and let Allie and Lewis have the Old Gentleman.

"You see," she explained, dropping her voice to the tones reserved for not very pretty subjects, "Allie and Lewis are—well, they haven't a great deal."

So it was gathered that the Old Gentleman would do big things for the Bains when he came to live with them. Not exactly by paying board—it is a little too much to ask your father to pay for his food and lodging, as if he were a stranger. But, as Mrs. Whittaker suggested, he could do a great deal in the way of buying needed things for the house and keeping everything going.

And the Old Gentleman did contribute to the Bain household. He bought an electric heater and an electric fan, new curtains, storm-windows, and light-fixtures, all for his bedroom; and had a nice little bathroom for his personal use made out of the small guest-room adjoining it.

He shopped for days until he found a coffee-cup large enough for his taste; he bought several large ash-trays, and a dozen extra-size bath-towels, that Mrs. Bain marked with his initials. And every Christmas and birthday he gave Mrs. Bain a round, new, shining ten-dollar gold piece. Of course, he presented gold pieces to Mrs. Whittaker, too, on like appropriate occasions. The Old Gentleman prided himself always on his fair-mindedness. He often said that he was not one to show any favoritism.

Mrs. Whittaker was Cordelia-like to her father during his declining years. She came to see him several times a month, bringing him jelly or potted hyacinths. Sometimes she sent her car and chauffeur for him, so that he might take an easy drive through the town, and Mrs. Bain might be afforded a chance to drop her cooking and accompany him. When Mrs. Whittaker was away on trips with her husband, she almost never neglected to send her father picture post-cards of various points of interest.

The Old Gentleman appreciated her affection, and took pride in her. He enjoyed being told that she was like him.

"That Hattie," he used to tell Mrs. Bain, "she's a fine woman—a fine woman."

As soon as she had heard that the Old Gentleman was dying Mrs. Whittaker had come right over, stopping only to change her dress and have her dinner. Her husband was away in the woods with some men, fishing. She explained to the Bains that there was no use in disturbing him—it would have been impossible for him to get back that night. As soon as—well, if anything happened she would telegraph him, and he could return in time for the funeral.

Mrs. Bain was sorry that he was away. She liked her ruddy, jovial, loud-voiced brother-in-law.

"It's too bad that Clint couldn't be here," she said, as she had said several times before. "He's so fond of cider," she added.

"Father," said Mrs. Whittaker, "was always very fond of Clint." Already the Old Gentleman had slipped into the past tense.

"Everybody likes Clint," Mr. Bain stated.

He was included in the "everybody." The last time he had failed in business, Clint had given him the clerical position he had since held over at the brush works. It was pretty generally understood that this had been brought about through Mrs. Whittaker's intervention, but still they were Clint's brush works, and it was Clint who paid him his salary. And forty dollars a week is indubitably forty dollars a week.

"I hope he'll be sure and be here in time for the funeral," said Mrs. Bain. "It will be Wednesday morning, I suppose, Hat?"

Mrs. Whittaker nodded.

"Or perhaps around two o'clock Wednesday afternoon," she amended. "I always think that's a nice time. Father has his frock coat, Allie?"

"Oh, yes," Mrs. Bain said eagerly. "And it's all clean and lovely. He has everything. Hattie, I noticed the other day at Mr. Newton's funeral they had more of a blue necktie on him, so I suppose they're wearing them—Mollie Newton always has everything just so. But I don't know——"

"I think," said Mrs. Whittaker firmly, "that there is nothing lovelier than black for an old gentleman."

"Poor Old Gentleman," said Mr. Bain, shaking his head. "He would have been eighty-five if he just could have lived till next September. Well, I suppose it's all for the best."

He took a small draft of cider and another cooky.

"A wonderful, wonderful life," summarized Mrs. Whittaker. "And a wonderful, wonderful old gentleman."

"Well, I should say so," said Mrs. Bain. "Why, up to the last year he was as interested in everything! It was, 'Allie, how much do you have to give for your eggs now?' and 'Allie, why don't you change your butcher?—this one's robbing you,' and 'Allie, who was that you were talking to on the telephone?' all day long! Everybody used to speak of it."

"And he used to come to the table right up to this stroke," Mr. Bain related, chuckling reminiscently. "My, he used to raise Cain when Allie didn't cut up his meat fast enough to suit him. Always had a temper, *I'll* tell you, the Old Gentleman did. Wouldn't stand for us having anybody in to meals—he didn't like that worth a cent. Eighty-four years old, and sitting right up there at the table with us!"

They vied in telling instances of the Old Gentleman's intelligence and liveliness, as parents cap one another's anecdotes of precocious children.

"It's only the past year that he had to be helped up- and downstairs," said Mrs. Bain. "Walked up-stairs all by himself, and more than eighty years old!"

Mrs. Whittaker was amused.

"I remember you said that once when Clint was here," she remarked, "and Clint said, 'Well, if you can't walk up-stairs by the time you're eighty, when are you going to learn?' "

Mrs. Bain smiled politely, because her brother-in-law had said it. Otherwise she would have been shocked and wounded.

"Yes, sir," said Mr. Bain. "Wonderful."

"The only thing I could have wished," Mrs. Bain said, after a pause—"I could have wished he'd been a little different about Paul. Somehow I've never felt quite right since Paul went into the navy."

Mrs. Whittaker's voice fell into the key used for the subject that has been gone over and over and over again.

"Now, Allie," she said, "you know yourself that was the best thing that could have happened. Father told you that himself, often and often. Paul was young, and he wanted to have all his young friends running in and out of the house, banging doors and making all sorts of racket, and it would have been a terrible nuisance for father. You must realize that father was more than eighty years old, Allie."

"Yes, I know," Mrs. Bain said. Her eyes went to the photograph of her son in his seaman's uniform, and she sighed.

"And besides," Mrs. Whittaker pointed out triumphantly, "now that Miss Chester's here in Paul's room, there wouldn't have been any room for him. So you see!"

There was rather a long pause. Then Mrs. Bain edged toward the other thing that had been weighing upon her.

"Hattie," she said, "I suppose—I suppose we'd ought to let Matt know?"

"I shouldn't," said Mrs. Whittaker composedly. She always took great pains with her "shall's" and "will's." "I only hope that he doesn't see it in the papers in time to come on for the funeral. If you want to have your brother turn up drunk at the services, Allie, *I* don't."

"But I thought he'd straightened up," said Mr. Bain. "Thought he was all right since he got married."

"Yes, I know, I know, Lewis," Mrs. Whittaker said wearily. "I've heard all about that. All I say is, *I* know what Matt is."

"John Loomis was telling me," reported Mr. Bain, "he was going through Akron, and he stopped off to see Matt. Said they had a nice little place, and he seemed to be getting along fine. Said she seemed like a cracker-jack housekeeper."

Mrs. Whittaker smiled.

"Yes," she said, "John Loomis and Matt were always two of a kind—you couldn't believe a word either of them said. Probably she did seem to be a good housekeeper. I've no doubt she acted the part very well. Matt never made any bones of the fact that she was on the stage once, for almost a year. Excuse me from having that woman come to Father's funeral. If you want to know what *I* think, *I* think that Matt marrying a woman like that had a good deal to do with hastening Father's death."

The Bains sat in awe.

"And after all Father did for Matt, too," added Mrs. Whittaker, her voice shaken.

"Well, I should think so," Mr. Bain was glad to agree. "I remember how the Old Gentleman used to try and help Matt get along. He'd go down, like it was to Mr. Fuller, that time Matt was working at the bank, and he'd explain to him, 'Now, Mr. Fuller,' he'd say, 'I don't know whether you know it, but this son of mine has always been what you might call the black sheep of the family. He's been kind of a drinker,' he'd say, 'and he's got himself into trouble a couple of times, and if you'd just keep an eye on him, so's to see he keeps straight, it'd be a favor to me.'

"Mr. Fuller told me about it himself. Said it was wonderful the way the Old Gentleman came right out and talked just as frankly to him. Said *he'd* never had any idea Matt was that way—wanted to hear all about it."

Mrs. Whittaker nodded sadly.

"Oh, I know," she said. "Time and again Father would do that. And then, as like as not, Matt would get one of his sulky fits, and not turn up at his work."

"And when Matt would be out of work," Mrs. Bain said, "the way Father'd hand him out his car-fare, and I don't know what all! When Matt was a grown man, going on thirty years old, Father would take him down to Newins & Malley's and buy him a whole new outfit—pick out everything himself. He always used to say Matt was the kind that would get cheated out of his eye-teeth if he went into a store alone."

"My, Father hated to see anybody make a fool of themselves about money," Mrs. Whittaker commented. "Remember how he always used to say, 'Anybody can make money, but it takes a wise man to keep it'?"

"I suppose he must be a pretty rich man," Mr. Bain said, abruptly restoring the Old Gentleman to the present.

"Oh—rich!" Mrs. Whittaker's smile was at its kindliest. "But he managed his affairs very well, Father did, right up to the last. Everything is in splendid shape, Clint says."

"He showed you the will, didn't he, Hat?" asked Mrs. Bain, forming bits of her sleeve into little plaits between her thin, hard fingers.

"Yes," said her sister. "Yes, he did. He showed me the will. A little over a year ago, I think it was, wasn't it? You know, just before he started to fail, that time."

She took a small bite of cooky.

"*Awfully* good," she said. She broke into a little bubbly laugh, the laugh she used at teas and wedding receptions and fairly formal dinners. "You know," she went on, as one sharing a good story, "he's gone and left all that old money to me. 'Why, Father!' I said, as soon as I'd read that part. But it seems he'd gotten some sort of idea in his head that Clint and I would be able to take care of it better than anybody else, and you know what Father was, once he made up that mind of his. You can just imagine how *I* felt. I couldn't say a thing."

She laughed again, shaking her head in amused bewilderment.

"Oh, and Allie," she said, "he's left you all the furniture he brought here with him, and all the things he bought since he came. And Lewis is to have his set of Thackeray. And that money he lent Lewis, to try and tide him over in the hardware business that time—that's to be regarded as a gift."

She sat back and looked at them, smiling.

"Lewis paid back most all of that money Father lent him that time," Mrs. Bain said. "There was only about two hundred dollars more, and then he would have had it all paid up."

"That's to be regarded as a gift," insisted Mrs. Whittaker. She leaned over and patted her brother-in-law's arm. "Father always liked you, Lewis," she said softly.

"Poor Old Gentleman," murmured Mr. Bain.

"Did it—did it say anything about Matt?" asked Mrs. Bain.

"Oh, Allie!" Mrs. Whittaker gently reproved her. "When you think of all the money Father spent and spent on Matt, it seems to me he did more than enough—more than enough. And then when Matt went way off there to live, and married that woman, and never a word about it—Father hearing it all through strangers—well, I don't think any of us realize how it hurt Father. He never said much about it, but I don't think he ever got over it. I'm always so thankful that poor dear mother didn't live to see how Matt turned out."

"Poor Mother," said Mrs. Bain shakily, and brought the grayish handkerchief into action once more. "I can hear her now, just as plain. 'Now, children,' she used to say, 'do for goodness' sake let's all try and keep your father in a good humor.' If I've heard her say it once, I've heard her say it a hundred times. Remember, Hat?"

"Do I remember!" said Mrs. Whittaker. "And do you remember how they used to play whist, and how furious Father used to get when he lost?"

"Yes," Mrs. Bain cried excitedly, "and how Mother used to have to cheat, so as to be sure and not win from him? She got so she used to be able to do it just as well!"

They laughed softly, filled with memories of the gone days. A pleasant, thoughtful silence fell around them.

Mrs. Bain patted a yawn to extinction, and looked at the clock.

"Ten minutes to eleven," she said. "Goodness, I had no idea it was anywhere near so late. I wish—" She stopped just in time, crimson at what her wish would have been.

"You see, Lew and I have got in the way of going to bed early," she explained. "Father slept so light, we couldn't have people in like we used to before he came here, to play a little bridge or anything, on account of disturbing him. And if we wanted to go to the movies or anywhere, he'd go on so about being left alone that we just kind of gave up going."

"Oh, the Old Gentleman always let you know what he wanted," said Mr. Bain, smiling. "He was a wonder, *I'll* tell you. Nearly eighty-five years old!"

"Think of it," said Mrs. Whittaker.

A door clicked open above them, and feet ran quickly and not lightly down the stairs. Miss Chester burst into the room.

"Oh, Mrs. Bain!" she cried. "Oh, the Old Gentleman! Oh, he's gone! I noticed him kind of stirring and whimpering a little, and he seemed to be trying to make motions at his warm milk, like as if he wanted some. So I put the cup up to his mouth, and he sort of fell over, and just like that he was gone, and the milk all over him."

Mrs. Bain instantly collapsed into passionate weeping. Her husband put his arm tenderly about her, and murmured a series of "Now-now's."

Mrs. Whittaker rose, set her cider-glass carefully on the table, shook out her handkerchief, and moved toward the door.

"A lovely death," she pronounced. "A wonderful, wonderful life, and now a beautiful, peaceful death. Oh, it's the best thing, Allie; it's the best thing."

"Oh, it is, Mrs. Bain; it's the best thing," Miss Chester said earnestly. "It's really a blessing. That's what it is."

Among them they got Mrs. Bain up the stairs.

A TELEPHONE CALL

PLEASE, God, let him telephone me now. Dear God, let him call me now. I won't ask anything else of You, truly I won't. It isn't very much to ask. It would be so little to You, God, such a little, little thing. Only let him telephone now. Please, God. Please, please, please.

If I didn't think about it, maybe the telephone might ring. Sometimes it does that. If I could think of something else. If I could think of something else. Maybe if I counted five hundred by fives, it might ring by that time. I'll count slowly. I won't cheat. And if it rings when I get to three hundred, I won't stop; I won't answer it until I get to five hundred. Five, ten, fifteen, twenty, twenty-five, thirty, thirty-five, forty, forty-five, fifty. . . . Oh, please ring. Please.

This is the last time I'll look at the clock. I will not look at it again. It's ten minutes past seven. He said he would telephone at five o'clock. "I'll call you at five, darling." I think that's where he said "darling." I'm almost sure he said it there. I know he called me "darling" twice, and the other time was when he said good-by. "Good-by, darling." He was busy, and he can't say much in the office, but he called me "darling" twice. He couldn't have minded my calling him up. I know you shouldn't keep telephoning them—I know they don't like that. When you do that, they know you are thinking about them and wanting them, and that makes them hate you. But I hadn't talked to him in three days—not in three days. And all I did was ask him how he was; it was just the way anybody might have called him up. He couldn't have minded that. He couldn't have thought I was bothering him. "No, of course you're not," he said. And he said he'd telephone me. He didn't have to say that. I didn't ask him to, truly I didn't. I'm sure I didn't. I don't think he would say he'd telephone me, and then just never do it. Please don't let him do that, God. Please don't.

"I'll call you at five, darling." "Good-by, darling." He was busy, and he was in a hurry, and there were people around him, but he called me "darling" twice. That's mine, that's mine. I have that, even if I never see him again. Oh, but that's so little. That isn't enough. Nothing's enough, if I never see him again. Please let me see him again, God. Please, I want him so much. I want him so much. I'll be good, God. I will try to be better, I will, if You will let me see him again. If You will let him telephone me. Oh, let him telephone me now.

Ah, don't let my prayer seem too little to You, God. You sit up there, so white and old, with all the angels about You and the stars slipping by. And I come to You with a prayer about a telephone call. Ah, don't laugh, God. You see, You don't know how it feels. You're so safe, there on Your throne, with the blue swirling under You. Nothing can touch You; no one can twist Your heart in his hands. This is suffering, God, this is bad, bad suffering. Won't You help me? For Your Son's sake, help me. You said You would do whatever was asked of You in His name. Oh, God, in the name of Thine only beloved Son, Jesus Christ, our Lord, let him telephone me now.

I must stop this. I mustn't be this way. Look. Suppose a young man says he'll call a girl up, and then something happens, and he doesn't. That isn't so terrible, is it? Why, it's going on all over the world, right this minute. Oh, what do I care what's going on all over the world? Why can't that telephone ring? Why can't it, why can't it? Couldn't you ring? Ah, please, couldn't you? You damned, ugly, shiny thing. It would hurt you to ring, wouldn't it? Oh, that would hurt you. Damn you, I'll pull your filthy roots out of the wall, I'll smash your smug black face in little bits. Damn you to hell.

No, no, no. I must stop. I must think about something else. This is what I'll do. I'll put the clock in the other room. Then I can't look at it. If I do have to look at it, then I'll have to walk into the bedroom, and that will be something to do. Maybe, before I look at it again, he will call me. I'll be so sweet to him, if he calls me. If he says he can't see me tonight, I'll say, "Why, that's all right, dear. Why, of course it's all right." I'll be the way I was when I first met him. Then maybe he'll like me again. I was always sweet, at first. Oh, it's so easy to be sweet to people before you love them.

I think he must still like me a little. He couldn't have called me "darling" twice today, if he didn't still like me a little. It isn't all gone, if he still likes me a little; even if it's only a little, little bit. You see, God, if You would just let him telephone me, I wouldn't have to ask You anything more. I would be sweet to him, I would be gay, I would be just the way I used to be, and then he would love me again. And then I would never have to ask You for anything more. Don't You see, God? So won't You please let him telephone me? Won't You please, please, please?

Are You punishing me, God, because I've been bad? Are You angry with me because I did that? Oh, but, God, there are so many bad people—You could not be hard only to me. And it wasn't very bad; it couldn't have been bad. We didn't hurt anybody, God. Things are only bad when they hurt people. We didn't hurt one single soul; You know that. You know it wasn't bad, don't You, God? So won't You let him telephone me now?

If he doesn't telephone me, I'll know God is angry with me. I'll count five hundred by fives, and if he hasn't called me then, I will know God isn't going to help me, ever again. That will be the sign. Five, ten, fifteen, twenty, twenty-five, thirty, thirty-five, forty, forty-five, fifty, fifty-five . . . It was bad. I knew it was bad. All right, God, send me to hell. You think You're frightening me with Your hell, don't You? You think Your hell is worse than mine.

I mustn't. I mustn't do this. Suppose he's a little late calling up—that's nothing to get hysterical about. Maybe he isn't going call—maybe he's coming straight up here without telephoning. He'll be cross if he sees I have been crying. They don't like you to cry. He doesn't cry. I wish to God I could make him cry. I wish I could make him cry and tread the floor and feel his heart heavy and big and festering in him. I wish I could hurt him like hell.

He doesn't wish that about me. I don't think he even knows how he makes me feel. I wish he could know, without my telling him. They don't like you to tell them they've made you cry. They don't like you to tell them you're unhappy because of them. If you do, they think you're possessive and exacting. And then they hate you. They hate you whenever you say anything you really think. You always have to keep playing little games. Oh, I thought we didn't have to; I thought this was so big I could say whatever I meant. I guess you can't, ever. I guess there isn't ever anything big enough for that. Oh, if he would just telephone, I wouldn't tell him I had been sad about him. They hate sad people. I would be so sweet and so gay, he couldn't help but like me. If he would only telephone. If he would only telephone.

Maybe that's what he is doing. Maybe he is coming on here without calling me up. Maybe he's on his way now. Something might have happened to him. No, nothing could ever happen to him. I can't picture anything happening to him. I never picture him run over. I never see him lying still and long and dead. I wish he were dead. That's a terrible wish. That's a lovely wish. If he were dead, he would be mine. If he were dead, I would never think of now and the last few weeks. I would remember only the lovely times. It would be all beautiful. I wish he were dead. I wish he were dead, dead, dead.

This is silly. It's silly to go wishing people were dead just because they don't call you up the very minute they said they would. Maybe the clock's fast; I don't know whether it's right. Maybe he's hardly late at all. Anything could have made him a little late. Maybe he had to stay at his office. Maybe he went home, to call me up from there, and somebody came in. He doesn't like to telephone me in front of people. Maybe he's worried, just a little, little bit, about keeping me waiting. He might even hope that I would call him up. I could do that. I could telephone him.

I mustn't. I mustn't, I mustn't. Oh, God, please don't let me telephone him. Please keep me from doing that. I know, God, just as well as You do, that if he were worried about me, he'd telephone no matter where he was or how many people there were around him. Please make me know that, God. I don't ask You to make it easy for me—You can't do that, for all that You could make a world. Only let me know it, God. Don't let me go on hoping. Don't let me say comforting things to myself. Please don't let me hope, dear God. Please don't.

I won't telephone him. I'll never telephone him again as long as I live. He'll rot in hell, before I'll call him up. You don't have to give me strength, God; I have it myself. If he wanted me, he could get me. He knows where I am. He knows I'm waiting here. He's so sure of me, so sure. I wonder why they hate you, as soon as they are sure of you. I should think it would be so sweet to be sure.

It would be so easy to telephone him. Then I'd know. Maybe it wouldn't be a foolish thing to do. Maybe he wouldn't mind. Maybe he'd like it. Maybe he has been trying to get me. Sometimes people try and try to get you on the telephone, and they say the number doesn't answer. I'm not just saying that to help myself; that really happens. You know that really happens, God. Oh, God, keep me away from that telephone. Keep me away. Let me still have just a little bit of pride. I think I'm going to need it, God. I think it will be all I'll have.

Oh, what does pride matter, when I can't stand it if I don't talk to him? Pride like that is such a silly, shabby little thing. The real pride, the big pride, is in having no pride. I'm not saying that just because I want to call him. I am not. That's true, I know that's true. I will be big. I will be beyond little prides.

Please, God, keep me from telephoning him. Please, God.

I don't see what pride has to do with it. This is such a little thing, for me to be bringing in pride, for me to be making such a fuss about. I may have misunderstood him. Maybe he said for me to call him up, at five. "Call me at five, darling." He could have said that, perfectly well. It's so possible that I didn't hear him right. "Call me at five, darling." I'm almost sure that's what he said. God, don't let me talk this way to myself. Make me know, please make me know.

I'll think about something else. I'll just sit quietly. If I could sit still. If I could sit still. Maybe I could read. Oh, all the books are about people who love each other, truly and sweetly. What do they want to write about that for? Don't they know it isn't true? Don't they know it's a lie, it's a God damned lie? What do they have to tell about that for, when they know how it hurts? Damn them, damn them, damn them.

I won't. I'll be quiet. This is nothing to get excited about. Look. Suppose he were someone I didn't know very well. Suppose he were another girl. Then I'd just telephone and say, "Well, for goodness' sake, what happened to you?" That's what I'd do, and I'd never even think about it. Why can't I be casual and natural, just because I love him? I can be. Honestly, I can be. I'll call him up, and be so easy and pleasant. You see if I won't, God. Oh, don't let me call him. Don't, don't, don't.

God, aren't You really going to let him call me? Are You sure, God? Couldn't You please relent? Couldn't You? I don't even ask You to let him telephone me this minute, God; only let him do it in a little while. I'll count five hundred by fives. I'll do it so slowly and so fairly. If he hasn't telephoned then, I'll call him. I will. Oh, please, dear God, dear kind God, my blessed Father in Heaven, let him call before then. Please, God. Please.

Five, ten, fifteen, twenty, twenty-five, thirty, thirty-five . . .

HERE WE ARE

THE young man in the new blue suit finished arranging the glistening luggage in tight corners of the Pullman compartment. The train had leaped at curves and bounced along straightaways, rendering balance a praiseworthy achievement and a sporadic one; and the young man had pushed and hoisted and tucked and shifted the bags with concentrated care.

Nevertheless, eight minutes for the settling of two suitcases and a hat-box is a long time.

He sat down, leaning back against bristled green plush, in the seat opposite the girl in beige. She looked as new as a peeled egg. Her hat, her fur, her frock, her gloves were glossy and stiff with novelty. On the arc of the thin, slippery sole of one beige shoe was gummed a tiny oblong of white paper, printed with the price set and paid for that slipper and its fellow, and the name of the shop that had dispensed them.

She had been staring raptly out of the window, drinking in the big weathered signboards that extolled the phenomena of codfish without bones and screens no rust could corrupt. As the young man sat down, she turned politely from the pane, met his eyes, started a smile and got it about half done, and rested her gaze just above his right shoulder.

"Well!" the young man said.

"Well!" she said.

"Well, here we are," he said.

"Here we are," she said. "Aren't we?"

"I should say we were," he said. "Eeyop. Here we are."

"Well!" she said.

"Well!" he said. "Well. How does it feel to be an old married lady?"

"Oh, it's too soon to ask me that," she said. "At least—I mean. Well, I mean, goodness, we've only been married about three hours, haven't we?"

The young man studied his wrist-watch as if he were just acquiring the knack of reading time.

"We have been married," he said, "exactly two hours and twenty-six minutes."

"My," she said. "It seems like longer."

"No," he said. "It isn't hardly half-past six yet."

"It seems like later," she said. "I guess it's because it starts getting dark so early."

"It does, at that," he said. "The nights are going to be pretty long from now on. I mean. I mean—well, it starts getting dark early."

"I didn't have any idea what time it was," she said. "Everything was so mixed up, I sort of don't know where I am, or what it's all about. Getting back from the church, and then all those people, and then changing all my clothes, and then everybody throwing things, and all. Goodness, I don't see how people do it every day."

"Do what?" he said.

"Get married," she said. "When you think of all the people, all over the world, getting married just as if it was nothing. Chinese people and everybody. Just as if it wasn't anything."

"Well, let's not worry about people all over the world," he said. "Let's don't think about a lot of Chinese. We've got something better to think about. I mean. I mean—well, what do we care about them?"

"I know," she said. "But I just sort of got to thinking of them, all of them, all over everywhere, doing it all the time. At least, I mean—getting married, you know. And it's—well, it's sort of such a big thing to do, it makes you feel queer. You think of them, all of them, all doing it just like it wasn't anything. And how does anybody know what's going to happen next?"

"Let them worry," he said. "We don't have to. We know darn well what's going to happen next. I mean. I mean—well, we know it's going to be great. Well, we know we're going to be happy. Don't we?"

"Oh, of course," she said. "Only you think of all the people, and you have to sort of keep thinking. It makes you feel funny. An awful lot of people that get married, it doesn't turn out so well. And I guess they all must have thought it was going to be great."

"Come on, now," he said. "This is no way to start a honeymoon, with all this thinking going on. Look at us—all married and everything done. I mean. The wedding all done and all."

"Ah, it was nice, wasn't it?" she said. "Did you really like my veil?"

"You looked great," he said. "Just great."

"Oh, I'm terribly glad," she said. "Ellie and Louise looked lovely, didn't they? I'm terribly glad they did finally decide on pink. They looked perfectly lovely."

"Listen," he said. "I want to tell you something. When I was standing up there in that old church waiting for you to come up, and I saw those two bridesmaids, I thought to myself, I thought, 'Well, I never knew Louise could look like that!' Why, she'd have knocked anybody's eye out."

"Oh, really?" she said. "Funny. Of course, everybody thought her dress and hat were lovely, but a lot of people seemed to think she looked sort of tired. People have been saying that a lot, lately. I tell them I think it's awfully mean of them to go around saying that about her. I tell them they've got to remember that Louise isn't so terribly young any more, and they've got to expect her to look like that. Louise can say she's twenty-three all she wants to, but she's a good deal nearer twenty-seven."

"Well, she was certainly a knock-out at the wedding," he said. "Boy!"

"I'm terribly glad you thought so," she said. "I'm glad some one did. How did you think Ellie looked?"

"Why, I honestly didn't get a look at her," he said.

"Oh, really?" she said. "Well, I certainly think that's too bad. I don't suppose I ought to say it about my own sister, but I never saw anybody look as beautiful as Ellie looked today. And always so sweet and unselfish, too. And you didn't even notice her. But you never pay attention to Ellie, anyway. Don't think I haven't noticed it. It makes me feel just terrible. It makes me feel just awful, that you don't like my own sister."

"I do so like her!" he said. "I'm crazy for Ellie. I think she's a great kid."

"Don't think it makes any difference to Ellie!" she said. "Ellie's got enough people crazy about her. It isn't anything to her whether you like her or not. Don't flatter yourself she cares! Only, the only thing is, it makes it awfully hard for me you don't like her, that's the only thing. I keep thinking, when we come back and get in the apartment and everything, it's going to be awfully hard for me that you won't want my own sister to come and see me. It's going to make it awfully hard for me that you won't ever want my family around. I know how you feel about my family. Don't think I haven't seen it. Only, if you don't ever want to see them, that's your loss. Not theirs. Don't flatter yourself!"

"Oh, now, come on!" he said. "What's all this talk about not wanting your family around? Why, you know how I feel about your family. I think your old lady—I think your mother's swell. And Ellie. And your father. What's all this talk?"

"Well, I've seen it," she said. "Don't think I haven't. Lots of people they get married, and they think it's going to be great and everything, and then it all goes to pieces because people don't like people's families, or something like that. Don't tell me! I've seen it happen."

"Honey," he said, "what is all this? What are you getting all angry about? Hey, look, this is our honeymoon. What are you trying to start a fight for? Ah, I guess you're just feeling sort of nervous."

"Me?" she said. "What have I got to be nervous about? I mean. I mean, goodness, I'm not nervous."

"You know, lots of times," he said, "they say that girls get kind of nervous and yippy on account of thinking about—I mean. I mean—

well, it's like you said, things are all so sort of mixed up and everything, right now. But afterwards, it'll be all right. I mean. I mean—well, look, honey, you don't look any too comfortable. Don't you want to take your hat off? And let's don't ever fight, ever. Will we?"

"Ah, I'm sorry I was cross," she said. "I guess I did feel a little bit funny. All mixed up, and then thinking of all those people all over everywhere, and then being sort of 'way off here, all alone with you. It's so sort of different. It's sort of such a big thing. You can't blame a person for thinking, can you? Yes, don't let's ever, ever fight. We won't be like a whole lot of them. We won't fight or be nasty or anything. Will we?"

"You bet your life we won't," he said.

"I guess I will take this darned old hat off," she said. "It kind of presses. Just put it up on the rack, will you, dear? Do you like it, sweetheart?"

"Looks good on you," he said.

"No, but I mean," she said, "do you really like it?"

"Well, I'll tell you," he said. "I know this is the new style and everything like that, and it's probably great. I don't know anything about things like that. Only I like the kind of a hat like that blue hat you had. Gee, I liked that hat."

"Oh, really?" she said. "Well, that's nice. That's lovely. The first thing you say to me, as soon as you get me off on a train away from my family and everything, is that you don't like my hat. The first thing you say to your wife is you think she has terrible taste in hats. That's nice, isn't it?"

"Now, honey," he said, "I never said anything like that. I only said——"

"What you don't seem to realize," she said, "is this hat cost twenty-two dollars. Twenty-two dollars. And that horrible old blue thing you think you're so crazy about, that cost three ninety-five."

"I don't give a darn what they cost," he said. "I only said—I said I liked that blue hat. I don't know anything about hats. I'll be crazy about this one as soon as I get used to it. Only it's kind of not like your other hats. I don't know about the new styles. What do I know about women's hats?"

"It's too bad," she said, "you didn't marry somebody that would get the kind of hats you'd like. Hats that cost three ninety-five. Why didn't you marry Louise? You always think she looks so beautiful. You'd love her taste in hats. Why didn't you marry her?"

"Ah, now, honey," he said. "For heaven's sakes!"

"Why didn't you marry her?" she said. "All you've done, ever since we got on this train, is talk about her. Here I've sat and sat, and just listened to you saying how wonderful Louise is. I suppose that's nice, getting me all off here alone with you, and then raving about Louise right in front of my face. Why didn't you ask her to marry you? I'm sure she would have jumped at the chance. There aren't so many people asking her to marry them. It's too bad you didn't marry her. I'm sure you'd have been much happier."

"Listen, baby," he said, "while you're talking about things like that, why didn't you marry Joe Brooks? I suppose he could have given you all the twenty-two-dollar hats you wanted, I suppose!"

"Well, I'm not so sure I'm not sorry I didn't," she said. "There! Joe Brooks wouldn't have waited until he got me all off alone and then sneered at my taste in clothes. Joe Brooks wouldn't ever hurt my feelings. Joe Brooks has always been fond of me. There!"

"Yeah," he said. "He's fond of you. He was so fond of you he didn't even send a wedding present. That's how fond of you he was."

"I happen to know for a fact," she said, "that he was away on business, and as soon as he comes back he's going to give me anything I want, for the apartment."

"Listen," he said. "I don't want anything he gives you in our apartment. Anything he gives you, I'll throw right out the window. That's what I think of your friend Joe Brooks. And how do you know where he is and what he's going to do, anyway? Has he been writing to you?"

"I suppose my friends can correspond with me," she said. "I didn't hear there was any law against that."

"Well, I suppose they can't!" he said. "And what do you think of that? I'm not going to have my wife getting a lot of letters from cheap traveling salesmen!"

"Joe Brooks is not a cheap traveling salesman!" she said. "He is not! He gets a wonderful salary."

"Oh yeah?" he said. "Where did you hear that?"

"He told me so himself," she said.

"Oh, he told you so himself," he said. "I see. He told you so himself."

"You've got a lot of right to talk about Joe Brooks," she said. "You and your friend Louise. All you ever talk about is Louise."

"Oh, for heaven's sakes!" he said. "What do I care about Louise? I just thought she was a friend of yours, that's all. That's why I ever even noticed her."

"Well, you certainly took an awful lot of notice of her today," she said. "On our wedding day! You said yourself when you were standing there in the church you just kept thinking of her. Right up at the altar. Oh, right in the presence of God! And all you thought about was Louise."

"Listen, honey," he said, "I never should have said that. How does anybody know what kind of crazy things come into their heads when they're standing there waiting to get married? I was just telling you that because it was so kind of crazy. I thought it would make you laugh."

"I know," she said. "I've been all sort of mixed up today, too. I told you that. Everything so strange and everything. And me all the time thinking about all those people all over the world, and now us here all alone, and everything. I know you get all mixed up. Only I did think, when you kept talking about how beautiful Louise looked, you did it with malice and forethought."

"I never did anything with malice and forethought!" he said. "I just told you that about Louise because I thought it would make you laugh."

"Well, it didn't," she said.

"No, I know it didn't," he said. "It certainly did not. Ah, baby, and we ought to be laughing, too. Hell, honey lamb, this is our honeymoon. What's the matter?"

"I don't know," she said. "We used to squabble a lot when we were going together and then engaged and everything, but I thought everything would be so different as soon as you were married. And now I feel so sort of strange and everything. I feel so sort of alone."

"Well, you see, sweetheart," he said, "we're not really married yet. I mean. I mean—well, things will be different afterwards. Oh, hell. I mean, we haven't been married very long."

"No," she said.

"Well, we haven't got much longer to wait now," he said. "I mean—well, we'll be in New York in about twenty minutes. Then we can have dinner, and sort of see what we feel like doing. Or I mean. Is there anything special you want to do tonight?"

"What?" she said.

"What I mean to say," he said, "would you like to go to a show or something?"

"Why, whatever you like," she said. "I sort of didn't think people went to theaters and things on their—I mean, I've got a couple of letters I simply must write. Don't let me forget."

"Oh," he said. "You're going to write letters tonight?"

"Well, you see," she said. "I've been perfectly terrible. What with all the excitement and everything. I never did thank poor old Mrs. Sprague for her berry spoon, and I never did a thing about those book ends the McMasters sent. It's just too awful of me. I've got to write them this very night."

"And when you've finished writing your letters," he said, "maybe I could get you a magazine or a bag of peanuts."

"What?" she said.

"I mean," he said, "I wouldn't want you to be bored."

"As if I could be bored with you!" she said. "Silly! Aren't we married? Bored!"

"What I thought," he said, "I thought when we got in, we could go right up to the Biltmore and anyway leave our bags, and maybe have a little dinner in the room, kind of quiet, and then do whatever we wanted. I mean. I mean—well, let's go right up there from the station."

"Oh, yes, let's," she said. "I'm so glad we're going to the Biltmore. I just love it. The twice I've stayed in New York we've always stayed there, Papa and Mamma and Ellie and I, and I was crazy about it. I always sleep so well there. I go right off to sleep the minute I put my head on the pillow."

"Oh, you do?" he said.

"At least, I mean," she said. " 'Way up high it's so quiet."

"We might go to some show or other tomorrow night instead of tonight," he said. "Don't you think that would be better?"

"Yes, I think it might," she said.

He rose, balanced a moment, crossed over and sat down beside her.

"Do you really have to write those letters tonight?" he said.

"Well," she said, "I don't suppose they'd get there any quicker than if I wrote them tomorrow."

There was a silence with things going on in it.

"And we won't ever fight any more, will we?" he said.

"Oh, no," she said. "Not ever! I don't know what made me do like that. It all got so sort of funny, sort of like a nightmare, the way I got thinking of all those people getting married all the time; and so many of them, everything spoils on account of fighting and everything. I got all mixed up thinking about them. Oh, I don't want to be like them. But we won't be, will we?"

"Sure we won't," he said.

"We won't go all to pieces," she said. "We won't fight. It'll all be different, now we're married. It'll all be lovely. Reach me down my hat, will you, sweetheart? It's time I was putting it on. Thanks. Ah, I'm sorry you don't like it."

"I do so like it!" he said.

"You said you didn't," she said. "You said you thought it was perfectly terrible."

"I never said any such thing," he said. "You're crazy."

"All right, I may be crazy," she said. "Thank you very much. But that's what you said. Not that it matters—it's just a little thing. But it makes you feel pretty funny to think you've gone and married somebody that says you have perfectly terrible taste in hats. And then goes and says you're crazy, beside."

"Now, listen here," he said. "Nobody said any such thing. Why, I love that hat. The more I look at it the better I like it. I think it's great."

"That isn't what you said before," she said.

"Honey," he said. "Stop it, will you? What do you want to start all this for? I love the damned hat. I mean, I love your hat. I love anything you wear. What more do you want me to say?"

"Well, I don't want you to say it like that," she said.

"I said I think it's great," he said. "That's all I said."

"Do you really?" she said. "Do you honestly? Ah, I'm so glad. I'd hate you not to like my hat. It would be—I don't know, it would be sort of such a bad start."

"Well, I'm crazy for it," he said. "Now we've got that settled, for heaven's sakes. Ah, baby. Baby lamb. We're not going to have any bad starts. Look at us—we're on our honeymoon. Pretty soon we'll be regular old married people. I mean. I mean, in a few minutes we'll be getting in to New York, and then we'll be going to the hotel, and then everything will be all right. I mean—well, look at us! Here we are married! Here we are!"

"Yes, here we are," she said. "Aren't we?"

LADY WITH A LAMP

WELL, Mona! Well, you poor sick thing, you! Ah, you look so little and white and *little,* you do, lying there in that great big bed. That's what you do—go and look so childlike and pitiful nobody'd have the heart to scold you. And I ought to scold you, Mona. Oh, yes, I should so, too. Never letting me know you were ill. Never a word to your oldest friend. Darling, you might have known I'd understand, no matter what you did. What do I mean? Well, what do you *mean* what do I mean, Mona? Of course, if you'd rather not talk about—Not even to your oldest friend. All I wanted to say was you might have known that I'm always for you, no matter what happens. I do admit, sometimes it's a little hard for me to understand how on earth you ever got into such—well. Goodness knows I don't want to nag you now, when you're so sick.

All right, Mona, then you're *not* sick. If that's what you want to say, even to me, why, all right, my dear. People who aren't sick have to stay in bed for nearly two weeks, I suppose; I suppose people who aren't sick look the way you do. Just your nerves? You were simply all tired out? I see. It's just your nerves. You were simply tired. Yes. Oh, Mona, Mona, why don't you feel you can trust me?

Well—if that's the way you want to be to me, that's the way you want to be. I won't say anything more about it. Only I do think you might have let me know that you had—well, that you were so *tired,* if that's what you want me to say. Why, I'd never have known a word about it if I hadn't run bang into Alice Patterson and she told me she'd called you up and that maid of yours said you had been sick in bed for ten days. Of course, I'd thought it rather funny I hadn't heard from you, but you know how you are—you simply let people go, and weeks can go by like, well, like *weeks,* and never a sign from you. Why, I could have been dead over and over again, for all you'd know. Twenty times over. Now, I'm not going to scold you when you're sick, but frankly and honestly, Mona, I said to myself this time, "Well, she'll have a good wait before I call her up. I've given in often enough, goodness knows. Now she can just call me first." Frankly and honestly, that's what I said!

And then I saw Alice, and I did feel mean, I really did. And now to see you lying there—well, I feel like a complete *dog*. That's what you do to people even when you're in the wrong the way you always are, you wicked little thing, you! Ah, the poor dear! Feels just so awful, doesn't it?

Oh, don't keep trying to be brave, child. Not with me. Just give in—it helps so much. Just tell me all about it. You know I'll never say a word. Or at least you ought to know. When Alice told me that maid of yours said you were all tired out and your nerves had gone bad, I naturally never said anything, but I thought to myself, "Well, maybe that's the only thing Mona could say was the matter. That's probably about the best excuse she could think of." And of course *I'll* never deny it—but perhaps it might have been better to have said you had influenza or ptomaine poisoning. After all, people don't stay in bed for ten whole days just because they're nervous. All right, Mona, then they *do*. Then they do. Yes, dear.

Ah, to think of you going through all this and crawling off here all alone like a little wounded animal or something. And with only that colored Edie to take care of you. Darling, oughtn't you have a trained nurse, I mean really oughtn't you? There must be so many things that have to be done for you. Why, Mona! Mona, please! Dear, you don't have to get so excited. Very well, my dear, it's just as you say—there isn't a single thing to be done. I was mistaken, that's all. I simply thought that after— Oh, now, you don't have to do that. You never have to say you're sorry, to *me*. I understand. As a matter of fact, I was glad to hear you lose your temper. It's a good sign when sick people are cross. It means they're on the way to getting better. Oh, I know! You go right ahead and be cross all you want to.

Look, where shall I sit? I want to sit some place where you won't have to turn around, so you can talk to me. You stay right the way you're lying, and I'll— Because you shouldn't move around, I'm sure. It must be terribly bad for you. All right, dear, you can move around all you want to. All right, I must be crazy. I'm crazy, then. We'll leave it like that. Only please, please don't excite yourself that way.

I'll just get this chair and put it over—oops, I'm sorry I joggled the bed—put it over here, where you can see me. There. But first I want to fix your pillows before I get settled. Well, they certainly are *not* all right, Mona. After the way you've been twisting them and pulling them, these last few minutes. Now look, honey, I'll help you raise yourself ve-ry, ve-ry slo-o-ow-ly. Oh. Of course you can sit up by yourself, dear. Of course you can. Nobody ever said you couldn't. Nobody ever thought of such a thing. There now, your pillows are all smooth and lovely, and you lie right down again, before you hurt yourself. Now, isn't that better? Well, I should think it was!

Just a minute, till I get my sewing. Oh, yes, I brought it along, so we'd be all cozy. Do you honestly, frankly and honestly, think it's pretty? I'm so glad. It's nothing but a tray-cloth, you know. But you simply can't have too many. They're a lot of fun to make, too, doing this edge—it goes so quickly. Oh, Mona dear, so often I think if you just had a home of your own, and could be all busy, making pretty little things like this for it, it would do so *much* for you. I worry so about you, living in a little furnished apartment, with nothing that belongs to you, no roots, no nothing. It's not right for a woman. It's all wrong for a woman like you. Oh, I wish you'd get over that Garry McVicker! If you could just meet some nice, sweet, considerate man, and get married to him, and have your own lovely place—and with your *taste*, Mona!—and maybe have a couple of children. You're so simply adorable with children.

Why, Mona Morrison, are you crying? Oh, you've got a cold? You've got a cold, *too*? I thought you were crying, there for a second. Don't you want my handkerchief, lamb? Oh, you have yours. Wouldn't you have a pink chiffon handkerchief, you nut! Why on earth don't you use cleansing tissues, just lying there in bed with no one to see you? You little idiot, you! Extravagant little fool!

No, but really, I'm serious. I've said to Fred so often, "Oh, if we could just get Mona married!" Honestly, you don't know the feeling it gives you, just to be all secure and safe with your own sweet home and your own blessed children, and your own nice husband coming back to you every night. That's a woman's *life,* Mona. What you've been doing is really horrible. Just drifting along, that's all. What's going to happen to you, dear, whatever is going to become of you? But no—you don't even think of it. You go, and go falling in love with that Garry. Well, my dear, you've got to give me credit—I said from the very first, "He'll never marry her." You know that. What? There was never any thought of marriage, with you and Garry? Oh, Mona, now listen! Every woman on earth thinks of marriage as soon as she's in love with a man. Every woman, I don't care who she is.

Oh, if you were only married! It would be all the difference in the world. I think a child would do everything for you, Mona. Goodness knows, I just can't speak *decently* to that Garry, after the way he's treated you—well, you know perfectly well, *none* of your friends can—but I can frankly and honestly say, if he married you, I'd absolutely let bygones be bygones, and I'd be just as happy as happy, for you. If he's what you want. And I will say, what with your lovely looks and what with good-looking as he is, you ought to have simply *gorgeous* children. Mona, baby, you really have got a rotten cold, haven't you? Don't you want me to get you another handkerchief? Really?

I'm simply sick that I didn't bring you any flowers. But I thought the place would be full of them. Well, I'll stop on the way home and send you some. It looks too dreary here, without a flower in the room. Didn't Garry send you any? Oh, he didn't know you were sick. Well, doesn't he send you flowers anyway? Listen, hasn't he called up, all this time, and found out whether you were sick or not? Not in ten days? Well, then, haven't you called him and told him? Ah, now, Mona, there *is* such a thing as being too much of a heroine. Let him worry a little, dear. It would be a very good thing for him. Maybe that's the trouble—you've always taken all the worry for both of you. Hasn't sent any flowers! Hasn't even telephoned! Well, I'd just like to talk to that young man for a few minutes. After all, this is all *his* responsibility.

He's away? He's *what*? Oh, he went to Chicago two weeks ago. Well, it seems to me I'd always heard that there were telephone wires running between here and Chicago, but of course— And you'd think since he's been back, the least he could do would be to do something. He's not back yet? He's not *back* yet? Mona, what are you trying to tell me? Why, just night before last— Said he'd let you know the minute he got home? Of all the rotten, low things I ever heard in my life, this is really the— Mona, dear, please lie down. Please. Why, I didn't mean anything. I don't know what I was going to say, honestly I don't, it couldn't have been anything. For goodness' sake, let's talk about something else.

Let's see. Oh, you really ought to see Julia Post's living-room, the way she's done it now. She has brown walls—not beige, you know, or tan or anything, but brown—and these cream-colored taffeta curtains and— Mona, I tell you I absolutely don't know what I was going to say, before. It's gone completely out of my head. So you see how unimportant it must have been. Dear, please just lie quiet and try to relax. Please forget about that man for a few minutes, anyway. No man's worth getting that worked up about. Catch me doing it! You know you can't expect to get well quickly, if you get yourself so excited. You know that.

What doctor did you have, darling? Or don't you want to say? Your own? Your own Doctor Britton? You don't mean it! Well, I certainly never thought he'd do a thing like— Yes, dear, of course he's a nerve specialist. Yes, dear. Yes, dear. Yes, dear, of course you have perfect confidence in him. I only wish you would in me, once in a while; after we went to school together and everything. You might know I absolutely sympathize with you. I don't see how you could possibly have done anything else. I know you've always talked about how you'd give anything to have a baby, but it would have been so terribly unfair to the child to bring it into the world without being married. You'd have had to go live abroad and never see anybody and— And even then, somebody would have been sure to have told it sometime. They always do. You did the only possible thing, *I* think. Mona, for heaven's sake! Don't scream like that. I'm not deaf, you know. All right, dear, all right, all right, all right. All right, of course I believe you. Naturally I take your word for anything. Anything you say. Only please do try to be quiet. Just lie back and rest, and have a nice talk.

Ah, now don't keep harping on that. I've told you a hundred times, if I've told you once, I wasn't going to say anything at all. I tell you I don't remember *what* I was going to say. "Night before last"? When did I mention "night before last"? I never said any such— Well. Maybe it's better this way, Mona. The more I think of it, the more I think it's much better for you to hear it from me. Because somebody's bound to tell you. These things always come out. And I know you'd rather hear it from your oldest friend, wouldn't you? And the good Lord knows, anything I could do to make you see what that man really is! Only do relax, darling. Just for me. Dear, Garry isn't in Chicago. Fred and I saw him night before last at the Comet Club, dancing. And Alice saw him Tuesday night at El Rhumba. And I don't know how many people have said they've seen him around at the theater and night clubs and things. Why, he couldn't have stayed in Chicago more than a day or so—if he went at all.

Well, he was with *her* when we saw him, honey. Apparently he's with her all the time; nobody ever sees him with anyone else. You really must make up your mind to it, dear; it's the only thing to do. I hear all over that he's just simply *pleading* with her to marry him, but I don't know how true that is. I'm sure I can't see why he'd want to, but then you never can tell what a man like that will do. It would be just good enough *for* him if he got her, that's what *I* say. Then he'd see. She'd never stand for any of his nonsense. She'd make him toe the mark. She's a smart woman.

But, oh, so *ordinary*. I thought, when we saw them the other night, "Well, she just looks cheap, that's all she looks." That must be what he likes, I suppose. I must admit he looked very well. I never saw him look better. Of course you know what I think of him, but I always had to say he's one of the handsomest men I ever saw in my life. I can understand how any woman would be attracted to him—at first. Until they found out what he's really like. Oh, if you could have seen him with that awful, common creature, never once taking his eyes off her, and hanging on every word she said, as if it was pearls! It made me just——

Mona, angel, are you *crying*? Now, darling, that's just plain silly. That man's not worth another thought. You've thought about him entirely too much, that's the trouble. Three years! Three of the best years of your life you've given him, and all the time he's been deceiving you with that woman. Just think back over what you've been through—all the times and times and times he promised you he'd give her up; and you, you poor little idiot, you'd believe him, and then he'd go right back to her again. And *everybody* knew about it. Think of that, and then try telling me that man's worth crying over! Really, Mona! I'd have more pride.

You know, I'm just glad this thing happened. I'm just glad you found out. This is a little too much, this time. In Chicago, indeed! Let you know the minute he came home! The kindest thing a person could possibly have done was to tell you, and bring you to your senses at last. I'm not sorry I did it, for a second. When I think of him out having the time of his life and you lying here deathly sick all on account of him, I could just— Yes, it is on account of him. Even if you didn't have an—well, even if I was mistaken about what I naturally thought was the matter with you when you made such a secret of your illness, he's driven you into a nervous breakdown, and that's plenty bad enough. All for that man! The skunk! You just put him right out of your head.

Why, of course you can, Mona. All you need to do is to pull yourself together, child. Simply say to yourself, "Well, I've wasted three years of my life, and that's that." Never worry about *him* any more. The Lord knows, darling, he's not worrying about you.

It's just because you're weak and sick that you're worked up like this, dear. I know. But you're going to be all right. You can make something of your life. You've got to, Mona, you know. Because after all—well, of course, you never looked sweeter, I don't mean that; but you're—well, you're not getting any younger. And here you've been throwing away your time, never seeing your friends, never going out, never meeting anybody new, just sitting here waiting for Garry to telephone, or Garry to come in—if he didn't have anything better to do. For three years, you've never had a thought in your head but that man. Now you just forget him.

Ah, baby, it isn't good for you to cry like that. Please don't. He's not even worth talking about. Look at the woman he's in love with, and you'll see what kind he is. You were much too good for him. You were much too sweet to him. You gave in too easily. The minute he had you, he didn't want you any more. That's what he's like. Why, he no more loved you than——

Mona, don't! Mona, stop it! Please, Mona! You mustn't talk like that, you mustn't say such things. You've got to stop crying, you'll be terribly sick. Stop, oh, stop it, oh, please stop! Oh, what am I going to do with her? Mona, dear—Mona! Oh, where in heaven's name is that fool maid?

Edie. Oh, Edie! Edie, I think you'd better get Dr. Britton on the telephone, and tell him to come down and give Miss Morrison something to quiet her. I'm afraid she's got herself a little bit upset.

TOO BAD

"My dear," Mrs. Marshall said to Mrs. Ames, "I never was so surprised in my life. Never in my life. Why, Grace and I were like that—just like *that*."

She held up her right hand, the upstanding first and second fingers rigidly close together, in illustration.

Mrs. Ames shook her head sadly, and offered the cinnamon toast.

"Imagine!" said Mrs. Marshall, refusing it though with a longing eye. "We were going to have dinner with them last Tuesday night, and then I got this letter from Grace from this little place up in Connecticut, saying she was going to be up there she didn't know how long, and she thought, when she came back, she'd probably take just one big room with a kitchenette. Ernest was living down at the club, she said."

"But what did they do about their apartment?" Mrs. Ames's voice was high with anxiety.

"Why, it seems his sister took it, furnished and all—by the way, remind me, I must go and see her," said Mrs. Marshall. "They wanted to move into town, anyway, and they were looking for a place."

"Doesn't she feel terribly about it—his sister?" asked Mrs. Ames.

"Oh—terribly." Mrs. Marshall dismissed the word as inadequate. "My dear, think how everybody that knew them feels. Think how I feel. I don't know when I've had a thing depress me more. If it had been anybody but the Weldons!"

Mrs. Ames nodded.

"That's what I said," she reported.

"That's what everybody says." Mrs. Marshall quickly took away any undeserved credit. "To think of the Weldons separating! Why, I always used to say to Jim. 'Well, there's one happily married couple, anyway,' I used to say, 'so congenial, and with that nice apartment, and all.' And then, right out of a clear sky, they go and separate. I simply can't understand what on earth made them do it. It just seems too awful!"

Again Mrs. Ames nodded, slowly and sadly.

"Yes, it always seems too bad, a thing like that does," she said. "It's too bad."

II

Mrs. Ernest Weldon wandered about the orderly living-room, giving it some of those little feminine touches. She was not especially good as a touch-giver. The idea was pretty, and appealing to her. Before she was married, she had dreamed of herself as moving softly about her new dwelling, deftly moving a vase here or straightening a flower there, and thus transforming it from a house to a home. Even now, after seven years of marriage, she liked to picture herself in the gracious act.

But, though she conscientiously made a try at it every night as soon as the rose-shaded lamps were lit, she was always a bit bewildered as to how one went about performing those tiny miracles that make all the difference in the world to a room. The living-room, it seemed to her, looked good enough as it was—as good as it would ever look, with that mantelpiece and the same old furniture. Delia, one of the most thoroughly feminine of creatures, had subjected it to a long series of emphatic touches earlier in the day, and none of her handiwork had since been disturbed. But the feat of making all the difference in the world, so Mrs. Weldon had always heard, was not a thing to be left to servants. Touch-giving was a wife's job. And Mrs. Weldon was not one to shirk the business she had entered.

With an almost pitiable air of uncertainty, she strayed over to the mantel, lifted a small Japanese vase, and stood with it in her hand, gazing helplessly around the room. The white-enameled bookcase caught her eye, and gratefully she crossed to it and set the vase upon it, carefully rearranging various ornaments to make room. To relieve the congestion, she took up a framed photograph of Mr. Weldon's sister in evening gown and eye-glasses, again looked all about, and then set it timidly on the piano. She smoothed the piano-cover ingratiatingly, straightened the copies of "A Day in Venice," "To a Wild Rose," and Kreisler's "Caprice Viennois," which stood ever upon the rack, walked over to the tea-table and effected a change of places between the cream-jug and the sugar-bowl.

Then she stepped back, and surveyed her innovations. It was amazing how little difference they made to the room.

Sighing, Mrs. Weldon turned her attention to a bowl of daffodils, slightly past their first freshness. There was nothing to be done there; the omniscient Delia had refreshed them with clear water, had clipped their stems, and removed their more passé sisters. Still Mrs. Weldon bent over them pulling them gently about.

She liked to think of herself as one for whom flowers would thrive, who must always have blossoms about her, if she would be truly happy. When her living-room flowers died, she almost never forgot to stop in at the florist's, the next day, and get a fresh bunch. She told people, in little bursts of confidence, that she loved flowers. There was something almost apologetic in her way of uttering her tender avowal, as if she would beg her listeners not to consider her too bizarre in her taste. It seemed rather as though she expected the hearer to fall back, startled, at her words, crying, "Not really! Well, what *are* we coming to?"

She had other little confessions of affection, too, that she made from time to time; always with a little hesitation, as if understandably delicate about baring her heart, she told her love for color, the country, a good time, a really interesting play, nice materials, well-made clothes, and sunshine. But it was her fondness for flowers that she acknowledged oftenest. She seemed to feel that this, even more than her other predilections, set her apart from the general.

Mrs. Weldon gave the elderly daffodils a final pat, now, and once more surveyed the room, to see if any other repairs suggested themselves. Her lips tightened as the little Japanese vase met her gaze; distinctly, it had been better off in the first place. She set it back, the irritation that the sight of the mantel always gave her welling within her.

She had hated the mantelpiece from the moment they had first come to look at the apartment. There were other things that she had always hated about the place, too—the long, narrow hall, the dark dining-room, the inadequate closets. But Ernest had seemed to like the apartment well enough, so she had said nothing, then or since. After all, what was the use of fussing? Probably there would always be drawbacks, wherever they lived. There were enough in the last place they had had.

So they had taken the apartment on a five-year lease—there were four years and three months to go. Mrs. Weldon felt suddenly weary. She lay down on the davenport, and pressed her thin hand against her dull brown hair.

Mr. Weldon came down the street, bent almost double in his battle with the wind from the river. His mind went over its nightly dark thoughts on living near Riverside Drive, five blocks from a subway station—two of those blocks loud with savage gales. He did not much like their apartment, even when he reached it. As soon as he had seen that dining-room, he had realized that they must always breakfast by artificial light—a thing he hated. But Grace had never appeared to notice it, so he had held his peace. It didn't matter much, anyway, he explained to himself. There was pretty sure to be something wrong, everywhere. The dining-room wasn't much worse than that bedroom on the court, in the last place. Grace had never seemed to mind that, either.

Mrs. Weldon opened the door at his ring.

"Well!" she said, cheerily.

They smiled brightly at each other.

"Hel-lo," he said. "Well! You home?"

They kissed, slightly. She watched with polite interest while he hung up his hat and coat, removed the evening papers from his pocket, and handed one to her.

"Bring the papers?" she said, taking it.

She preceded him along the narrow hall to the living-room, where he let himself slowly down into his big chair, with a sound between a sigh and a groan. She sat opposite him, on the davenport. Again they smiled brightly at each other.

"Well, what have you been doing with yourself today?" he inquired.

She had been expecting the question. She had planned before he came in, how she would tell him all the little events of her day—how the woman in the grocer's shop had had an argument with the cashier, and how Delia had tried out a new salad for lunch with but moderate success, and how Alice Marshall had come to tea and it was quite true that Norma Matthews was going to have another baby. She had woven them into a lively little narrative, carefully choosing amusing phrases of description; had felt that she was going to tell it well and with spirit, and that he might laugh at the account of the occurrence in the grocer's. But now, as she considered it, it seemed to her a long, dull story. She had not the energy to begin it. And he was already smoothing out his paper.

"Oh, nothing," she said, with a gay little laugh. "Did you have a nice day?"

"Why—" he began. He had had some idea of telling her how he had finally put through that Detroit thing, and how tickled J. G. had seemed to be about it. But his interest waned, even as he started to speak. Besides, she was engrossed in breaking off a loose thread from the wool fringe on one of the pillows beside her.

"Oh, pretty fair," he said.

"Tired?" she asked.

"Not so much," he answered. "Why—want to do anything tonight?"

"Why, not unless you do," she said, brightly. "Whatever you say."

"Whatever *you* say," he corrected her.

The subject closed. There was a third exchange of smiles, and then he hid most of himself behind his paper.

Mrs. Weldon, too, turned to the newspaper. But it was an off night for news—a long speech of somebody's, a plan for a garbage dump, a proposed dirigible, a four-day-old murder mystery. No one she knew had died or become engaged or married, or had attended any social functions. The fashions depicted on the woman's page were for Miss Fourteen-to-Sixteen. The advertisements ran mostly to bread, and sauces, and men's clothes and sales of kitchen utensils. She put the paper down.

She wondered how Ernest could get so much enjoyment out of a newspaper. He could occupy himself with one for almost an hour, and then pick up another and go all through the same news with unabated interest. She wished that she could. She wished, even more than that, that she could think of something to say. She glanced around the room for inspiration.

"See my pretty daffy-down-dillies?" she said, finding it. To anyone else, she would have referred to them as daffodils.

Mr. Weldon looked in the direction of the flowers.

"M-m-mm," he said in admission, and returned to the news.

She looked at him, and shook her head despondently. He did not see, behind the paper; nor did she see that he was not reading. He was waiting, his hands gripping the printed sheet till their knuckles were blue-white, for her next remark.

It came.

"I love flowers," she said, in one of her little rushes of confidence.

Her husband did not answer. He sighed, his grip relaxed, and he went on reading.

Mrs. Weldon searched the room for another suggestion.

"Ernie," she said, "I'm so comfortable. Wouldn't you like to get up and get my handkerchief off the piano for me?"

He rose instantly. "Why, certainly," he said.

The way to ask people to fetch handkerchiefs, he thought as he went back to his chair, was to ask them to do it, and not try to make them think that you were giving them a treat. Either come right out and ask them, would they or wouldn't they, or else get up and get your handkerchief yourself.

"Thank you ever so much," his wife said with enthusiasm.

Delia appeared in the doorway. "Dinner," she murmured bashfully, as if it were not quite a nice word for a young woman to use, and vanished.

"Dinner, Ern," cried Mrs. Weldon gaily, getting up.

"Just minute," issued indistinctly from behind the newspaper.

Mrs. Weldon waited. Then her lips compressed, and she went over and playfully took the paper from her husband's hands. She smiled carefully at him, and he smiled back at her.

"You go ahead in," he said, rising. "I'll be right with you. I've just got to wash up."

She looked after him, and something like a volcanic eruption took place within her. You'd think that just one night—just one little night—he might go and wash before dinner was announced. Just one night—it didn't seem much to ask. But she said nothing. God knew it was aggravating, but after all, it wasn't worth the trouble of fussing about.

She was waiting, cheerful and bright, courteously refraining from beginning her soup, when he took his place at the table.

"Oh, tomato soup, eh?" he said.

"Yes," she answered. "You like it, don't you?"

"Who—me?" he said. "Oh, yes. Yes, indeed."

She smiled at him.

"Yes, I thought you liked it," she said.

"You like it, too, don't you?" he inquired.

"Oh, yes," she assured him. "Yes, I like it ever so much. I'm awfully fond of tomato soup."

"Yes," he said, "there's nothing much better than tomato soup on a cold night."

She nodded.

"I think it's nice, too," she confided.

They had had tomato soup for dinner probably three times a month during their married life.

The soup was finished, and Delia brought in the meat.

"Well, that looks pretty good," said Mr. Weldon, carving it. "We haven't had steak for a long time."

"Why, yes, we have, too, Ern," his wife said eagerly. "We had it—let me see, what night were the Baileys here?—we had it Wednesday night—no, Thursday night. Don't you remember?"

"Did we?" he said. "Yes, I guess you're right. It seemed longer, somehow."

Mrs. Weldon smiled politely. She could not think of any way to prolong the discussion.

What did married people talk about, anyway, when they were alone together? She had seen married couples—not dubious ones but people she really knew were husbands and wives—at the theater or in trains, talking together as animatedly as if they were just acquaintances. She always watched them, marvelingly, wondering what on earth they found to say.

She could talk well enough to other people. There never seemed to be enough time for her to finish saying all she wanted to to her friends; she recalled how she had run on to Alice Marshall, only that afternoon. Both men and women found her attractive to listen to; not brilliant, not particularly funny, but still amusing and agreeable. She was never at a loss for something to say, never conscious of groping around for a topic. She had a good memory for bits of fresh gossip, or little stories of some celebrity that she had read or heard somewhere, and a knack of telling them entertainingly. Things people said to her stimulated her to quick replies, and more amusing narratives. They weren't especially scintillating people, either; it was just that they talked to her.

That was the trick of it. If nobody said anything to you, how were you to carry on a conversation from there? Inside, she was always bitter and angry at Ernest for not helping her out.

Ernest, too, seemed to be talkative enough when he was with others. People were always coming up and telling her how much they had enjoyed meeting her husband, and what fun he was. They weren't just being polite. There was no reason why they should go out of their way to say it.

Even when she and Ernest had another couple in to dinner or bridge, they both talked and laughed easily, all evening long. But as soon as the guests said good-night and what an awfully nice evening it had been, and the door had closed behind them, there the Weldons were again, without a word to say to each other. It would have been intimate and amusing to have talked over their guests' clothes and skill at bridge and probable domestic and financial affairs, and she would do it the next day, with great interest, too, to Alice Marshall, or some other one of her friends. But she couldn't do it with Ernest. Just as she started to, she found she simply couldn't make the effort.

So they would put away the card-table and empty the ash-receivers, with many "Oh, I beg your pardon's" and "No, no—I was in your way's," and then Ernest would say, "Well, I guess I'll go along to bed," and she would answer, "All right—I'll be in in a minute," and they would smile cheerfully at each other, and another evening would be over.

She tried to remember what they used to talk about before they were married, when they were engaged. It seemed to her that they never had had much to say to each other. But she hadn't worried about it then; indeed, she had felt the satisfaction of the correct, in their courtship, for she had always heard that true love was inarticulate. Then, besides, there had been always kissing and things, to take up your mind. But it had turned out that true marriage was apparently equally dumb. And you can't depend on kisses and all the rest of it to while away the evenings, after seven years.

You'd think that you would get used to it, in seven years, would realize that that was the way it was, and let it go at that. You don't, though. A thing like that gets on your nerves. It isn't one of those cozy, companionable silences that people occasionally fall into together. It makes you feel as if you must do something about it, as if you weren't performing your duty. You have the feeling a hostess has when her party is going badly, when her guests sit in corners and refuse to mingle. It makes you nervous and self-conscious, and you talk desperately about tomato soup, and say things like "daffy-down-dilly."

Mrs. Weldon cast about in her mind for a subject to offer her husband. There was Alice Marshall's new system of reducing—no, that was pretty dull. There was the case she had read in the morning's paper about the man of eighty-seven who had taken, as his fourth wife, a girl of twenty—he had probably seen that, and as long as he hadn't thought it worth repeating, he wouldn't think it worth hearing. There was the thing the Baileys' little boy had said about Jesus—no, she had told him that the night before.

She looked over at him, desultorily eating his rhubarb pie. She wished he wouldn't put that greasy stuff on his head. Perhaps it was necessary, if his hair really was falling out, but it did seem that he might find some more attractive remedy, if he only had the consideration to look around for one. Anyway, why must his hair fall out? There was something a little disgusting about people with falling hair.

"Like your pie, Ernie?" she asked vivaciously.

"Why, I don't know," he said, thinking it over. "I'm not so crazy about rhubarb, I don't think. Are you?"

"No, I'm not so awfully crazy about it," she answered. "But then, I'm not really crazy about any kind of pie."

"Aren't you really?" he said, politely surprised. "I like pie pretty well—some kinds of pie."

"Do you?" The polite surprise was hers now.

"Why, yes," he said. "I like a nice huckleberry pie, or a nice lemon meringue pie, or a—" He lost interest in the thing himself, and his voice died away.

He avoided looking at her left hand, which lay on the edge of the table, palm upward. The long, grey-white ends of her nails protruded beyond the tips of her fingers, and the sight made him uncomfortable. Why in God's name must she wear her finger nails that preposterous length, and file them to those horrible points? If there was anything that he hated, it was a woman with pointed finger nails.

They returned to the living-room, and Mr. Weldon again eased himself down into his chair, reaching for the second paper.

"Quite sure there isn't anything you'd like to do tonight?" he asked solicitously. "Like to go to the movies or anything?"

"Oh, no," she said. "Unless there's something you want to do."

"No, no," he answered. "I just thought maybe you wanted to."

"Not unless you do," she said.

He began on his paper, and she wandered aimlessly about the room. She had forgotten to get a new book from the library, and it had never in her life occurred to her to reread a book that she had once completed. She thought vaguely of playing solitaire, but she did not care enough about it to go to the trouble of getting out the cards, and setting up the table. There was some sewing that she could do, and she thought that she might presently go into the bedroom and fetch the nightgown that she was making for herself. Yes, she would probably do that, in a little while.

Ernest would read industriously, and, along toward the middle of the paper, he would start yawning aloud. Something happened inside Mrs. Weldon when he did this. She would murmur that she had to speak to Delia, and hurry to the kitchen. She would stay there rather a long time, looking vaguely into jars and inquiring half-heartedly about laundry lists, and, when she returned, he would have gone in to get ready for bed.

In a year, three hundred of their evenings were like this. Seven times three hundred is more than two thousand.

Mrs. Weldon went into the bedroom, and brought back her sewing. She sat down, pinned the pink satin to her knee, and began whipping narrow lace along the top of the half-made garment. It was fussy work. The fine thread knotted and drew, and she could not get the light adjusted so that the shadow of her head did not fall on her work. She grew a little sick, from the strain on her eyes.

Mr. Weldon turned a page, and yawned aloud. "Wah-huh-huh-huh-huh," he went, on a descending scale. He yawned again, and this time climbed the scale.

III

"My dear," Mrs. Ames said to Mrs. Marshall, "don't you really think that there must have been some other woman?"

"Oh, I simply couldn't think it was anything like that," said Mrs. Marshall. "Not Ernest Weldon. So devoted—home every night at half-past six, and such good company, and so jolly, and all. I don't see how there *could* have been."

"Sometimes," observed Mrs. Ames, "those awfully jolly men at home are just the kind."

"Yes, I know," Mrs. Marshall said. "But not Ernest Weldon. Why, I used to say to Jim, 'I never saw such a devoted husband in my life,' I said. Oh, not Ernest Weldon."

"I don't suppose," began Mrs. Ames, and hesitated. "I don't suppose," she went on, intently pressing the bit of sodden lemon in her cup with her teaspoon, "that Grace—that there was ever anyone—or anything like that?"

"Oh, Heavens, no," cried Mrs. Marshall. "Grace Weldon just gave her whole life to that man. It was Ernest this and Ernest that every minute. I simply can't understand it. If there was one earthly reason—if they ever fought, or if Ernest drank, or anything like that. But they got along so beautifully together—why, it just seems as if they must have been crazy to go and do a thing like this. Well, I can't begin to tell you how blue it's made me. It seems so awful!"

"Yes," said Mrs. Ames, "it certainly is too bad."

MR. DURANT

Not for some ten days had Mr. Durant known any such ease of mind. He gave himself up to it, wrapped himself, warm and soft, as in a new and an expensive cloak. God, for Whom Mr. Durant entertained a good-humored affection, was in His heaven, and all was again well with Mr. Durant's world.

Curious how this renewed peace sharpened his enjoyment of the accustomed things about him. He looked back at the rubber works, which he had just left for the day, and nodded approvingly at the solid red pile, at the six neat stories rising impressively into the darkness. You would go far, he thought, before you would find a more up-and-coming outfit, and there welled in him a pleasing, proprietary sense of being a part of it.

He gazed amiably down Center Street, noting how restfully the lights glowed. Even the wet, dented pavement, spotted with thick puddles, fed his pleasure by reflecting the discreet radiance above it. And to complete his comfort, the car for which he was waiting, admirably on time, swung into view far down the track. He thought, with a sort of jovial tenderness, of what it would bear him to; of his dinner—it was fish-chowder night—of his children, of his wife, in the order named. Then he turned his kindly attention to the girl who stood near him, obviously awaiting the Center Street car, too. He was delighted to feel a sharp interest in her. He regarded it as being distinctly creditable to himself that he could take a healthy notice of such matters once more. Twenty years younger—that's what he felt.

Rather shabby, she was, in her rough coat with its shagginess rubbed off here and there. But there was a something in the way her cheaply smart turban was jammed over her eyes, in the way her thin young figure moved under the loose coat. Mr. Durant pointed his tongue, and moved it delicately along his cool, smooth upper lip.

The car approached, clanged to a stop before them. Mr. Durant stepped gallantly aside to let the girl get in first. He did not help her to enter, but the solicitous way in which he superintended the process gave all the effect of his having actually assisted her.

Her tight little skirt slipped up over her thin, pretty legs as she took the high step. There was a run in one of her flimsy silk stockings. She was doubtless unconscious of it; it was well back toward the seam, extending, probably from her garter, half-way down the calf. Mr. Durant had an odd desire to catch his thumbnail in the present end of the run, and to draw it on down until the slim line of the dropped stitches reached to the top of her low shoe. An indulgent smile at his whimsy played about his mouth, broadening to a grin of affable evening greeting for the conductor, as he entered the car and paid his fare.

The girl sat down somewhere far up at the front. Mr. Durant found a desirable seat toward the rear, and craned his neck to see her. He could catch a glimpse of a fold of her turban and a bit of her brightly rouged cheek, but only at a cost of holding his head in a strained, and presently painful, position. So, warmed by the assurance that there would always be others, he let her go, and settled himself restfully. He had a ride of twenty minutes or so before him. He allowed his head to fall gently back, to let his eyelids droop, and gave himself to his thoughts. Now that the thing was comfortably over and done with, he could think of it easily, almost laughingly. Last week, now, and even part of the week before, he had had to try with all his strength to force it back every time it wrenched itself into his mind. It had positively affected his sleep. Even though he was shielded by his newly acquired amused attitude, Mr. Durant felt indignation flood within him when he recalled those restless nights.

He had met Rose for the first time about three months before. She had been sent up to his office to take some letters for him. Mr. Durant was assistant manager of the rubber company's credit department; his wife was wont to refer to him as one of the officers of the company, and, though she often spoke thus of him to people in his presence, he never troubled to go more fully into detail about his position. He rated a room, a desk, and a telephone to himself; but not a stenographer. When he wanted to give dictation or to have some letters typewritten, he telephoned around to the various other offices until he found a girl who was not busy with her own work. That was how Rose had come to him.

She was not a pretty girl. Distinctly, no. But there was a rather sweet fragility about her, and an almost desperate timidity that Mr. Durant had once found engaging, but that he now thought of with a prickling irritation. She was twenty, and the glamour of youth was around her. When she bent over her work, her back showing white through her sleazy blouse, her clean hair coiled smoothly on her thin neck, her straight, childish legs crossed at the knee to support her pad, she had an undeniable appeal.

But not pretty—no. Her hair wasn't the kind that went up well, her eyelashes and lips were too pale, she hadn't much knack about choosing and wearing her cheap clothes. Mr. Durant, in reviewing the thing, felt a surprise that she should ever have attracted him. But it was a tolerant surprise, not an impatient one. Already he looked back on himself as being just a big boy in the whole affair.

It did not occur to him to feel even a flicker of astonishment that Rose should have responded so eagerly to him, an immovably married man of forty-nine. He never thought of himself in that way. He used to tell Rose, laughingly, that he was old enough to be her father, but neither of them ever really believed it. He regarded her affection for him as the most natural thing in the world—there she was, coming from a much smaller town, never the sort of girl to have had admirers; naturally, she was dazzled at the attentions of a man who, as Mr. Durant put it, was approaching the prime. He had been charmed with the idea of there having been no other men in her life; but lately, far from feeling flattered at being the first and only one, he had come to regard it as her having taken a sly advantage of him, to put him in that position.

It had all been surprisingly easy. Mr. Durant knew it would be almost from the first time he saw her. That did not lessen its interest in his eyes. Obstacles discouraged him, rather than led him on. Elimination of bother was the main thing.

Rose was not a coquettish girl. She had that curious directness that some very timid people possess. There were her scruples, of course, but Mr. Durant readily reasoned them away. Not that he was a master of technique, either. He had had some experiences, probably a third as many as he habitually thought of himself as having been through, but none that taught him much of the delicate shadings of wooing. But then, Rose's simplicity asked exceedingly little.

She was never one to demand much of him, anyway. She never thought of stirring up any trouble between him and his wife, never besought him to leave his family and go away with her, even for a day. Mr. Durant valued her for that. It did away with a lot of probable fussing.

It was amazing how free they were, how little lying there was to do. They stayed in the office after hours—Mr. Durant found many letters that must be dictated. No one thought anything of that. Rose was busy most of the day, and it was only considerate that Mr. Durant should not break in on her employer's time, only natural that he should want as good a stenographer as she was to attend to his correspondence.

Rose's only relative, a married sister, lived in another town. The girl roomed with an acquaintance named Ruby, also employed at the rubber works, and Ruby, who was much taken up with her own affairs of the emotions, never appeared to think it strange if Rose was late to dinner, or missed the meal entirely. Mr.

Durant readily explained to his wife that he was detained by a rush of business. It only increased his importance, to her, and spurred her on to devising especially pleasing dishes, and solicitously keeping them hot for his return. Sometimes, important in their guilt, Rose and he put out the light in the little office and locked the door, to trick the other employees into thinking that they had long ago gone home. But no one ever so much as rattled the doorknob, seeking admission.

It was all so simple that Mr. Durant never thought of it as anything outside the usual order of things. His interest in Rose did not blunt his appreciation of chance attractive legs or provocative glances. It was an entanglement of the most restful, comfortable nature. It even held a sort of homelike quality, for him.

And then everything had to go and get spoiled. "Wouldn't you know?" Mr. Durant asked himself, with deep bitterness.

Ten days before, Rose had come weeping to his office. She had the sense to wait till after hours, for a wonder, but anybody might have walked in and seen her blubbering there; Mr. Durant felt it to be due only to the efficient management of his personal God that no one had. She wept, as he sweepingly put it, all over the place. The color left her cheeks and collected damply in her nose, and rims of vivid pink grew around her pale eyelashes. Even her hair became affected; it came away from the pins, and stray ends of it wandered limply over her neck. Mr. Durant hated to look at her, could not bring himself to touch her.

All his energies were expended in urging her for God's sake to keep quiet; he did not ask her what was the matter. But it came out, between bursts of unpleasant-sounding sobs. She was "in trouble." Neither then nor in the succeeding days did she and Mr. Durant ever use any less delicate phrase to describe her condition. Even in their thoughts, they referred to it that way.

She had suspected it, she said, for some time, but she hadn't wanted to bother him about it until she was absolutely sure. "Didn't want to bother me!" thought Mr. Durant.

Naturally, he was furious. Innocence is a desirable thing, a dainty thing, an appealing thing, in its place; but carried too far, it is merely ridiculous. Mr. Durant wished to God that he had never seen Rose. He explained this desire to her.

But that was no way to get things done. As he had often jovially remarked to his friends, he knew "a thing or two." Cases like this could be what people of the world called "fixed up"—New York society women, he understood, thought virtually nothing of it. This case could be fixed up, too. He got Rose to go home, telling her not to worry, he would see that everything was all right. The main thing was to get her out of sight, with that nose and those eyes.

But knowing a thing or two and putting the knowledge into practice turned out to be vastly different things. Mr. Durant did not know whom to seek for information. He pictured himself inquiring of his intimates if they could tell him of "someone that this girl he had heard about could go to." He could hear his voice uttering the words, could hear the nervous laugh that would accompany them, the terrible flatness of them as they left his lips. To confide in one person would be confiding in at least one too many. It was a progressing town, but still small enough for gossip to travel like a typhoon. Not that he thought for a moment that his wife would believe any such thing, if it reached her; but where would be the sense in troubling her?

Mr. Durant grew pale and jumpy over the thing as the days went by. His wife worried herself into one of her sick spells over his petulant refusals of second helpings. There daily arose in him an increasing anger that he should be drawn into conniving to find a way to break the law of his country—probably the law of every country in the world. Certainly of every decent, Christian place.

It was Ruby, finally, who got them out of it. When Rose confessed to him that she had broken down and told Ruby, his rage leaped higher than any words. Ruby was secretary to the vice-president of the rubber company. It would be pretty, wouldn't it, if she let it out? He had lain wide-eyed beside his wife all that night through. He shuddered at the thought of chance meetings with Ruby in the hall.

But Ruby had made it delightfully simple, when they did meet. There were no reproachful looks, no cold turnings away of the head. She had given him her usual smiling "good-morning," and added a little upward glance, mischievous, understanding, with just the least hint of admiration in it. There was a sense of intimacy, of a shared secret binding them cozily together. A fine girl, that Ruby!

Ruby had managed it all without any fuss. Mr. Durant was not directly concerned in the planning. He heard of it only through Rose, on the infrequent occasions when he had had to see her. Ruby knew, through some indistinct friends of hers, of "a woman." It would be twenty-five dollars. Mr. Durant had gallantly insisted upon giving Rose the money. She had started to sniffle about taking it, but he had finally prevailed. Not that he couldn't have used the twenty-five very nicely himself, just then, with Junior's teeth, and all!

Well, it was all over now. The invaluable Ruby had gone with Rose to "the woman"; had that very afternoon taken her to the station and put her on a train for her sister's. She had even thought of wiring the sister beforehand that Rose had had influenza and must have a rest.

Mr. Durant had urged Rose to look on it as just a little vacation. He promised, moreover, to put in a good word for her whenever she wanted her job back. But Rose had gone pink about the nose again at the thought. She had sobbed her rasping sobs, then had raised her face from her stringy handkerchief and said, with an entirely foreign firmness, that she never wanted to see the rubber works or Ruby or Mr. Durant again. He had laughed indulgently, had made himself pat her thin back. In his relief at the outcome of things, he could be generous to the pettish.

He chuckled inaudibly, as he reviewed that last scene. "I suppose she thought she'd make me sore, saying she was never coming back," he told himself. "I suppose I was supposed to get down on my knees and coax her."

It was fine to dwell on the surety that it was all done with. Mr. Durant had somewhere picked up a phrase that seemed ideally suited to the occasion. It was to him an admirably dashing expression. There was something stylish about it; it was the sort of thing you would expect to hear used by men who wore spats and swung canes without self-consciousness. He employed it now, with satisfaction.

"Well, that's that," he said to himself. He was not sure that he didn't say it aloud.

The car slowed, and the girl in the rough coat came down toward the door. She was jolted against Mr. Durant—he would have sworn she did it purposely—uttered a word of laughing apology, gave him what he interpreted as an inviting glance. He half rose to follow her, then sank back again. After all, it was a wet night, and his corner was five blocks farther on. Again there came over him the cozy assurance that there would always be others.

In high humor, he left the car at his street, and walked in the direction of his house. It was a mean night, but the insinuating cold and the black rain only made more graphic his picture of the warm, bright house, the great dish of steaming fish chowder, the well-behaved children and wife that awaited him. He walked rather slowly to make them seem all the better for the wait, humming a little on his way down the neat sidewalk, past the solid, reputably shabby houses.

Two girls ran past him, holding their hands over their heads to protect their hats from the wet. He enjoyed the click of their heels on the pavement, their little bursts of breathless laughter, their arms upraised in a position that brought out all the neat lines of their bodies. He knew who they were—they lived three doors down from him, in the house with the lamp-post in front of it. He had often lingeringly noticed their fresh prettiness. He hurried, so that he might see them run up the steps, their narrow skirts sliding up over their legs. His mind went back to the girl with the run in her stocking, and amusing thoughts filled him as he entered his own house.

His children rushed, clamoring, to meet him, as he unlocked the door. There was something exciting going on, for Junior and Charlotte were usually too careful-mannered to cause people discomfort by rushing and babbling. They were nice, sensible children, good at their lessons, and punctilious about brushing their teeth, speaking the truth, and avoiding playmates who used bad words. Junior would be the very picture of his father, when they got the bands off his teeth, and little Charlotte strongly resembled her mother. Friends often commented on what a nice arrangement it was.

Mr. Durant smiled good-naturedly through their racket, carefully hanging up his coat and hat. There was even pleasure for him in the arrangement of his apparel on the cool, shiny knob of the hatrack. Everything was pleasant, tonight. Even the children's noise couldn't irritate him.

Eventually he discovered the cause of the commotion. It was a little stray dog that had come to the back door. They were out in the kitchen helping Freda, and Charlotte thought she heard something scratching, and Freda said nonsense, but Charlotte went to the door, anyway, and there was this little dog, trying to get in out of the wet. Mother helped them give it a bath, and Freda fed it, and now it was in the living-room. Oh, Father, couldn't they keep it, please, couldn't they, couldn't they, please, Father, couldn't they? It didn't have any collar on it—so you see it didn't belong to anybody. Mother said all right, if he said so, and Freda liked it fine.

Mr. Durant still smiled his gentle smile. "We'll see," he said.

The children looked disappointed, but not despondent. They would have liked more enthusiasm, but "we'll see," they knew by experience, meant a leaning in the right direction.

Mr. Durant proceeded to the living-room, to inspect the visitor. It was not a beauty. All too obviously, it was the living souvenir of a mother who had never been able to say no. It was a rather stocky little beast with shaggy white hair and occasional, rakishly placed patches of black. There was a suggestion of Sealyham terrier about it, but that was almost blotted out by hosts of reminiscences of other breeds. It looked, on the whole, like a composite photograph of Popular Dogs. But you could tell at a glance that it had a way with it. Scepters have been tossed aside for that.

It lay, now, by the fire, waving its tragically long tail wistfully, its eyes pleading with Mr. Durant to give it a fair trial. The children had told it to lie down there, and so it did not move. That was something it could do toward repaying them.

Mr. Durant warmed to it. He did not dislike dogs, and he somewhat fancied the picture of himself as a soft-hearted fellow who extended shelter to friendless animals. He bent, and held out a hand to it.

"Well, sir," he said, genially. "Come here, good fellow."

The dog ran to him, wriggling ecstatically. It covered his cold hand with joyous, though respectful kisses, then laid its warm, heavy head on his palm. "You are beyond a doubt the greatest man in America," it told him with its eyes.

Mr. Durant enjoyed appreciation and gratitude. He patted the dog graciously.

"Well, sir, how'd you like to board with us?" he said. "I guess you can plan to settle down." Charlotte squeezed Junior's arm wildly. Neither of them, though, thought it best to crowd their good fortune by making any immediate comment on it.

Mrs. Durant entered from the kitchen, flushed with her final attentions to the chowder. There was a worried line between her eyes. Part of the worry was due to the dinner, and part to the disturbing entrance of the little dog into the family life. Anything not previously included in her day's schedule threw Mrs. Durant into a state resembling that of one convalescing from shellshock. Her hands jerked nervously, beginning gestures that they never finished.

Relief smoothed her face when she saw her husband patting the dog. The children, always at ease with her, broke their silence and jumped about her, shrieking that Father said it might stay.

"There, now—didn't I tell you what a dear, good father you had?" she said in the tone parents employ when they have happened to guess right. "That's fine, Father. With that big yard and all, I think we'll make out all right. She really seems to be an awfully good little——"

Mr. Durant's hand stopped sharply in its patting motions, as if the dog's neck had become red-hot to his touch. He rose, and looked at his wife as at a stranger who had suddenly begun to behave wildly.

"She?" he said. He maintained the look and repeated the word. "She?"

Mrs. Durant's hands jerked.

"Well—" she began, as if about to plunge into a recital of extenuating circumstances. "Well—yes," she concluded.

The children and the dog looked nervously at Mr. Durant, feeling something was gone wrong. Charlotte whimpered wordlessly.

"Quiet!" said her father, turning suddenly upon her. "I said it could stay, didn't I? Did you ever know Father to break a promise?"

Charlotte politely murmured, "No, Father," but conviction was not hers. She was a philosophical child, though, and she decided to leave the whole issue to God, occasionally jogging Him up a bit with prayer.

Mr. Durant frowned at his wife, and jerked his head backward. This indicated that he wished to have a few words with her, for adults only, in the privacy of the little room across the hall, known as "Father's den."

He had directed the decoration of his den, had seen that it had been made a truly masculine room. Red paper covered its walls, up to the wooden rack on which were displayed ornamental steins, of domestic manufacture. Empty pipe-racks—Mr. Durant smoked cigars—were nailed against the red paper at frequent intervals. On one wall was an indifferent reproduction of a drawing of a young woman with wings like a vampire bat, and on another, a water-colored photograph of "September Morn," the tints running a bit beyond the edges of the figure as if the artist's emotions had rendered his hand unsteady. Over the table was carefully flung a tanned and fringed hide with the profile of an unknown Indian maiden painted on it, and the rocking-chair held a leather pillow bearing the picture, done by pyrography, of a girl in a fencing costume which set off her distressingly dated figure.

Mr. Durant's books were lined up behind the glass of the bookcase. They were all tall, thick books, brightly bound, and they justified his pride in their showing. They were mostly accounts of favorites of the French court, with a few volumes on odd personal habits of various monarchs, and the adventures of former Russian monks. Mrs. Durant, who never had time to get around to reading, regarded them with awe, and thought of her husband as one of the country's leading bibliophiles. There were books, too, in the living-room, but those she had inherited or been given. She had arranged a few on the living-room table; they looked as if they had been placed there by the Gideons.

Mr. Durant thought of himself as an indefatigable collector and an insatiable reader. But he was always disappointed in his books, after he had sent for them. They were never so good as the advertisements had led him to believe.

Into his den Mr. Durant preceded his wife, and faced her, still frowning. His calm was not shattered, but it was punctured. Something annoying always had to go and come up. Wouldn't you know?

"Now you know perfectly well, Fan, we can't have that dog around," he told her. He used the low voice reserved for underwear and bathroom articles and kindred shady topics. There was all the kindness in his tones that one has for a backward child, but a Gibraltar-like firmness was behind it. "You must be crazy to even think we could for a minute. Why, I wouldn't give a she-dog houseroom, not for any amount of money. It's disgusting, that's what it is."

"Well, but, Father—" began Mrs. Durant, her hands again going off into their convulsions.

"Disgusting," he repeated. "You have a female around, and you know what happens. All the males in the neighborhood will be running after her. First thing you know, she'd be having puppies—and the way they look after they've had them, and all! That would be nice for the children to see, wouldn't it? I should think you'd think of the children, Fan. No, sir, there'll be nothing like that around here, not while I know it. Disgusting!"

"But the children," she said. "They'll be just simply——"

"Now you just leave all that to me," he reassured her. "I told them the dog could stay, and I've never broken a promise yet, have I? Here's what I'll do—I'll wait till they're asleep, and then I'll just take this little dog and put it out. Then, in the morning, you can tell them it ran away during the night, see?"

She nodded. Her husband patted her shoulder, in its crapy-smelling black silk. His peace with the world was once more intact, restored by this simple solution of the little difficulty. Again his mind wrapped itself in the knowledge that everything was all fixed, all ready for a nice, fresh start. His arm was still about his wife's shoulder as they went on in to dinner.

JUST A LITTLE ONE

I LIKE this place, Fred. This is a nice place. How did you ever find it? I think you're perfectly marvelous, discovering a speakeasy in the year 1928. And they let you right in, without asking you a single question. I bet you could get into the subway without using anybody's name. Couldn't you, Fred?

Oh, I like this place better and better, now that my eyes are getting accustomed to it. You mustn't let them tell you this lighting system is original with them, Fred; they got the idea from the Mammoth Cave. This is you sitting next to me, isn't it? Oh, you can't fool me. I'd know that knee anywhere.

You know what I like about this place? It's got atmosphere. That's what it's got. If you would ask the waiter to bring a fairly sharp knife, I could cut off a nice little block of the atmosphere, to take home with me. It would be interesting to have for my memory book. I'm going to start keeping a memory book tomorrow. Don't let me forget.

Why, I don't know, Fred—what are you going to have? Then I guess I'll have a highball, too; please, just a little one. Is it really real Scotch? Well, that will be a new experience for me. You ought to see the Scotch I've got home in my cupboard; at least it was in the cupboard this morning—it's probably eaten its way out by now. I got it for my birthday. Well, it was something. The birthday before, all I got was a year older.

This is a nice highball, isn't it? Well, well, well, to think of me having real Scotch; I'm out of the bush leagues at last. Are you going to have another one? Well, I shouldn't like to see you drinking all by yourself, Fred. Solitary drinking is what causes half the crime in the country. That's what's responsible for the failure of prohibition. But please, Fred, tell him to make mine just a little one. Make it awfully weak; just cambric Scotch.

It will be nice to see the effect of veritable whisky upon one who has been accustomed only to the simpler forms of entertainment. You'll like that, Fred. You'll stay by me if anything happens, won't you? I don't think there will be anything spectacular, but I want to ask you one thing, just in case. Don't let me take any horses home with me. It doesn't matter so much about stray dogs and kittens, but elevator boys get awfully stuffy when you try to bring in a horse. You might just as well know that about me now, Fred. You can always tell that the crash is coming when I start getting tender about Our Dumb Friends. Three highballs, and I think I'm St. Francis of Assisi.

But I don't believe anything is going to happen to me on these. That's because they're made of real stuff. That's what the difference is. This just makes you feel fine. Oh, I feel swell, Fred. You do too, don't you? I knew you did, because you look better. I love that tie you have on. Oh, did Edith give it to you? Ah, wasn't that nice of her? You know, Fred, most people are really awfully nice. There are darn few that aren't pretty fine at heart. You've got a beautiful heart, Fred. You'd be the first person I'd go to if I were in trouble. I guess you are just about the best friend I've got in the world. But I worry about you, Fred. I do so, too. I don't think you take enough care of yourself. You ought to take care of yourself for your friends' sake. You oughtn't to drink all this terrible stuff that's around; you owe it to your friends to be careful. You don't mind my talking to you like this, do you? You see, dear, it's because I'm your friend that I hate to see you not taking care of yourself. It hurts me to see you batting around the way you've been doing. You ought to stick to this place, where they have real Scotch that can't do you any harm. Oh, darling, do you really think I ought to? Well, you tell him just a little bit of a one. Tell him, sweet.

Do you come here often, Fred? I shouldn't worry about you so much if I knew you were in a safe place like this. Oh, is this where you were Thursday night? I see. Why, no, it didn't make a bit of difference, only you told me to call you up, and like a fool I broke a date I had, just because I thought I was going to see you. I just sort of naturally thought so, when you said to call you up. Oh, good Lord, don't make all that fuss about it. It really didn't make the slightest difference. It just didn't seem a very friendly way to behave, that's all. I don't know—I'd been believing we were such good friends. I'm an awful idiot about people, Fred. There aren't many who are really your friend at heart. Practically anybody would play you dirt for a nickel. Oh, yes, they would.

Was Edith here with you, Thursday night? This place must be very becoming to her. Next to being in a coal mine, I can't think of anywhere she could go that the light would be more flattering to that pan of hers. Do you really know a lot of people that say she's good-looking? You must have a wide acquaintance among the astigmatic, haven't you, Freddie, dear? Why, I'm not being any way at all—it's simply one of those things, either you can see it or you can't. Now to me, Edith looks like something that would eat her young. Dresses well? *Edith* dresses well? Are you trying to kid me, Fred, at my age? You mean you mean it? Oh, my God. You mean those clothes of hers are *intentional*? My heavens, I always thought she was on her way out of a burning building.

Well, we live and learn. Edith dresses well! Edith's got good taste! Yes, she's got sweet taste in neckties. I don't suppose I ought to say it about such a dear friend of yours, Fred, but she is the lousiest necktie-picker-out I ever saw. I never saw anything could touch that thing you have around your neck. All right, suppose I did say I liked it. I just said that because I felt sorry for you. I'd feel sorry for anybody with a thing like that on. I just wanted to try to make you feel good, because I thought you were my friend. My friend! I haven't got a friend in the world. Do you know that, Fred? Not one single friend in this world.

All right, what do you care if I'm crying, I can cry if I want to, can't I? I guess you'd cry, too, if you didn't have a friend in the world. Is my face very bad? I suppose that damned mascara has run all over it. I've got to give up using mascara, Fred; life's too sad. Isn't life terrible? Oh, my God, isn't life awful? Ah, don't cry, Fred. Please don't. Don't you care, baby. Life's terrible, but don't you care. You've got friends. I'm the one that hasn't got any friends. I am so. No, it's me. I'm the one.

I don't think another drink would make me feel any better. I don't know whether I want to feel any better. What's the sense of feeling good, when life's so terrible? Oh, all right, then. But please tell him just a little one, if it isn't too much trouble. I don't want to stay here much longer. I don't like this place. It's all dark and stuffy. It's the kind of place Edith would be crazy about—that's all I can say about this place. I know I oughtn't to talk about your best friend, Fred, but that's a terrible woman. That woman is the louse of this world. It makes me feel just awful that you trust that woman, Fred. I hate to see anybody play you dirt. I'd hate to see you get hurt. That's what makes me feel so terrible. That's why I'm getting mascara all over my face. No, please don't, Fred. You mustn't hold my hand. It wouldn't be fair to Edith. We've got to play fair with the big louse. After all, she's your best friend, isn't she?

Honestly? Do you honestly mean it, Fred? Yes, but how could I help thinking so, when you're with her all the time—when you bring her here every night in the week? Really, only Thursday? Oh, I know—I know how those things are. You simply can't help it, when you get stuck with a person that way. Lord, I'm glad you realize what an awful thing that woman is. I was worried about it, Fred. It's because I'm your friend. Why, of course I am, darling. You know I am. Oh, that's just silly, Freddie. You've got heaps of friends. Only you'll never find a better friend than I am. No, I know that. I know I'll never find a better friend than you are to me. Just give me back my hand a second, till I get this damned mascara out of my eye.

Yes, I think we ought to, honey. I think we ought to have a little drink, on account of our being friends. Just a little one, because it's real Scotch, and we're real friends. After all, friends are the greatest things in the world, aren't they, Fred? Gee, it makes you feel good to know you have a friend. I feel great, don't you, dear? And you look great, too. I'm proud to have you for a friend. Do you realize, Fred, what a rare thing a friend is, when you think of all the terrible people there are in this world? Animals are much better than people. God, I love animals. That's what I like about you, Fred. You're so fond of animals.

Look, I'll tell you what let's do, after we've had just a little highball. Let's go out and pick up a lot of stray dogs. I never had enough dogs in my life, did you? We ought to have more dogs. And maybe there'd be some cats around, if we looked. And a horse, I've never had one single horse, Fred. Isn't that rotten? Not one single horse. Ah, I'd like a nice old cab-horse, Fred. Wouldn't you? I'd like to take care of it and comb its hair and everything. Ah, don't be stuffy about it, Fred, please don't. I need a horse, honestly I do. Wouldn't you like one? It would be so sweet and kind. Let's have a drink and then let's you and I go out and get a horsie, Freddie—just a little one, darling, just a little one.

HORSIE

WHEN young Mrs. Gerald Cruger came home from the hospital, Miss Wilmarth came along with her and the baby. Miss Wilmarth was an admirable trained nurse, sure and calm and tireless, with a real taste for the arranging of flowers in bowls and vases. She had never known a patient to receive so many flowers, or such uncommon ones; yellow violets and strange lilies and little white orchids poised like a bevy of delicate moths along green branches. Care and thought must have been put into their selection that they, like all the other fragile and costly things she kept about her, should be so right for young Mrs. Cruger. No one who knew her could have caught up the telephone and lightly bidden the florist to deliver her one of his five-dollar assortments of tulips, stock, and daffodils. Camilla Cruger was no complement to garden blooms.

Sometimes, when she opened the shiny boxes and carefully grouped the cards, there would come a curious expression upon Miss Wilmarth's face. Playing over shorter features, it might almost have been one of wistfulness. Upon Miss Wilmarth, it served to perfect the strange resemblance that she bore through her years; her face was truly complete with that look of friendly melancholy peculiar to the gentle horse. It was not, of course, Miss Wilmarth's fault that she looked like a horse. Indeed, there was nowhere to attach any blame. But the resemblance remained.

She was tall, pronounced of bone, and erect of carriage; it was somehow impossible to speculate upon her appearance undressed. Her long face was innocent, indeed ignorant, of cosmetics, and its color stayed steady. Confusion, heat, or haste caused her neck to flush crimson. Her mild hair was pinned with loops of nicked black wire into a narrow knot, practical to support her little high cap, like a charlotte russe from a bake-shop. She had big, trustworthy hands, scrubbed and dry, with nails cut short and so deeply cleaned with some small sharp instrument that the ends stood away from the spatulate finger-tips. Gerald Cruger, who nightly sat opposite her at his own dinner table, tried not to see her hands. It irritated him to be reminded by their sight that they must feel like straw matting and smell of white soap. For him, women who were not softly lovely were simply not women.

He tried, too, so far as it was possible to his beautiful manners, to keep his eyes from her face. Not that it was unpleasant—a kind face, certainly. But, as he told Camilla, once he looked he stayed fascinated, awaiting the toss and the whinny.

"I love horses, myself," he said to Camilla, who lay all white and languid on her apricot satin chaise-longue. "I'm a fool for a horse. Ah, what a noble animal, darling! All I say is, nobody has any business to go around looking like a horse and behaving as if it were all right. You don't catch horses going around looking like people, do you?"

He did not dislike Miss Wilmarth; he only resented her. He had no bad wish in the world for her, but he waited with longing the day she would leave. She was so skilled and rhythmic in her work that she disrupted the household but little. Nevertheless, her presence was an onus. There was that thing of dining with her every evening. It was a chore for him, certainly, and one that did not ease with repetition, but there was no choice. Everyone had always heard of trained nurses' bristling insistence that they be not treated as servants; Miss Wilmarth could not be asked to dine with the maids. He would not have dinner out; be away from *Camilla*? It was too much to expect the maids to institute a second dinner service or to carry trays, other than Camilla's, up and down the stairs. There were only three servants and they had work enough.

"Those children," Camilla's mother was wont to say, chuckling. "Those two kids. The independence of them! Struggling along on cheese and kisses. Why, they hardly let me pay for the trained nurse. And it was all we could do, last Christmas, to make Camilla take the Packard and the chauffeur."

So Gerald dined each night with Miss Wilmarth. The small dread of his hour with her struck suddenly at him in the afternoon. He would forget it for stretches of minutes, only to be smitten sharper as the time drew near. On his way home from his office, he found grim entertainment in rehearsing his table talk, and plotting desperate innovations to it.

Cruger's Compulsory Conversations: Lesson I, a Dinner with a Miss Wilmarth, a Trained Nurse. Good evening, Miss Wilmarth. Well! And how were the patients all day? That's good, that's fine. Well! The baby gained two ounces, did she? That's fine. Yes, that's right, she will be before we know it. That's right. Well! Mrs. Cruger seems to be getting stronger every day, doesn't she? That's good, that's fine. That's right, up and about before we know it. Yes, she certainly will. Well! Any visitors today? That's good. Didn't stay too long, did they? That's fine. Well! No, no, no, Miss Wilmarth—*you* go ahead. I wasn't going to say anything at all, really. No, really. Well! Well! I see where they found those two aviators after all. Yes, they certainly do run risks. That's right. Yes. Well! I see where they've been having a regular old-fashioned blizzard out west. Yes, we certainly have had a mild winter. That's right. Well! I see where they held up that jeweler's shop right in broad daylight on Fifth Avenue. Yes, I certainly don't know what we're coming to. That's right. Well! I see the cat. Do you see the cat? The cat is on the mat. It certainly is. Well! Pardon me, Miss Wilmarth, but must you look so much like a horse? Do you like to look like a horse, Miss Wilmarth? That's good, Miss Wilmarth, that's fine. You certainly do, Miss Wilmarth. That's right. Well! Will you for God's sake finish your oats, Miss Wilmarth, and let me get out of this?

Every evening he reached the dining-room before Miss Wilmarth and stared gloomily at silver and candle-flame until she was upon him. No sound of footfall heralded her coming, for her ample canvas oxfords were soled with rubber; there would be a protest of parquet, a trembling of ornaments, a creak, a rustle, and the authoritative smell of stiff linen; and there she would be, set for her ritual of evening cheer.

"Well, Mary," she would cry to the waitress, "you know what they say—better late than never!"

But no smile would mellow Mary's lips, no light her eyes. Mary, in converse with the cook, habitually referred to Miss Wilmarth as "that one." She wished no truck with Miss Wilmarth or any of the others of her guild; always in and out of a person's pantry.

Once or twice Gerald saw a strange expression upon Miss Wilmarth's face as she witnessed the failure of her adage with the maid. He could not quite classify it. Though he did not know, it was the look she sometimes had when she opened the shiny white boxes and lifted the exquisite, scentless blossoms that were sent to Camilla. Anyway, whatever it was, it increased her equine resemblance to such a point that he thought of proffering her an apple.

But she always had her big smile turned toward him when she sat down. Then she would look at the thick watch strapped to her wrist and give a little squeal that brought the edges of his teeth together.

"Mercy!" she would say. "My good mercy! Why, I had no more idea it was so late. Well, you mustn't blame me, Mr. Cruger. Don't you scold *me*. You'll just have to blame that daughter of yours. She's the one that keeps us all busy."

"She certainly is," he would say. "That's right."

He would think, and with small pleasure, of the infant Diane, pink and undistinguished and angry, among the ruffles and *choux* of her bassinet. It was her doing that Camilla had stayed so long away from him in the odorous limbo of the hospital, her doing that Camilla lay all day upon her apricot satin chaise-longue. "We must take our time," the doctor said, "just ta-a-ake our ti-yem." Yes; well, that would all be because of young Diane. It was because of her, indeed, that night upon night he must face Miss Wilmarth and comb up conversation. All right, young Diane, there you are and nothing to do about it. But you'll be an only child, young woman, that's what you'll be.

Always Miss Wilmarth followed her opening pleasantry about the baby with a companion piece. Gerald had come to know it so well he could have said it in duet with her.

"You wait," she would say. "Just you wait. You're the one that's going to be kept busy when the beaux start coming around. You'll see. That young lady's going to be a heart-breaker if ever I saw one."

"I guess that's right," Gerald would say, and he would essay a small laugh and fail at it. It made him uncomfortable, somehow embarrassed him to hear Miss Wilmarth banter of swains and conquest. It was unseemly, as rouge would have been unseemly on her long mouth and perfume on her flat bosom.

He would hurry her over to her own ground. "Well!" he would say. "Well! And how were the patients all day?"

But that, even with the baby's weight and the list of the day's visitors, seldom lasted past the soup.

"Doesn't that woman ever go out?" he asked Camilla. "Doesn't our Horsie ever rate a night off?"

"Where would she want to go?" Camilla said. Her low, lazy words had always the trick of seeming a little weary of their subject.

"Well," Gerald said, "she might take herself a moonlight canter around the park."

"Oh, she doubtless gets a thrill out of dining with you," Camilla said. "You're a man, they tell me, and she can't have seen many. Poor old horse. She's not a bad soul."

"Yes," he said. "And what a round of pleasure it is, having dinner every night with Not a Bad Soul."

"What makes you think," Camilla said, "that I am caught up in any whirl of gaiety, lying here?"

"Oh, darling," he said. "Oh, my poor darling. I didn't mean it, honestly I didn't. Oh, *lord,* I didn't mean it. How could I complain, after all you've been through, and I haven't done a thing? Please, sweet, please. Ah, Camilla, say you know I didn't mean it."

"After all," Camilla said, "you just have her at dinner. I have her around all day."

"Sweetheart, please," he said. "Oh, poor angel."

He dropped to his knees by the chaise-longue and crushed her limp, fragrant hand against his mouth. Then he remembered about being very, very gentle. He ran little apologetic kisses up and down her fingers and murmured of gardenias and lilies and thus exhausted his knowledge of white flowers.

Her visitors said that Camilla looked lovelier than ever, but they were mistaken. She was only as lovely as she had always been. They spoke in hushed voices of the new look in her eyes since her motherhood; but it was the same far brightness that had always lain there. They said how white she was and how lifted above other people; they forgot that she had always been pale as moonlight and had always worn a delicate disdain, as light as the lace that covered her breast. Her doctor cautioned tenderly against hurry, besought her to take recovery slowly—Camilla, who had never done anything quickly in her life. Her friends gathered, adoring, about the apricot satin chaise-longue where Camilla lay and moved her hands as if they hung heavy from her wrists; they had been wont before to gather and adore at the white satin sofa in the drawing-room where Camilla reclined, her hands like heavy lilies in a languid breeze. Every night, when Gerald crossed the threshold of her fragrant room, his heart leaped and his words caught in his throat; but those things had always befallen him at the sight of her. Motherhood had not brought perfection to Camilla's loveliness. She had had that before.

Gerald came home early enough, each evening, to have a while with her before dinner. He made his cocktails in her room, and watched her as she slowly drank one. Miss Wilmarth was in and out, touching flowers, patting pillows. Sometimes she brought Diane in on display, and those would be minutes of real discomfort for Gerald. He could not bear to watch her with the baby in her arms, so acute was his vicarious embarrassment at her behavior. She would bring her long head down close to Diane's tiny, stern face and toss it back again high on her rangy neck, all the while that strange words, in a strange high voice, came from her.

"Well, her wuzza booful dirl. Ess, her wuzza. Her wuzza, wuzza, wuzza. Ess, her *wuzz*." She would bring the baby over to him. "See, Daddy. Isn't us a gate, bid dirl? Isn't us booful? Say 'nigh-nigh,' Daddy. Us doe teepy-bye, now. Say 'nigh-nigh.' "

Oh, God.

Then she would bring the baby to Camilla. "Say 'nigh-nigh,' " she would cry. " 'Nigh-nigh,' Mummy."

"If that brat ever calls you 'Mummy,' " he told Camilla once, fiercely, "I'll turn her out in the snow."

Camilla would look at the baby, amusement in her slow glance. "Good night, useless," she would say. She would hold out a finger, for Diane's pink hand to curl around. And Gerald's heart would quicken, and his eyes sting and shine.

Once he tore his gaze from Camilla to look at Miss Wilmarth, surprised by the sudden cessation of her falsetto. She was no longer lowering her head and tossing it back. She was standing quite still, looking at him over the baby; she looked away quickly, but not before he had seen that curious expression on her face again. It puzzled him, made him vaguely uneasy. That night, she made no further exhortations to Diane's parents to utter the phrase "nigh-nigh." In silence she carried the baby out of the room and back to the nursery.

One evening, Gerald brought two men home with him; lean, easily dressed young men, good at golf and squash rackets, his companions through his college and in his clubs. They had cocktails in Camilla's room, grouped about the chaise-longue. Miss Wilmarth, standing in the nursery adjoining, testing the temperature of the baby's milk against her wrist, could hear them all talking lightly and swiftly, tossing their sentences into the air to hang there unfinished. Now and again she could distinguish Camilla's lazy voice; the others stopped immediately when she spoke, and when she was done there were long peals of laughter. Miss Wilmarth pictured her lying there, in golden chiffon and deep lace, her light figure turned always a little away from those about her, so that she must move her head and speak her slow words over her shoulder to them. The trained nurse's face was astoundingly equine as she looked at the wall that separated them.

They stayed in Camilla's room a long time, and there was always more laughter. The door from the nursery into the hall was open, and presently she heard the door of Camilla's room being opened, too. She had been able to hear only voices before, but now she could distinguish Gerald's words as he called back from the threshold; they had no meaning to her.

"Only wait, fellers," he said. "Wait till you see Seabiscuit."

He came to the nursery door. He held a cocktail shaker in one hand and a filled glass in the other.

"Oh, Miss Wilmarth," he said. "Oh, good evening, Miss Wilmarth. Why, I didn't know this door was open—I mean, I hope we haven't been disturbing you."

"Oh, not the least little bit," she said. "Goodness."

"Well!" he said. "I—we were wondering if you wouldn't have a little cocktail. Won't you please?" He held out the glass to her.

"Mercy," she said, taking it. "Why, thank you ever so much. Thank you, Mr. Cruger."

"And, oh, Miss Wilmarth," he said, "would you tell Mary there'll be two more to dinner? And ask her not to have it before half an hour or so, will you? Would you mind?"

"Not the least little bit," she said. "Of course I will."

"Thank you," he said. "Well! Thank you, Miss Wilmarth. Well! See you at dinner."

"Thank *you*," she said. "I'm the one that ought to thank *you*. For the lovely little cockytail."

"Oh," he said, and failed at an easy laugh. He went back into Camilla's room and closed the door behind him.

Miss Wilmarth set her cocktail upon a table, and went down to inform Mary of the impending guests. She felt light and quick, and she told Mary gaily, awaiting a flash of gaiety in response. But Mary received the news impassively, made a grunt but no words, and slammed out through the swinging doors into the kitchen. Miss Wilmarth stood looking after her. Somehow servants never seemed to—She should have become used to it.

Even though the dinner hour was delayed, Miss Wilmarth was a little late. The three young men were standing in the dining-room, talking all at once and laughing all together. They stopped their noise when Miss Wilmarth entered, and Gerald moved forward to perform introductions. He looked at her, and then looked away. Prickling embarrassment tormented him. He introduced the young men, with his eyes away from her.

Miss Wilmarth had dressed for dinner. She had discarded her linen uniform and put on a frock of dark blue taffeta, cut down to a point at the neck and given sleeves that left bare the angles of her elbows. Small, stiff ruffles occurred about the hips, and the skirt was short for its year. It revealed that Miss Wilmarth had clothed her ankles in roughened gray silk and her feet in black, casket-shaped slippers, upon which little bows quivered as if in lonely terror at the expanse before them. She had been busied with her hair; it was crimped and loosened, and ends that had escaped the tongs were already sliding from their pins. All the length of her nose and chin was heavily powdered; not with a perfumed dust, tinted to praise her skin, but with coarse, bright white talcum.

Gerald presented his guests; Miss Wilmarth, Mr. Minot; Miss Wilmarth, Mr. Forster. One of the young men, it turned out, was Freddy, and one, Tommy. Miss Wilmarth said she was pleased to meet each of them. Each of them asked her how she did.

She sat down at the candle-lit table with the three beautiful young men. Her usual evening vivacity was gone from her. In silence she unfolded her napkin and took up her soup spoon. Her neck glowed crimson, and her face, even with its powder, looked more than ever as if it should have been resting over the top rail of a paddock fence.

"Well!" Gerald said.

"Well!" Mr. Minot said.

"Getting much warmer out, isn't it?" Mr. Forster said. "Notice it?"

"It is, at that," Gerald said. "Well. We're about due for warm weather."

"Yes, we ought to expect it now," Mr. Minot said. "Any day now."

"Oh, it'll be here," Mr. Forster said. "It'll come."

"I love spring," said Miss Wilmarth. "I just love it."

Gerald looked deep into his soup plate. The two young men looked at her.

"Darn good time of year," Mr. Minot said. "Certainly is."

"And how it is!" Mr. Forster said.

They ate their soup.

There was champagne all through dinner. Miss Wilmarth watched Mary fill her glass, none too full. The wine looked gay and pretty. She looked about the table before she took her first sip. She remembered Camilla's voice and the men's laughter.

"Well," she cried. "Here's a health, everybody!"

The guests looked at her. Gerald reached for his glass and gazed at it as intently as if he beheld a champagne goblet for the first time. They all murmured and drank.

"Well!" Mr. Minot said. "Your patients seem to be getting along pretty well, Miss Witmark. Don't they?"

"I should say they do," she said. "And they're pretty nice patients, too. Aren't they, Mr. Cruger?"

"They certainly are," Gerald said. "That's right."

"They certainly are," Mr. Minot said. "That's what they are. Well. You must meet all sorts of people in your work, I suppose. Must be pretty interesting."

"Oh, sometimes it is," Miss Wilmarth said. "It depends on the people." Her words fell from her lips clear and separate, sterile as if each had been freshly swabbed with boracic acid solution. In her ears rang Camilla's light, insolent drawl.

"That's right," Mr. Forster said. "Everything depends on the people, doesn't it? Always does, wherever you go. No matter what you do. Still, it must be wonderfully interesting work. Wonderfully."

"Wonderful the way this country's come right up in medicine," Mr. Minot said. "They tell me we have the greatest doctors in the world, right here. As good as any in Europe. Or Harley Street."

"I see," Gerald said, "where they think they've found a new cure for spinal meningitis."

"*Have* they really?" Mr. Minot said.

"Yes, I saw that, too," Mr. Forster said. "Wonderful thing. Wonderfully interesting."

"Oh, say, Gerald," Mr. Minot said, and he went from there into an account, hole by hole, of his most recent performance at golf. Gerald and Mr. Forster listened and questioned him.

The three young men left the topic of golf and came back to it again, and left it and came back. In the intervals, they related to Miss Wilmarth various brief items that had caught their eyes in the newspapers. Miss Wilmarth answered in exclamations, and turned her big smile readily to each of them. There was no laughter during dinner.

It was a short meal, as courses went. After it, Miss Wilmarth bade the guests good-night and received their bows and their "*Good* night, Miss Witmark." She said she was awfully glad to have met them. They murmured.

"Well, good night, then, Mr. Cruger," she said. "See you tomorrow!"

"Good night, Miss Wilmarth," Gerald said.

The three young men went and sat with Camilla. Miss Wilmarth could hear their voices and their laughter as she hung up her dark blue taffeta dress.

Miss Wilmarth stayed with the Crugers for five weeks. Camilla was pronounced well—so well that she could have dined downstairs on the last few nights of Miss Wilmarth's stay, had she been able to support the fardel of dinner at the table with the trained nurse.

"I really couldn't dine opposite that face," she told Gerald. "You go amuse Horsie at dinner, stupid. You must be good at it, by now."

"All right, I will, darling," he said. "But God keep me, when she asks for another lump of sugar, from holding it out to her on my palm."

"Only two more nights," Camilla said, "and then Thursday Nana'll be here, and she'll be gone forever."

" 'Forever,' sweet, is my favorite word in the language," Gerald said.

Nana was the round and competent Scottish woman who had nursed Camilla through her childhood and was scheduled to engineer the unknowing Diane through hers. She was a comfortable woman, easy to have in the house; a servant, and knew it.

Only two more nights. Gerald went down to dinner whistling a good old tune.

"The old gray mare, she ain't what she used to be,
Ain't what she used to be, ain't what she used to be——"

The final dinners with Miss Wilmarth were like all the others. He arrived first, and stared at the candles until she came.

"Well, Mary," she cried on her entrance, "you know what they say—better late than never."

Mary, to the last, remained unamused.

Gerald was elated all the day of Miss Wilmarth's departure. He had a holiday feeling, a last-day-of-school jubilation with none of its faint regret. He left his office early, stopped at a florist's shop, and went home to Camilla.

Nana was installed in the nursery, but Miss Wilmarth had not yet left. She was in Camilla's room, and he saw her for the second time out of uniform. She wore a long brown coat and a brown rubbed velvet hat of no definite shape. Obviously, she was in the middle of the embarrassments of farewell. The melancholy of her face made it so like a horse's that the hat above it was preposterous.

"Why, there's Mr. Cruger!" she cried.

"Oh, good evening, Miss Wilmarth," he said. "Well! Ah, hello, darling. How are you, sweet? Like these?"

He laid a florist's box in Camilla's lap. In it were strange little yellow roses, with stems and leaves and tiny, soft thorns all of blood red. Miss Wilmarth gave a little squeal at the sight of them.

"Oh, the darlings!" she cried. "Oh, the boo-fuls!"

"And these are for you, Miss Wilmarth," he said. He made himself face her and hold out to her a square, smaller box.

"Why, Mr. Cruger," she said. "For me, really? Why, really, Mr. Cruger."

She opened the box and found four gardenias, with green foil and pale green ribbon holding them together.

"Oh, now, really, Mr. Cruger," she said. "Why, I never in all my life—Oh, now, you shouldn't have done it. Really, you shouldn't. My good mercy! Well, I never saw anything so lovely in all my life. Did you, Mrs. Cruger? They're *lovely*. Well, I just don't know how to *begin* to thank you. Why, I just—well, I just adore them."

Gerald made sounds designed to convey the intelligence that he was glad she liked them, that it was nothing, that she was welcome. Her squeaks of thanks made red rise in back of his ears.

"They're nice ones," Camilla said. "Put them on, Miss Wilmarth. And these are awfully cunning, Jerry. Sometimes you have your points."

"Oh, I didn't think I'd *wear* them," Miss Wilmarth said. "I thought I'd just take them in the box like this, so they'd keep better. And it's such a nice box—I'd like to have it. I—I'd like to keep it."

She looked down at the flowers. Gerald was in sudden horror that she might bring her head down close to them and toss it back high, crying "wuzza, wuzza, wuzza" at them the while.

"Honestly," she said, "I just can't take my eyes *off* them."

"The woman is mad," Camilla said. "It's the effect of living with us, I suppose. I hope we haven't ruined you for life, Miss Wilmarth."

"Why, Mrs. Cruger," Miss Wilmarth cried. "Now, really! I was just telling Mrs. Cruger, Mr. Cruger, that I've never been on a pleasanter case. I've just had the time of my life, all the time I was here. I don't know when I—honestly, I can't stop looking at my posies, they're so lovely. Well, I just can't thank you for all you've done."

"Well, we ought to thank you, Miss Wilmarth," Gerald said. "We certainly ought."

"I really hate to say 'good-by,' " Miss Wilmarth said. "I just hate it."

"Oh, don't say it," Camilla said. "I never dream of saying it. And remember, you must come in and see the baby, any time you can."

"Yes, you certainly must," Gerald said. "That's right."

"Oh, I will," Miss Wilmarth said. "Mercy, I just don't dare go take another look at her, or I wouldn't be able to leave, ever. Well, what am I thinking of! Why, the car's been waiting all this time. Mrs. Cruger simply insists on sending me home in the car, Mr. Cruger. Isn't she terrible?"

"Why, not at all," he said. "Why, of course."

"Well, it's only five blocks down and over to Lexington," she said, "or I really couldn't think of troubling you."

"Why, not at all," Gerald said. "Well! Is that where you live, Miss Wilmarth?"

She lived in some place of her own sometimes? She wasn't always disarranging somebody else's household?

"Yes," Miss Wilmarth said. "I have Mother there."

Oh. Now Gerald had never thought of her having a mother. Then there must have been a father, too, some time. And Miss Wilmarth existed because two people once had loved and known. It was not a thought to dwell upon.

"My aunt's with us, too," Miss Wilmarth said. "It makes it nice for Mother—you see, Mother doesn't get around very well any more. It's a little bit crowded for the three of us—I sleep on the davenport when I'm home, between cases. But it's so nice for Mother, having my aunt there."

Even in her leisure, then, Miss Wilmarth was a disruption and a crowd. Never dwelling in a room that had been planned only for her occupancy; no bed, no corner of her own; dressing before other people's mirrors, touching other people's silver, never looking out one window that was hers. Well. Doubtless she had known nothing else for so long that she did not mind or even ponder.

"Oh, yes," Gerald said. "Yes, it certainly must be fine for your mother. Well! Well! May I close your bags for you, Miss Wilmarth?"

"Oh, that's all done," she said. "The suitcase is downstairs. I'll just go get my hat-box. Well, good-by, then, Mrs. Cruger, and take care of yourself. And thank you a thousand times."

"Good luck, Miss Wilmarth," Camilla said. "Come see the baby."

Miss Wilmarth looked at Camilla and at Gerald standing beside her, touching one long white hand. She left the room to fetch her hat-box.

"I'll take it down for you, Miss Wilmarth," Gerald called after her.

He bent and kissed Camilla gently, very, very gently.

"Well, it's nearly over, darling," he said. "Sometimes I am practically convinced that there is a God."

"It was darn decent of you to bring her gardenias," Camilla said. "What made you think of it?"

"I was so crazed at the idea that she was really going," he said, "that I must have lost my head. No one was more surprised than I, buying gardenias for Horsie. Thank the Lord she didn't put them on. I couldn't have stood that sight."

"She's not really at her best in her street clothes," Camilla said. "She seems to lack a certain *chic.*" She stretched her arms slowly above her head and let them sink slowly back. "That was a fascinating glimpse of her home life she gave us. Great fun."

"Oh, I don't suppose she minds," he said. "I'll go down now and back her into the car, and that'll finish it."

He bent again over Camilla.

"Oh, you look so lovely, sweet," he said. "So *lovely.*"

Miss Wilmarth was coming down the hall, when Gerald left the room, managing a pasteboard hat-box, the florist's box, and a big leather purse that had known service. He took the boxes from her, against her protests, and followed her down the stairs and out to the motor at the curb. The chauffeur stood at the open door. Gerald was glad of that presence.

"Well, good luck, Miss Wilmarth," he said. "And thank you so much."

"Thank *you,* Mr. Cruger," she said. "I—I can't tell you how I've enjoyed it all the time I was here. I never had a pleasanter— And the flowers, and everything. I just don't know what to say. I'm the one that ought to thank *you.*"

She held out her hand, in a brown cotton glove. Anyway, worn cotton was easier to the touch than dry, corded flesh. It was the last moment of her. He scarcely minded looking at the long face on the red, red neck.

"Well!" he said. "Well! Got everything? Well, good luck, again, Miss Wilmarth, and don't forget us."

"Oh, I won't," she said. "I—oh, I won't do that."

She turned from him and got quickly into the car, to sit upright against the pale gray cushions. The chauffeur placed her hat-box at her feet and the florist's box on the seat beside her, closed the door smartly, and returned to his wheel. Gerald waved cheerily as the car slid away. Miss Wilmarth did not wave to him.

When she looked back, through the little rear window, he had already disappeared in the house. He must have run across the sidewalk—run, to get back to the fragrant room and the little yellow roses and Camilla. Their little pink baby would lie sleeping in its bed. They would be alone together; they would dine alone together by candlelight; they would be alone together in the night. Every morning and every evening Gerald would drop to his knees beside her to kiss her perfumed hand and call her sweet. Always she would be perfect, in scented chiffon and deep lace. There would be lean, easy young men, to listen to her drawl and give her their laughter. Every day there would be shiny white boxes for her, filled with curious blooms. It was perhaps fortunate that no one looked in the limousine. A beholder must have been startled to learn that a human face could look as much like that of a weary mare as did Miss Wilmarth's.

Presently the car swerved, in a turn of the traffic. The florist's box slipped against Miss Wilmarth's knee. She looked down at it. Then she took it on her lap, raised the lid a little and peeped at the waxy white bouquet. It would have been all fair then for a chance spectator; Miss Wilmarth's strange resemblance was not apparent, as she looked at her flowers. They were her flowers. A man had given them to her. She had been given flowers. They might not fade maybe for days. And she could keep the box.

CLOTHE THE NAKED

Big Lannie went out by the day to the houses of secure and leisured ladies, to wash their silks and their linens. She did her work perfectly; some of the ladies even told her so. She was a great, slow mass of a woman, colored a sound brown-black save for her palms and the flat of her fingers that were like gutta-percha from steam and hot suds. She was slow because of her size, and because the big veins in her legs hurt her, and her back ached much of the time. She neither cursed her ills nor sought remedies for them. They had happened to her; there they were.

Many things had happened to her. She had had children, and the children had died. So had her husband, who was a kind man, cheerful with the little luck he found. None of their children had died at birth. They had lived to be four or seven or ten, so that they had had their ways and their traits and their means of causing love; and Big Lannie's heart was always wide for love. One child had been killed in a street accident and two others had died of illnesses that might have been no more than tedious, had there been fresh food and clear spaces and clean air behind them. Only Arlene, the youngest, lived to grow up.

Arlene was a tall girl, not so dark as her mother but with the same firm flatness of color. She was so thin that her bones seemed to march in advance of her body. Her little pipes of legs and her broad feet with jutting heels were like things a child draws with crayons. She carried her head low, her shoulders scooped around her chest, and her stomach slanted forward. From the time that she was tiny, there were men after her.

Arlene was a bad girl always; that was one of the things that had happened to Big Lannie. There it was, and Big Lannie could only keep bringing her presents, surprises, so that the girl would love her mother and would want to stay at home. She brought little bottles of sharp perfume, and pale stockings of tinny silk, and rings set with bits of green and red glass; she tried to choose what Arlene would like. But each time Arlene came home she had bigger rings and softer stockings and stronger perfume than her mother could buy for her. Sometimes she would stay with her mother over a night, and sometimes more than a week; and then Big Lannie would come back from work one evening, and the girl would be gone, and no word of her. Big Lannie would go on bringing surprises, and setting them out along Arlene's bed to wait a return.

Big Lannie did not know it, when Arlene was going to have a baby. Arlene had not been home in nearly half a year; Big Lannie told the time in days. There was no news at all of the girl until the people at the hospital sent for Big Lannie to come to her daughter and grandson. She was there to hear Arlene say the baby must be named Raymond, and to see the girl die. For whom Raymond was called, or if for anyone, Big Lannie never knew.

He was a long, light-colored baby, with big, milky eyes that looked right back at his grandmother. It was several days before the people at the hospital told her he was blind.

Big Lannie went to each of the ladies who employed her and explained that she could not work for some while; she must take care of her grandson. The ladies were sharply discommoded, after her steady years, but they dressed their outrage in shrugs and cool tones. Each arrived, separately, at the conclusion that she had been too good to Big Lannie, and had been imposed upon, therefore. "Honestly, those niggers!" each said to her friends. "They're all alike."

Big Lannie sold most of the things she lived with, and took one room with a stove in it. There, as soon as the people at the hospital would let her, she brought Raymond and tended him. He was all her children to her.

She had always been a saving woman, with few needs and no cravings, and she had been long alone. Even after Arlene's burial, there was enough left for Raymond and Big Lannie to go on for a time. Big Lannie was slow to be afraid of what must come; fear did not visit her at all, at first, and then it slid in only when she waked, when the night hung motionless before another day.

Raymond was a good baby, a quiet, patient baby, lying in his wooden box and stretching out his delicate hands to the sounds that were light and color to him. It seemed but a little while, so short to Big Lannie, before he was walking about the room, his hands held out, his feet quick and sure. Those of Big Lannie's friends who saw him for the first time had to be told that he could not see.

Then, and it seemed again such a little while, he could dress himself, and open the door for his granny, and unlace the shoes from her tired feet, and talk to her in his soft voice. She had occasional employment—now and then a neighbor would hear of a day's scrubbing she could do, or sometimes she might work in the stead of a friend who was sick—infrequent, and not to be planned on. She went to the ladies for whom she had worked, to ask if they might not want her back again; but there was little hope in her, after she had visited the first one. Well, now, really, said the ladies; well, really, now.

The neighbors across the hall watched over Raymond while Big Lannie looked for work. He was no trouble to them, nor to himself. He sat and crooned at his chosen task. He had been given a wooden spool around the top of which were driven little brads, and over these with a straightened hairpin he looped bright worsted, working faster than sight until a long tube of woven wool fell through the hole in the spool. The neighbors threaded big, blunt needles for him, and he coiled the woolen tubes and sewed them into mats. Big Lannie called them beautiful, and it made Raymond proud to have her tell him how readily she sold them. It was hard for her, when he was asleep at night, to unravel the mats and wash the worsted and stretch it so straight that even Raymond's shrewd fingers could not tell, when he worked with it next day, that it was not new.

Fear stormed in Big Lannie and took her days and nights. She might not go to any organization dispensing relief, for dread that Raymond would be taken from her and put in—she would not say the word to herself, and she and her neighbors lowered their voices when they said it to one another—an institution. The neighbors wove lingering tales of what happened inside certain neat, square buildings on the cindery skirts of the town, and, if they must go near them, hurried as if passing graveyards, and came home heroes. When they got you in one of those places, whispered the neighbors, they laid your spine open with whips, and then when you dropped, they kicked your head in. Had anyone come into Big Lannie's room to take Raymond away to an asylum for the blind, the neighbors would have fought for him with stones and rails and boiling water.

Raymond did not know about anything but good. When he grew big enough to go alone down the stairs and into the street, he was certain of delight each day. He held his head high, as he came out into the little yard in front of the flimsy wooden house, and slowly turned his face from side to side, as if the air were soft liquid in which he bathed it. Trucks and wagons did not visit the street, which ended in a dump for rusted bedsprings and broken boilers and staved-in kettles; children played over its cobbles, and men and women sat talking in open windows and called across to one another in gay, rich voices. There was always laughter for Raymond to hear, and he would laugh back, and hold out his hands to it.

At first, the children stopped their play when he came out, and gathered quietly about him, and watched him, fascinated. They had been told of his affliction, and they had a sort of sickened pity for him. Some of them spoke to him, in soft, careful tones. Raymond would laugh with pleasure, and stretch his hands, the curious smooth, flat hands of the blind, to their voices. They would draw sharply back, afraid that his strange hands might touch them. Then, somehow ashamed because they had shrunk from him and he could not see that they had done so, they said gentle good-bys to him, and backed away into the street again, watching him steadily.

When they were gone, Raymond would start on his walk to the end of the street. He guided himself by lightly touching the broken fences along the dirt sidewalk, and as he walked he crooned little songs with no words to them. Some of the men and women at the windows would call hello to him, and he would call back and wave and smile. When the children, forgetting him, laughed again at their games, he stopped and turned to the sound as if it were the sun.

In the evening, he would tell Big Lannie about his walk, slapping his knee and chuckling at the memory of the laughter he had heard. When the weather was too hard for him to go out in the street, he would sit at his worsted work, and talk all day of going out the next day.

The neighbors did what they could for Raymond and Big Lannie. They gave Raymond clothes their own children had not yet worn out, and they brought food, when they had enough to spare and other times. Big Lannie would get through a week, and would pray to get through the next one; and so the months went. Then the days on which she could find work fell farther and farther apart, and she could not pray about the time to come because she did not dare to think of it.

It was Mrs. Ewing who saved Raymond's and Big Lannie's lives, and let them continue together. Big Lannie said that then and ever after; daily she blessed Mrs. Ewing, and nightly she would have prayed for her, had she not known, in some dimmed way, that any intercession for Mrs. Delabarre Ewing must be impudence.

Mrs. Ewing was a personage in the town. When she went to Richmond for a visit, or when she returned from viewing the azalea gardens in Charleston, the newspaper always printed the fact. She was a woman rigorously conscious of her noble obligation; she was prominent on the Community Chest committee, and it was she who planned and engineered the annual Bridge Drive to raise funds for planting salvia around the cannon in front of the D.A.R. headquarters. These and many others were her public activities, and she was no less exacting of herself in her private life. She kept a model, though childless, house for her husband and herself, relegating the supervision of details to no domestic lieutenant, no matter how seemingly trustworthy.

Back before Raymond was born, Big Lannie had worked as laundress for Mrs. Ewing. Since those days, the Ewing wash tubs had witnessed many changes, none for the better. Mrs. Ewing took Big Lannie back into her employment. She apologized for this step to her friends by the always winning method of self-deprecation. She knew she was a fool, she said, after all that time, and after the way that Big Lannie had treated her. But still, she said—and she laughed a little at her own ways—anyone she felt kind of sorry for could always get round her, she said. She knew it was awful foolish, but that, she said, was the way she was. Mr. Ewing, she said behind her husband's hearing, always called her just a regular little old easy mark.

Big Lannie had no words in which to thank Mrs. Ewing, nor to tell her what two days' assured employment every week could mean. At least, it was fairly assured. Big Lannie, as Mrs. Ewing pointed out to her, had got no younger, and she had always been slow. Mrs. Ewing kept her in a state of stimulating insecurity by referring, with perfect truth, to the numbers of stronger, quicker women who were also in need of work.

Two days' work in the week meant money for rent and stovewood and almost enough food for Raymond and Big Lannie. She must depend, for anything further, on whatever odd jobs she could find, and she must not stop seeking them. Pressed on by fear and gratitude, she worked so well for Mrs. Ewing that there was sometimes expressed satisfaction at the condition of the lady's household linen and her own and her husband's clothing. Big Lannie had a glimpse of Mr. Ewing occasionally, leaving the house as she came, or entering it as she was leaving. He was a bit of a man, not much bigger than Raymond.

Raymond grew so fast that he seemed to be taller each morning. Every day he had his walk in the street to look forward to and experience, and tell Big Lannie about at night. He had ceased to be a sight of the street; the children were so used to him that they did not even look at him, and the men and women at the windows no longer noticed him enough to hail him. He did not know. He would wave to any gay cry he heard, and go on his way, singing his little songs and turning toward the sound of laughter.

Then his lovely list of days ended as sharply as if ripped from some bright calendar. A winter came, so sudden and savage as to find no comparison in the town's memories, and Raymond had no clothes to wear out in the street. Big Lannie mended his outgrown garments as long as she could, but the stuff had so rotted with wear that it split in new places when she tried to sew together the ragged edges of rents.

The neighbors could give no longer; all they had they must keep for their own. A demented colored man in a near-by town had killed the woman who employed him, and terror had spread like brush fire. There was a sort of panic of reprisal; colored employees were dismissed from their positions, and there was no new work for them. But Mrs. Ewing, admittedly soft-hearted certainly to a fault and possibly to a peril, kept her black laundress on. More than ever Big Lannie had reason to call her blessed.

All winter, Raymond stayed indoors. He sat at his spool and worsted, with Big Lannie's old sweater about his shoulders and, when his tattered knickerbockers would no longer hold together, a calico skirt of hers lapped around his waist. He lived, at his age, in the past; in the days when he had walked, proud and glad, in the street, with laughter in his ears. Always, when he talked of it, he must laugh back at that laughter.

Since he could remember, he had not been allowed to go out when Big Lannie thought the weather unfit. This he had accepted without question, and so he accepted his incarceration through the mean weeks of the winter. But then one day it was spring, so surely that he could tell it even in the smoky, stinking rooms of the house, and he cried out with joy because now he might walk in the street again. Big Lannie had to explain to him that his rags were too thin to shield him, and that there were no odd jobs for her, and so no clothes and shoes for him.

Raymond did not talk about the street any more, and his fingers were slow at his spool.

Big Lannie did something she had never done before; she begged of her employer. She asked Mrs. Ewing to give her some of Mr. Ewing's old clothes for Raymond. She looked at the floor and mumbled so that Mrs. Ewing requested her to talk *up*. When Mrs. Ewing understood, she was, she said, surprised. She had, she said, a great, great many demands on her charity, and she would have supposed that Big Lannie, of all people, might have known that she did everything she could, and, in fact, a good deal more. She spoke of inches and ells. She said that if she found she could spare anything, Big Lannie was kindly to remember it was to be just for this once.

When Big Lannie was leaving at the end of her day's work, Mrs. Ewing brought her a package with her own hands. There, she said, was a suit and a pair of shoes; beautiful, grand things that people would think she was just a crazy to go giving away like that. She simply didn't know, she said, what Mr. Ewing would say to her for being such a crazy. She explained that that was the way she was when anyone got around her, all the while Big Lannie was trying to thank her.

Big Lannie had never before seen Raymond behave as he did when she brought him home the package. He jumped and danced and clapped his hands, he tried to speak and squealed instead, he tore off the paper himself, and ran his fingers over the close-woven cloth and held it to his face and kissed it. He put on the shoes and clattered about in them, digging with his toes and heels to keep them on; he made Big Lannie pin the trousers around his waist and roll them up over his shins. He babbled of the morrow when he would walk in the street, and could not say his words for laughing.

Big Lannie must work for Mrs. Ewing the next day, and she had thought to bid Raymond wait until she could stay at home and dress him herself in his new garments. But she heard him laugh again; she could not tell him he must wait. He might go out at noon next day, she said, when the sun was so warm that he would not take cold at his first outing; one of the neighbors across the hall would help him with the clothes. Raymond chuckled and sang his little songs until he went to sleep.

After Big Lannie left in the morning, the neighbor came in to Raymond, bringing a pan of cold pork and corn bread for his lunch. She had a call for a half-day's work, and she could not stay to see him start out for his walk. She helped him put on the trousers and pinned and rolled them for him, and she laced the shoes as snug as they would go on his feet. Then she told him not to go out till the noon whistles blew, and kissed him, and left.

Raymond was too happy to be impatient. He sat and thought of the street and smiled and sang. Not until he heard the whistles did he go to the drawer where Big Lannie had laid the coat, and take it out and put it on. He felt it soft on his bare back, he twisted his shoulders to let it fall warm and loose from them. As he folded the sleeves back over his thin arms, his heart beat so that the cloth above it fluttered.

The stairs were difficult for him to manage, in the big shoes, but the very slowness of the descent was delicious to him. His anticipation was like honey in his mouth.

Then he came out into the yard, and turned his face in the gentle air. It was all good again; it was all given back again. As quickly as he could, he gained the walk and set forth, guiding himself by the fence. He could not wait; he called out, so that he would hear gay calls in return, he laughed so that laughter would answer him.

He heard it. He was so glad that he took his hand from the fence and turned and stretched out his arms and held up his smiling face to welcome it. He stood there, and his smile died on his face, and his welcoming arms stiffened and shook.

It was not the laughter he had known; it was not the laughter he had lived on. It was like great flails beating him flat, great prongs tearing his flesh from his bones. It was coming at him, to kill him. It drew slyly back, and then it smashed against him. It swirled around and over him, and he could not breathe. He screamed and tried to run out through it, and fell, and it licked over him, howling higher. His clothes unrolled, and his shoes flapped on his feet. Each time he could rise, he fell again. It was as if the street were perpendicular before him, and the laughter leaping at his back. He could not find the fence, he did not know which way he was turned. He lay screaming, in blood and dust and darkness.

When Big Lannie came home, she found him on the floor in a corner of the room, moaning and whimpering. He still wore his new clothes, cut and torn and dusty, and there was dried blood on his mouth and his palms. Her heart had leapt in alarm when he had not opened the door at her footstep, and she cried out so frantically to ask what had happened that she frightened him into wild weeping. She could not understand what he said; it was something about the street, and laughing at him, and make them go away, and don't let him go in the street no more, never in the street no more. She did not try to make him explain. She took him in her arms and rocked him, and told him, over and over, never mind, don't care, everything's all right. Neither he nor she believed her words.

But her voice was soft and her arms warm. Raymond's sobs softened, and trembled away. She held him, rocking silently and rhythmically, a long time. Then gently she set him on his feet, and took from his shoulders Mr. Ewing's old full-dress coat.

THE WALTZ

WHY, *thank you so much. I'd adore to.*

I don't want to dance with him. I don't want to dance with anybody. And even if I did, it wouldn't be him. He'd be well down among the last ten. I've seen the way he dances; it looks like something you do on Saint Walpurgis Night. Just think, not a quarter of an hour ago, here I was sitting, feeling so sorry for the poor girl he was dancing with. And now *I'm* going to be the poor girl. Well, well. Isn't it a small world?

And a peach of a world, too. A true little corker. Its events are so fascinatingly unpredictable, are not they? Here I was, minding my own business, not doing a stitch of harm to any living soul. And then he comes into my life, all smiles and city manners, to sue me for the favor of one memorable mazurka. Why, he scarcely knows my name, let alone what it stands for. It stands for Despair, Bewilderment, Futility, Degradation, and Premeditated Murder, but little does he wot. I don't wot his name, either; I haven't any idea what it is. Jukes, would be my guess from the look in his eyes. How do you do, Mr. Jukes? And how is that dear little brother of yours, with the two heads?

Ah, now why did he have to come around me, with his low requests? Why can't he let me lead my own life? I ask so little—just to be left alone in my quiet corner of the table, to do my evening brooding over all my sorrows. And he must come, with his bows and his scrapes and his may-I-have-this-ones. And I had to go and tell him that I'd adore to dance with him. I cannot understand why I wasn't struck right down dead. Yes, and being struck dead would look like a day in the country, compared to struggling out a dance with this boy. But what could I do? Everyone else at the table had got up to dance, except him and me. There was I, trapped. Trapped like a trap in a trap.

What can you say, when a man asks you to dance with him? I most certainly will *not* dance with you, I'll see you in hell first. Why, thank you, I'd like to awfully, but I'm having labor pains. Oh, yes, *do* let's dance together—it's so nice to meet a man who isn't a scaredy-cat about catching my beri-beri. No. There was nothing for me to do, but say I'd adore to. Well, we might as well get it over with. All right, Cannonball, let's run out on the field. You won the toss; you can lead.

Why, I think it's more of a waltz, really. Isn't it? We might just listen to the music a second. Shall we? Oh, yes, it's a waltz. Mind? Why, I'm simply thrilled. I'd love to waltz with you.

I'd love to waltz with you. I'd love to waltz with you. I'd love to have my tonsils out, I'd love to be in a midnight fire at sea. Well, it's too late now. We're getting under way. *Oh*. Oh, dear. Oh, dear, dear, dear. Oh, this is even worse than I thought it would be. I suppose that's the one dependable law of life—everything is always worse than you thought it was going to be. Oh, if I had any real grasp of what this dance would be like, I'd have held out for sitting it out. Well, it will probably amount to the same thing in the end. We'll be sitting it out on the floor in a minute, if he keeps this up.

I'm so glad I brought it to his attention that this is a waltz they're playing. Heaven knows what might have happened, if he had thought it was something fast; we'd have blown the sides right out of the building. Why does he always want to be somewhere that he isn't? Why can't we stay in one place just long enough to get acclimated? It's this constant rush, rush, rush, that's the curse of American life. That's the reason that we're all of us so—*Ow!* For God's sake, don't *kick*, you idiot; this is only second down. Oh, my shin. My poor, poor shin, that I've had ever since I was a little girl!

Oh, no, no, no. Goodness, no. It didn't hurt the least little bit. And anyway it was my fault. Really it was. Truly. Well, you're just being sweet, to say that. It really was all my fault.

I wonder what I'd better do—kill him this instant, with my naked hands, or wait and let him drop in his traces. Maybe it's best not to make a scene. I guess I'll just lie low, and watch the pace get him. He can't keep this up indefinitely—he's only flesh and blood. Die he must, and die he shall, for what he did to me. I don't want to be of the over-sensitive type, but you can't tell me that kick was unpremeditated. Freud says there are no accidents. I've led no cloistered life, I've known dancing partners who have spoiled my slippers and torn my dress; but when it comes to kicking, I am Outraged Womanhood. When you kick me in the shin, *smile*.

Maybe he didn't do it maliciously. Maybe it's just his way of showing his high spirits. I suppose I ought to be glad that one of us is having such a good time. I suppose I ought to think myself lucky if he brings me back alive. Maybe it's captious to demand of a practically strange man that he leave your shins as he found them. After all, the poor boy's doing the best he can. Probably he grew up in the hill country, and never had no larnin'. I bet they had to throw him on his back to get shoes on him.

Yes, it's lovely, isn't it? It's simply lovely. It's the loveliest waltz. Isn't it? Oh, I think it's lovely, too.

Why, I'm getting positively drawn to the Triple Threat here. He's my hero. He has the heart of a lion, and the sinews of a buffalo. Look at him—never a thought of the consequences, never afraid of his face, hurling himself into every scrimmage, eyes shining, cheeks ablaze. And shall it be said that I hung back? No, a thousand times no. What's it to me if I have to spend the next couple of years in a plaster cast? Come on, Butch, right through them! Who wants to live forever?

Oh. Oh, dear. Oh, he's all right, thank goodness. For a while I thought they'd have to carry him off the field. Ah, I couldn't bear to have anything happen to him. I love him. I love him better than anybody in the world. Look at the spirit he gets into a dreary, commonplace waltz; how effete the other dancers seem, beside him. He is youth and vigor and courage, he is strength and gaiety and—*Ow!* Get off my instep, you hulking peasant! What do you think I am, anyway—a gangplank? *Ow!*

No, of course it didn't hurt. Why, it didn't a bit. Honestly. And it was all my fault. You see, that little step of yours—well, it's perfectly lovely, but it's just a tiny bit tricky to follow at first. Oh, did you work it up yourself? You really did? Well, aren't you amazing! Oh, now I think I've got it. Oh, I think it's lovely. I was watching you do it when you were dancing before. It's awfully effective when you look at it.

It's awfully effective when you look at it. I bet I'm awfully effective when you look at me. My hair is hanging along my cheeks, my skirt is swaddled about me, I can feel the cold damp of my brow. I must look like something out of "The Fall of the House of Usher." This sort of thing takes a fearful toll of a woman my age. And he worked up his little step himself, he with his degenerate cunning. And it was just a tiny bit tricky at first, but now I think I've got it. Two stumbles, slip, and a twenty-yard dash; yes. I've got it. I've got several other things, too, including a split shin and a bitter heart. I hate this creature I'm chained to. I hated him the moment I saw his leering, bestial face. And here I've been locked in his noxious embrace for the thirty-five years this waltz has lasted. Is that orchestra never going to stop playing? Or must this obscene travesty of a dance go on until hell burns out?

Oh, they're going to play another encore. Oh, goody. Oh, that's lovely. Tired? I should say I'm not tired. I'd like to go on like this forever.

I should say I'm not tired. I'm dead, that's all I am. Dead, and in what a cause! And the music is never going to stop playing, and we're going on like this, Double-Time Charlie and I, throughout eternity. I suppose I won't care any more, after the first hundred thousand years. I suppose nothing will matter then, not heat nor pain nor broken heart nor cruel, aching weariness. Well. It can't come too soon for me.

I wonder why I didn't tell him I was tired. I wonder why I didn't suggest going back to the table. I could have said let's just listen to the music. Yes, and if he would, that would be the first bit of attention he has given it all evening. George Jean Nathan said that the lovely rhythms of the waltz should be listened to in stillness and not be accompanied by strange gyrations of the human body. I think that's what he said. I think it was George Jean Nathan. Anyhow, whatever he said and whoever he was and whatever he's doing now, he's better off than I am. That's safe. Anybody who isn't waltzing with this Mrs. O'Leary's cow I've got here is having a good time.

Still if we were back at the table, I'd probably have to talk to him. Look at him—what could you say to a thing like that! Did you go to the circus this year, what's your favorite kind of ice cream, how do you spell cat? I guess I'm as well off here. As well off as if I were in a cement mixer in full action.

I'm past all feeling now. The only way I can tell when he steps on me is that I can hear the splintering of bones. And all the events of my life are passing before my eyes. There was the time I was in a hurricane in the West Indies, there was the day I got my head cut open in the taxi smash, there was the night the drunken lady threw a bronze ash-tray at her own true love and got me instead, there was that summer that the sailboat kept capsizing. Ah, what an easy, peaceful time was mine, until I fell in with Swifty, here. I didn't know what trouble was, before I got drawn into this *danse macabre*. I think my mind is beginning to wander. It almost seems to me as if the orchestra were stopping. It couldn't be, of course; it could never, never be. And yet in my ears there is a silence like the sound of angel voices. . . .

Oh, they've stopped, the mean things. They're not going to play any more. Oh, darn. Oh, do you think they would? Do you really think so, if you gave them twenty dollars? Oh, that would be lovely. And look, do tell them to play this same thing. I'd simply adore to go on waltzing.

LITTLE CURTIS

Mrs. Matson paused in the vestibule of G. Fosdick's Sons' Department Store. She transferred a small parcel from her right hand to the crook of her left arm, gripped her shopping-bag firmly by its German-silver frame, opened it with a capable click, and drew from its orderly interior a little black-bound book and a neatly sharpened pencil.

Shoppers passing in and out jostled her as she stood there, but they neither shared in Mrs. Matson's attention nor hurried her movements. She made no answer to the "Oh, I *beg* your pardons" that bubbled from the lips of the more tender-hearted among them. Calm, sure, gloriously aloof, Mrs. Matson stood, opened her book, poised her pencil, and wrote in delicate, prettily slanting characters: "4 crepe-paper candy-baskets, $.28."

The dollar-sign was gratifyingly decorative, the decimal point clear and deep, the 2 daintily curled, the 8 admirably balanced. Mrs. Matson looked approvingly at her handiwork. Still unhurried, she closed the book, replaced it and the pencil in the bag, tested the snap to see that it was indisputably shut, and took the parcel once more in her right hand. Then, with a comfortable air of duty well done, she passed impressively, and with a strong push, from G. Fosdick's Sons' Department Store by means of a portal which bore a placard with the request, "Please Use Other Door."

Slowly Mrs. Matson made her way down Maple Street. The morning sunshine that flooded the town's main thoroughfare caused her neither to squint nor to lower her face. She held her head high, looking about her as one who says, "Our good people, we are pleased with you."

She stopped occasionally by a shop-window, to inspect thoroughly the premature autumn costumes there displayed. But her heart was unfluttered by the envy which attacked the lesser women around her. Though her long black coat, of that vintage when coats were puffed of sleeve and cut sharply in at the waist, was stained and shiny, and her hat had the general air of indecision and lack of spirit that comes with age, and her elderly black gloves were worn in patches of rough gray, Mrs. Matson had no yearnings for the fresh, trim costumes set temptingly before her. Snug in her was the thought of the rows of recent garments, each one in its flowered cretonne casing, occupying the varnished hangers along the poles of her bedroom closet.

She had her unalterable ideas about such people as gave or threw away garments that might still be worn, for warmth and modesty, if not for style. She found it distinctly lower-class to wear one's new clothes "for every day"; there was an unpleasant suggestion of extravagance and riotous living in the practice. The working classes, who, as Mrs. Matson often explained to her friends, went and bought themselves electric ice-boxes and radios the minute they got a little money, did such things.

No morbid thought of her possible sudden demise before the clothes in her closet could be worn or enjoyed irked her. Life's uncertainty was not for those of her position. Mrs. Matsons pass away between seventy and eighty; sometimes later, never before.

A blind colored woman, a tray of pencils hung about her neck, with a cane tapping the pavement before her, came down the street. Mrs. Matson swerved sharply to the curb to avoid her, wasting a withering glance upon her. It was Mrs. Matson's immediate opinion that the woman could see as well as *she* could. She never bought of the poor on the streets, and was angry if she saw others do so. She frequently remarked that these beggars all had big bank-accounts.

She crossed to the car-tracks to await the trolley that would bear her home, her calm upset by her sight of the woman. "Probably owns an apartment-house," she told herself, and shot an angry glance after the blind woman.

However, her poise was restored by the act of tendering her fare to the courteous conductor. Mrs. Matson rather enjoyed small and legitimate disbursements to those who were appropriately grateful. She gave him her nickel with the manner of one presenting a park to a city, and swept into the car to a desirable seat.

Settled, with the parcel securely wedged between her hip and the window, against loss or robbery, Mrs. Matson again produced the book and pencil. "Car-fare, $.05," she wrote. Again the exquisite handwriting, the neat figures, gave her a flow of satisfaction.

Mrs. Matson, regally without acknowledgment, accepted the conductor's aid in alighting from the car at her corner. She trod the sun-splashed pavement, bowing now and again to neighbors knitting on their porches or bending solicitously over their iris-beds. Slow, stately bows she gave, unaccompanied by smile or word of greeting. After all, she was Mrs. Albert Matson; she had been Miss Laura Whitmore, of the Drop Forge and Tool Works Whitmores. One does not lose sight of such things.

She always enjoyed the first view of her house as she walked toward it. It amplified in her her sense of security and permanence. There it stood, in its tidy, treeless lawns, square and solid and serviceable. You thought of steel-engravings and rows of Scott's novels behind glass, and Sunday dinner in the middle of the day, when you looked at it. You knew immediately that within it no one ever banged a door, no one clattered up- and down-stairs, no one spilled crumbs or dropped ashes or left the light burning in the bathroom.

Expectancy pervaded Mrs. Matson as she approached her home. She spoke of it always as her home. "You must come to see me in my home some time," she graciously commanded new acquaintances. There was a large, institutional sound to it that you didn't get in the word "house."

She liked to think of its cool, high-ceilinged rooms, of its busy maids, of little Curtis waiting to deliver her his respectful kiss. She had adopted him almost a year ago, when he was four. She had, she told her friends, never once regretted it.

In her absence her friends had been wont to comment sadly upon what a shame it was that the Albert Matsons had no child—and with all the Matson and Whitmore money, too. Neither of them, the friends pointed out, could live forever; it would all have to go to the Henry Matsons' children. And they were but quoting Mrs. Albert Matson's own words when they observed that those children would be just the kind that would run right through it.

Mr. and Mrs. Matson held a joint view of the devastation that would result if their nephews and nieces were ever turned loose among the Matson and Whitmore money. As is frequent in such instances, their worry led them to pay the other Matson family the compliment of the credit for schemes and desires that had never edged into their thoughts.

The Albert Matsons saw their relatives as waiting, with a sort of stalking patience, for the prayed-for moment of their death. For years they conjured up ever more lurid pictures of the Matson children going through their money like Sherman to the sea; for years they carried about with them the notion that their demise was being eagerly awaited, was being made, indeed, the starting-point of bacchanalian plans.

The Albert Matsons were as one in everything, as in this. Their thoughts, their manners, their opinions, their very locutions were phenomena of similarity. People even pointed out that Mr. and Mrs. Matson looked alike. It was regarded as the world's misfortune that so obviously Heaven-made a match was without off-spring. And of course—you always had to come back to it, it bulked so before you—there was all that Matson and Whitmore money.

No one, though, ever directly condoled with Mrs. Matson upon her childlessness. In her presence one didn't speak of things like having children. She accepted the fact of babies when they were shown to her; she fastidiously disregarded their mode of arrival.

She had told none of her friends of her decision to adopt a little boy. No one knew about it until the papers were signed and he was established in the Matson house. Mrs. Matson had got him, she explained, "at the best place in New York." No one was surprised at that. Mrs. Matson always went to the best places when she shopped in New York. You thought of her selecting a child as she selected all her other belongings: a good one, one that would last.

She stopped abruptly now, as she came to her gate, a sudden frown creasing her brow. Two little boys, too absorbed to hear her steps, were playing in the hot sun by the hedge—two little boys much alike in age, size, and attire, compact, pink-and-white, good little boys, their cheeks flushed with interest, the backs of their necks warm and damp. They played an interminable, mysterious game with pebbles and twigs and a small tin trolley-car.

Mrs. Matson entered the yard.

"Curtis!" she said.

Both little boys looked up, startled. One of them rose and hung his head before her frown.

"And who," said Mrs. Matson deeply, "who told Georgie he could come here?"

No answer. Georgie, still squatting on his heels, looked inquiringly from her to Curtis. He was interested and unalarmed.

"Was it you, Curtis?" asked Mrs. Matson.

Curtis nodded. You could scarcely tell that he did, his head hung so low.

"Yes, mother dear!" said Mrs. Matson.

"Yes, mother dear," whispered Curtis.

"And how many times," Mrs. Matson inquired, "have I told you that you were not to play with Georgie? How many times, Curtis?"

Curtis murmured vaguely. He wished that Georgie would please go.

"You don't know?" said Mrs. Matson incredulously. "You don't know? After all mother does for you, you don't know how many times she has told you not to play with Georgie? Don't you remember what mother told you she'd have to do if you ever played with Georgie again?"

A pause. Then the nod.

"Yes, mother dear!" said Mrs. Matson.

"Yes, mother dear," said Curtis.

"Well!" Mrs. Matson said. She turned to the enthralled Georgie. "You'll have to go home now, Georgie—go right straight home. And you're not to come here any more, do you understand me? Curtis is not allowed to play with you—not ever."

Georgie rose.

" 'By," he said philosophically, and walked away, his farewell unanswered.

Mrs. Matson gazed upon Curtis. Grief disarranged her features.

"Playing!" she said, her voice broken with emotion. "Playing with a furnaceman's child! After all mother does for you!"

She took him by a limp arm and led him, unresisting, along the walk to the house; led him past the maid that opened the door, up the stairs to his little blue bedroom. She put him in it and closed the door.

Then she went to her own room, placed her package carefully on the table, removed her gloves, and laid them, with her bag, in an orderly drawer. She entered her closet, hung up her coat, then stooped for one of the felt slippers that were set scrupulously, in the first dancing position, on the floor beneath her nightgown. It was a lavender slipper, with scallops and a staid rosette; it had a light, flexible leather sole, across which was stamped its name, "Kumfy-Toes."

Mrs. Matson grasped it firmly by the heel and flicked it back and forth. Carrying it, she went to the little boy's room. She began to speak as she turned the door-knob.

"And before mother had time to take her hat off, too," she said. The door closed behind her.

She came out again presently. A scale of shrieks followed her.

"That will do!" she announced, looking back from the door. The shrieks faded obediently to sobs. "That's quite enough of that, thank you. Mother's had just about plenty for one morning. And today, too, with the ladies coming this afternoon, and all mother has to attend to! Oh, I'd be ashamed, Curtis, if I were you—that's what I'd be."

She closed the door, and retired, to remove her hat.

The ladies came in mid-afternoon. There were three of them. Mrs. Kerley, gray and brittle and painstaking, always thoughtful about sending birthday-cards and carrying glass jars of soup to the sick. Mrs. Swan, her visiting sister-in-law, younger, and given to daisied hats and crocheted lace collars, with her transient's air of bright, determined interest in her hostess's acquaintances and activities. And Mrs. Cook. Only she did not count very much. She was extremely deaf, and so pretty well out of things.

She had visited innumerable specialists, spent uncounted money, endured agonizing treatments, in her endeavors to be able to hear what went on about her and to have a part in it. They had finally fitted her out with a long, coiling, corrugated speaking-tube, rather like a larger intestine. One end of this she placed in her better ear, and the other she extended to those who would hold speech with her. But the shining black mouthpiece seemed to embarrass people and intimidate them; they could think of nothing better to call into it than "Getting colder out," or "You keeping pretty well?" To hear such remarks as these she had gone through years of suffering.

Mrs. Matson, in her last spring's blue taffeta, assigned her guests to seats about the living-room. It was an afternoon set apart for fancy-work and conversation. Later there would be tea, and two triangular sandwiches apiece made from the chopped remnants of last night's chicken, and a cake which was a high favorite with Mrs. Matson, for its formula required but one egg. She had gone, in person, to the kitchen to supervise its making. She was not entirely convinced that her cook was wasteful of materials, but she felt that the woman would bear watching.

The crepe-paper baskets, fairly well filled with disks of peppermint creams were to enliven the corners of the tea-table. Mrs. Matson trusted her guests not to regard them as favors and take them home.

The conversation dealt, and favorably, with the weather. Mrs. Kerley and Mrs. Swan vied with each other in paying compliments to the day.

"So clear," said Mrs. Kerley.

"Not a cloud in the sky," augmented Mrs. Swan. "Not a one."

"The air was just lovely this morning," reported Mrs. Kerley. "I said to myself, 'Well, this is a beautiful day if there ever *was* one.' "

"There's something so balmy about it," said Mrs. Swan.

Mrs. Cook spoke suddenly and overloudly, in the untrustworthy voice of the deaf.

"Phew, this is a scorcher!" she said. "Something terrible out."

The conversation went immediately to literature. It developed that Mrs. Kerley had been reading a lovely book. Its name and that of its author escaped her at the moment, but her enjoyment of it was so keen that she had lingered over it till 'way past ten o'clock the night before. Particularly did she commend its descriptions of some of those Italian places; they were, she affirmed, just like a picture. The book had been drawn to her attention by the young woman at the Little Booke Nooke. It was, on her authority, one of the new ones.

Mrs. Matson frowned at her embroidery. Words flowed readily from her lips. She seemed to have spoken on the subject before.

"I haven't any use for all these new books," she said. "I wouldn't give them house-room. I don't see why a person wants to sit down and write any such stuff. I often think, I don't believe they know what they're writing about themselves half the time. I don't know who they think wants to read those kind of things. I'm sure *I* don't."

She paused to let her statements sink deep.

"Mr. Matson," she continued–she always spoke of her husband thus; it conveyed an aristocratic sense of aloofness, did away with any suggestion of carnal intimacy between them– "Mr. Matson isn't any hand for these new books, either. He always says, if he could find another book like *David Harum*, he'd read it in a minute. I wish," she added longingly, "I had a dollar for every time I've heard him say that."

Mrs. Kerley smiled. Mrs. Swan threw a rippling little laugh into the pause.

"Well, it's true, you know, it really is true," Mrs. Kerley told Mrs. Swan.

"Oh, it is," Mrs. Swan hastened to reassure her.

"I don't know what we're coming to, *I'm* sure," announced Mrs. Matson.

She sewed, her thread twanging through the tight-stretched circle of linen in her embroidery-hoop.

The stoppage of conversation weighed upon Mrs. Swan. She lifted her head and looked out the window.

"My, what a lovely lawn you have!" she said. "I couldn't help noticing it, first thing. We've been living in New York, you know."

"I often say I don't see what people want to shut themselves up in a place like that for," Mrs. Matson said. "You know, you exist, in New York–we live, out here."

Mrs. Swan laughed a bit nervously. Mrs. Kerley nodded. "That's right," she said. "That's pretty good."

Mrs. Matson herself thought it worthy of repetition. She picked up Mrs. Cook's speaking-tube.

"I was just saying to Mrs. Swan," she cried, and called her epigram into the mouthpiece.

"Live where?" asked Mrs. Cook.

Mrs. Matson smiled at her patiently. "New York. You know, that's where I got my little adopted boy."

"Oh, yes," said Mrs. Swan. "Carrie told me. Now, wasn't that lovely of you!"

Mrs. Matson shrugged. "Yes," she said, "I went right to the best place for him. Miss Codman's nursery—it's absolutely reliable. You can get awfully nice children there. There's quite a long waiting-list, they tell me."

"Goodness, just think how it must seem to him to be up here," said Mrs. Swan, "with this big house, and that lovely, smooth lawn, and everything."

Mrs. Matson laughed slightly. "Oh—well," she said.

"I hope he appreciates it," remarked Mrs. Swan.

"I think he will," Mrs. Matson said capably. "Of course," she conceded, "he's pretty young right now."

"So lovely," murmured Mrs. Swan. "So sweet to get them young like this and have them grow up."

"Yes, I think that's the nicest way," agreed Mrs. Matson. "And, you know, I really enjoy training him. Naturally, now that we have him here with us, we want him to act like a little gentleman."

"Just think of it," cried Mrs. Swan, "a child like that having all this! And will you have him go to school later on?"

"Oh, yes," Mrs. Matson replied. "Yes, we want him to be educated. You take a child going to some nice little school near here, say, where he'll meet only the best children, and he'll make friends that it will be a pretty good thing for him to know some day."

Mrs. Swan waxed arch. "I suppose you've got it all settled what he's going to be when he grows up," she said.

"Why, certainly," said Mrs. Matson. "He's to go right straight into Mr. Matson's business. My husband," she informed Mrs. Swan, "is the Matson Adding Machines."

"Oh-h-h," said Mrs. Swan on a descending scale.

"I think Curtis will do very well in school," prophesied Mrs. Matson. "He's not at all stupid—picks up everything. Mr. Matson is anxious to have him brought up to be a good, sensible business man—he says that's what this country needs, you know. So I've been trying to teach him the value of money. I've bought him a little bank. I don't think you can begin too early. Because probably some day Curtis is going to have—well——"

Mrs. Matson drifted into light, anecdotal mood.

"Oh, it's funny the way children are," she remarked. "The other day Mrs. Newman brought her little Amy down to play with Curtis, and when I went up to look at them, there he was, trying to give her his brand-new flannel rabbit. So I just took him into my room, and I sat him down, and I said to him, 'Now, Curtis,' I said, 'you must realize that mother had to pay almost two dollars for that rabbit—nearly two hundred pennies,' I said. 'It's very nice to be generous, but you must learn that it isn't a good idea to give things away to people. Now you go in to Amy,' I said, 'and you tell her you're sorry, but she'll have to give that rabbit right back to you.' "

"And did he do it?" asked Mrs. Swan.

"Why, I told him to," Mrs. Matson said.

"Isn't it splendid?" Mrs. Swan asked of the company at large. "Really, when you think of it. A child like that, just suddenly having everything all at once. And probably coming of poor people, too. Are his parents—living?"

"Oh, no, no," Mrs. Matson said briskly. "I couldn't be bothered with anything like that. Of course, I found out all about them. They were really quite nice, clean people—the father was a college man. Curtis really comes of a very nice family, for an orphan."

"Do you think you'll ever tell him that you aren't—that he isn't—tell him about it?" inquired Mrs. Kerley.

"Dear me, yes, just as soon as he's a little older," Mrs. Matson answered. "I think it's so much nicer for him to know. He'll appreciate everything so much more."

"Does the little thing remember his father and mother at all?" Mrs. Swan asked.

"*I* really don't know if he does or not," said Mrs. Matson.

"Tea," announced the maid, appearing abruptly at the door.

"Tea is served, Mrs. Matson," said Mrs. Matson, her voice lifted.

"Tea is served, Mrs. Matson," echoed the maid.

"I don't know what I'm going to do with her," Mrs. Matson told her guests when the girl had disappeared. "Here last night she had company in the kitchen till nearly eleven o'clock at night. The trouble with me is I'm too good to servants. The only way to do is to treat them like cattle."

"They don't appreciate anything else," said Mrs. Kerley.

Mrs. Matson placed her embroidery in her sweet-grass work-basket, and rose.

"Well, shall we go have a cup of tea?" she said.

"Why, how lovely!" cried Mrs. Swan.

Mrs. Cook, who had been knitting doggedly, was informed, via the speaking-tube, of the readiness of tea. She dropped her work instantly, and led the way to the dining-room.

The talk, at the tea-table, was of stitches and patterns. Praise, benignly accepted by Mrs. Matson, was spread by Mrs. Swan and Mrs. Kerley upon the sandwiches, the cake, the baskets, the table-linen, the china, and the design of the silver.

A watch was glanced at, and there arose cries of surprise at the afternoon's flight. There was an assembling of workbags, a fluttering exodus to the hall to put on hats. Mrs. Matson watched her guests.

"Well, it's been just too lovely," Mrs. Swan declared, clasping her hand. "I can't *tell* you how much I've enjoyed it, hearing about the dear little boy, and all. I *hope* you're going to let me see him some time."

"Why, you can see him now, if you'd like," said Mrs. Matson. She went to the foot of the stairs and sang, "*Cur*-tis, *Cur*-tis."

Curtis appeared in the hall above, clean in the gray percale sailor-suit that had been selected in the thrifty expectation of his "growing into it." He looked down at them, caught sight of Mrs. Cook's speaking-tube, and watched it intently, his eyes wide open.

"Come down and see the ladies, Curtis," commanded Mrs. Matson.

Curtis came down, his warm hand squeaking along the banister. He placed his right foot upon a step, brought his left foot carefully down to it, then started his right one off again. Eventually he reached them.

"Can't you say how-do-you-do to the ladies?" asked Mrs. Matson.

He gave each guest, in turn, a small, flaccid hand.

Mrs. Swan squatted suddenly before him, so that her face was level with his.

"My, what a nice boy!" she cried. "I just love little boys like you, do you know it? Ooh, I could just eat you up! I could!"

She squeezed his arms. Curtis, in alarm, drew his head back from her face.

"And what's *your* name?" she asked him. "Let's see if you can tell me what your name is. I just *bet* you can't!"

He looked at her.

"Can't you tell the lady your name, Curtis?" demanded Mrs. Matson.

"Curtis," he told the lady.

"Why, what a *pretty* name!" she cried. She looked up at Mrs. Matson. "Was that his real name?" she asked.

"No," Mrs. Matson said, "they had him called something else. But I named him as soon as I got him. My mother was a Curtis."

Thus might one say, "My name was Guelph before I married."

Mrs. Cook spoke sharply. "Lucky!" she said. "Pretty lucky, that young one!"

"Well, I should say so," echoed Mrs. Swan. "Aren't you a pretty lucky little boy? Aren't you, aren't you, aren't you?" She rubbed her nose against his.

"Yes, Mrs. Swan." Mrs. Matson pronounced and frowned at Curtis.

He murmured something.

"Ooh—*you!*" said Mrs. Swan. She rose from her squatting posture. "I'd like to *steal* you, in your little sailor-suit, and all!"

"Mother bought that suit for you, didn't she?" asked Mrs. Matson of Curtis. "Mother bought him all his nice things."

"Oh, he calls you mother? Now, isn't that sweet!" cried Mrs. Swan.

"Yes, I think it's nice," said Mrs. Matson.

There was a brisk, sure step on the porch; a key turned in the lock. Mr. Matson was among them.

"Well," said Mrs. Matson upon seeing her mate. It was her invariable evening greeting to him.

"Ah," said Mr. Matson. It was his to her.

Mrs. Kerley cooed. Mrs. Swan blinked vivaciously. Mrs. Cook applied her speaking-tube to her ear in the anticipation of hearing something good.

"I don't think you've met Mrs. Swan, Albert," remarked Mrs. Matson. He bowed.

"Oh, I've heard so much about Mr. Matson," cried Mrs. Swan.

Again he bowed.

"We've been making friends with your dear little boy," Mrs. Swan said. She pinched Curtis's cheek. "You sweetie, you!"

"Well, Curtis," said Mr. Matson, "haven't you got a good-evening for me?"

Curtis gave his hand to his present father with a weak smile of politeness. He looked modestly down.

"That's more like it," summarized Mr. Matson. His parental duties accomplished, he turned to fulfill his social obligations. Boldly he caught up Mrs. Cook's speaking-tube. Curtis watched.

"Getting cooler out," roared Mr. Matson. "I thought it would."

Mrs. Cook nodded. "That's good!" she shouted.

Mr. Matson pressed forward to open the door for her. He was of generous proportions, and the hall was narrow. One of the buttons-of-leisure on his coat-sleeve caught in Mrs. Cook's speaking-tube. It fell, with a startling crash, to the floor, and writhed about.

Curtis's control went. Peal upon peal of high, helpless laughter came from him. He laughed on, against Mrs. Matson's cry of "Curtis!" against Mr. Matson's frown. He doubled over with his hands on his little brown knees, and laughed mad laughter.

"Curtis!" bellowed Mr. Matson. The laughter died. Curtis straightened himself, and one last little moan of enjoyment escaped him.

Mr. Matson pointed with a magnificent gesture. "Upstairs!" he boomed.

Curtis turned and climbed the stairs. He looked small beside the banister.

"Well, of all the—" said Mrs. Matson. "I never knew him to do a thing like that since he's been here. I never heard him do such a thing!"

"That young man," pronounced Mr. Matson, "needs a good talking to."

"He needs more than that," his spouse said.

Mr. Matson stooped with a faint creaking, retrieved the speaking-tube, and presented it to Mrs. Cook. "Not at all," he said in anticipation of the thanks which she left unspoken. He bowed. "Pardon me," he ordered, and mounted the stairs.

Mrs. Matson moved to the door in the wake of her guests. She was bewildered and, it seemed, grieved.

"I never," she affirmed, "never knew that child to go on that way."

"Oh, children," Mrs. Kerley assured her, "they're funny sometimes—especially a little boy like that. You can't expect so much. My goodness, you'll fix all that! I always say I don't know any child that's getting any better bringing up than that young one—just as if he was your own."

Peace returned to the breast of Mrs. Matson. "Oh—goodness!" she said. There was almost a coyness in her smile as she closed the door on the departing.

THE LITTLE HOURS

Now what's this? What's the object of all this darkness all over me? They haven't gone and buried me alive while my back was turned, have they? Ah, now would you think they'd do a thing like that! Oh, no, I know what it is. I'm awake. That's it. I've waked up in the middle of the night. Well, isn't that nice. Isn't that simply ideal. Twenty minutes past four, sharp, and here's Baby wide-eyed as a marigold. Look at this, will you? At the time when all decent people are just going to bed, I must wake up. There's no way things can ever come out even, under this system. This is as rank as injustice is ever likely to get. This is what brings about hatred and bloodshed, that's what *this* does.

Yes, and you want to know what got me into this mess? Going to bed at ten o'clock, that's what. That spells ruin. T-e-n-space-o-apostrophe-c-l-o-c-k: ruin. Early to bed, and you'll wish you were dead. Bed before eleven, nuts before seven. Bed before morning, sailors give warning. Ten o'clock, after a quiet evening of reading. Reading—there's an institution for you. Why, I'd turn on the light and read, right this minute, if reading weren't what contributed toward driving me here. I'll show it. God, the bitter misery that reading works in this world! Everybody knows that—everybody who *is* everybody. All the best minds have been off reading for years. Look at the swing La Rochefoucauld took at it. He said that if nobody had ever learned to read, very few people would be in love. There was a man for you, and that's what *he* thought of it. Good for you, La Rochefoucauld; nice going, boy. I wish I'd never learned to read. I wish I'd never learned to take off my clothes. Then I wouldn't have been caught in this jam at half-past four in the morning. If nobody had ever learned to undress, very few people would be in love. No, his is better. Oh, well, it's a man's world.

La Rochefoucauld, indeed, lying quiet as a mouse, and me tossing and turning here! This is no time to be getting all steamed up about La Rochefoucauld. It's only a question of minutes before I'm going to be pretty darned good and sick of La Rochefoucauld, once and for all. La Rochefoucauld this and La Rochefoucauld that. Yes, well, let me tell you that if nobody had ever learned to quote, very few people would be in love with La Rochefoucauld. I bet you I don't know ten souls who read him without a middle-man. People pick up those scholarly little essays that start off "Was it not that lovable old cynic, La Rochefoucauld, who said . . ." and then they go around claiming to know the master backwards. Pack of illiterates, that's all they are. All right, let them keep their La Rochefoucauld, and see if I care. I'll stick to La Fontaine. Only I'd be better company if I could quit thinking that La Fontaine married Alfred Lunt.

I don't know what I'm doing mucking about with a lot of French authors at this hour, anyway. First thing you know, I'll be reciting *Fleurs du Mal* to myself, and then I'll be little more good to anybody. And I'll stay off Verlaine too; he was always chasing Rimbauds. A person would be better off with La Rochefoucauld, even. Oh, damn La Rochefoucauld. The big Frog. I'll thank him to keep out of my head. What's he doing there, anyhow? What's La Rochefoucauld to me, or he to Hecuba? Why, I don't even know the man's first name, that's how close I ever was to *him*. What am I supposed to be, a hostess to La Rochefoucauld? That's what *he* thinks. Sez he. Well, he's only wasting his time, hanging around here. I can't help him. The only other thing I can remember his saying is that there is always something a little pleasing to us in the misfortunes of even our dearest friends. That cleans me all up with Monsieur La Rochefoucauld. *Maintenant c'est fini, ça.*

Dearest friends. A sweet lot of dearest friends *I've* got. All of them lying in swinish stupors, while I'm practically up and about.

All of them stretched sodden through these, the fairest hours of the day, when man should be at his most productive. Produce, produce, produce, for I tell you the night is coming. Carlyle said that. Yes, and a fine one *he* was, to go shooting off his face on production. *Oh*, Thomas Car*li*-yill, what *I* know about *you*-oo! No, that will be enough of that. I'm not going to start fretting about Carlyle, at this stage of the game. What did he ever do that was so great, besides founding a college for Indians? (That one ought to make him spin.) Let him keep his face out of this, if he knows what's good for him. I've got enough trouble with that lovable old cynic, La Rochefoucauld—him and the misfortunes of his dearest friends!

The first thing I've got to do is get out and whip me up a complete new set of dearest friends; that's the first thing. Everything else can wait. And will somebody please kindly be so good as to inform me how I am ever going to meet up with any new people when my entire scheme of living is out of joint—when I'm the only living being awake while the rest of the world lies sleeping? I've got to get this thing adjusted. I must try to get back to sleep right now. I've got to conform to the rotten little standards of this sluggard civilization. People needn't feel that they have to change their ruinous habits and come my way. Oh, no, no; no, indeed. Not at all. I'll go theirs. If that isn't the woman of it for you! Always having to do what somebody else wants, like it or not. Never able to murmur a suggestion of her own.

And what suggestion has anyone to murmur as to how I am going to drift lightly back to slumber? Here I am, awake as high noon what with all this milling and pitching around with La Rochefoucauld. I really can't be expected to drop everything and start counting sheep, at my age. I hate sheep. Untender it may be in me, but all my life I've hated sheep. It amounts to a phobia, the way I hate them. I can tell the minute there's one in the room. They needn't think that I am going to lie here in the dark and count their unpleasant little faces for them; I wouldn't do it if I didn't fall asleep again until the middle of next August. Suppose they never get counted—what's the worst that can happen? If the number of imaginary sheep in this world remains a matter of guesswork, who is richer or poorer for it? No, sir; *I'm* not their scorekeeper. Let them count themselves, if they're so crazy mad after mathematics. Let them do their own dirty work. Coming around here, at this time of day, and asking me to count them! And not even *real* sheep, at that. Why, it's the most preposterous thing I ever heard in my life.

But there must be *something* I could count. Let's see. No, I already know by heart how many fingers I have. I could count my bills, I suppose. I could count the things I didn't do yesterday that I should have done. I could count the things I should do today that I'm not going to do. I'm never going to accomplish anything; that's perfectly clear to me. I'm never going to be famous. My name will never be writ large on the roster of Those Who Do Things. I don't do anything. Not one single thing. I used to bite my nails, but I don't even do that any more. I don't amount to the powder to blow me to hell. I've turned out to be nothing but a bit of flotsam. Flotsam and leave 'em—that's me from now on. Oh, it's all terrible.

Well. This way lies galloping melancholia. Maybe it's because this is the zero hour. This is the time the swooning soul hangs pendant and vertiginous between the new day and the old, nor dares confront the one or summon back the other. This is the time when all things, known and hidden, are iron to weight the spirit; when all ways, traveled or virgin, fall away from the stumbling feet, when all before the straining eyes is black. Blackness now, everywhere is blackness. This is the time of abomination, the dreadful hour of the victorious dark. For it is always darkest— Was it not that lovable old cynic, La Rochefoucauld, who said that it is always darkest before the deluge?

There. Now you see, don't you? Here we are again, practically back where we started. La Rochefoucauld, we are here. Ah, come on, son—how about your going your way and letting me go mine?

I've got my work cut out for me right here; I've got all this sleeping to do. Think how I am going to look by daylight if this keeps up. I'll be a seamy sight for all those rested, clear-eyed, fresh-faced dearest friends of mine—the rats! My *dear*, whatever have you been doing; I thought you were so good lately. Oh, I was helling around with La Rochefoucauld till all hours; we couldn't stop laughing about your misfortunes. No, this is getting too thick, really. It isn't right to have this happen to a person, just because she went to bed at ten o'clock once in her life. Honest, I won't ever do it again. I'll go straight, after this. I'll never go to bed again, if I can only sleep now. If I can tear my mind away from a certain French cynic, *circa* 1650, and slip into lovely oblivion. 1650. I bet I look as if I'd been awake since then.

How do people go to sleep? I'm afraid I've lost the knack. I might try busting myself smartly over the temple with the night-light. I might repeat to myself, slowly and soothingly, a list of quotations beautiful from minds profound; if I can remember any of the damn things. That might do it. And it ought effectually to bar that visiting foreigner that's been hanging around ever since twenty minutes past four. Yes, that's what I'll do. Only wait till I turn the pillow; it feels as if La Rochefoucauld had crawled inside the slip.

Now let's see—where shall we start? Why—er—let's see. Oh, yes, I know one. This above all, to thine own self be true and it must follow, as the night the day, thou canst not then be false to any man. Now they're off. And once they get started, they ought to come like hot cakes. Let's see. Ah, what avail the sceptered race and what the form divine, when every virtue, every grace, Rose Aylmer, all were thine. Let's see. They also serve who only stand and wait. If Winter comes, can Spring be far behind? Lilies that fester smell far worse than weeds. Silent upon a peak in Darien. Mrs. Porter and her daughter wash their feet in soda-water. And Agatha's Arth is a hug-the-hearth, but my true love is false. Why did you die when lambs were cropping, you should have died when apples were dropping. Shall be together, breathe and ride, so one day more am I deified, who knows but the world will end tonight. And he shall hear the stroke of eight and not the stroke of nine. They are not long, the weeping and the laughter; love and desire and hate I think will have no portion in us after we pass the gate. But none, I think, do there embrace. I think that I shall never see a poem lovely as a tree. I think I will not hang myself today. Ay tank Ay go home now.

Let's see. Solitude is the safeguard of mediocrity and the stern companion of genius. Consistency is the hobgoblin of little minds. Something is emotion remembered in tranquillity. A cynic is one who knows the price of everything and the value of nothing. That lovable old cynic is one who—oops, there's King Charles's head again. I've got to watch myself. Let's see. Circumstantial evidence is a trout in the milk. Any stigma will do to beat a dogma. If you would learn what God thinks about money, you have only to look at those to whom He has given it. If nobody had ever learned to read, very few people—

All right. That fixes it. I throw in the towel right now. I know when I'm licked. There'll be no more of this nonsense; I'm going to turn on the light and read my head off. Till the next ten o'clock, if I feel like it. And what does La Rochefoucauld want to make of that? Oh, he *will*, eh? Yes, he will! He and who else? La Rochefoucauld and *what* very few people?

BIG BLONDE

HAZEL MORSE was a large, fair woman of the type that incites some men when they use the word "blonde" to click their tongues and wag their heads roguishly. She prided herself upon her small feet and suffered for her vanity, boxing them in snub-toed, high-heeled slippers of the shortest bearable size. The curious things about her were her hands, strange terminations to the flabby white arms splattered with pale tan spots—long, quivering hands with deep and convex nails. She should not have disfigured them with little jewels.

She was not a woman given to recollections. At her middle thirties, her old days were a blurred and flickering sequence, an imperfect film, dealing with the actions of strangers.

In her twenties, after the deferred death of a hazy widowed mother, she had been employed as a model in a wholesale dress establishment—it was still the day of the big woman, and she was then prettily colored and erect and high-breasted. Her job was not onerous, and she met numbers of men and spent numbers of evenings with them, laughing at their jokes and telling them she loved their neckties. Men liked her, and she took it for granted that the liking of many men was a desirable thing. Popularity seemed to her to be worth all the work that had to be put into its achievement. Men liked you because you were fun, and when they liked you they took you out, and there you were. So, and successfully, she was fun. She was a good sport. Men like a good sport.

No other form of diversion, simpler or more complicated, drew her attention. She never pondered if she might not be better occupied doing something else. Her ideas, or, better, her acceptances, ran right along with those of the other substantially built blondes in whom she found her friends.

When she had been working in the dress establishment some years she met Herbie Morse. He was thin, quick, attractive, with shifting lines about his shiny, brown eyes and a habit of fiercely biting at the skin around his finger nails. He drank largely; she found that entertaining. Her habitual greeting to him was an allusion to his state of the previous night.

"Oh, what a peach you had," she used to say, through her easy laugh. "I thought I'd die, the way you kept asking the waiter to dance with you."

She liked him immediately upon their meeting. She was enormously amused at his fast, slurred sentences, his interpolations of apt phrases from vaudeville acts and comic strips; she thrilled at the feel of his lean arm tucked firm beneath the sleeve of her coat; she wanted to touch the wet, flat surface of his hair. He was as promptly drawn to her. They were married six weeks after they had met.

She was delighted at the idea of being a bride; coquetted with it, played upon it. Other offers of marriage she had had, and not a few of them, but it happened that they were all from stout, serious men who had visited the dress establishment as buyers; men from Des Moines and Houston and Chicago and, in her phrase, even funnier places. There was always something immensely comic to her in the thought of living elsewhere than New York. She could not regard as serious proposals that she share a western residence.

She wanted to be married. She was nearing thirty now, and she did not take the years well. She spread and softened, and her darkening hair turned her to inexpert dabblings with peroxide. There were times when she had little flashes of fear about her job. And she had had a couple of thousand evenings of being a good sport among her male acquaintances. She had come to be more conscientious than spontaneous about it.

Herbie earned enough, and they took a little apartment far uptown. There was a Mission-furnished dining-room with a hanging central light globed in liver-colored glass; in the living-room were an "over-stuffed suite," a Boston fern, and a reproduction of the Henner "Magdalene" with the red hair and the blue draperies; the bedroom was in gray enamel and old rose, with Herbie's photograph on Hazel's dressing-table and Hazel's likeness on Herbie's chest of drawers.

She cooked—and she was a good cook—and marketed and chatted with the delivery boys and the colored laundress. She loved the flat, she loved her life, she loved Herbie. In the first months of their marriage, she gave him all the passion she was ever to know.

She had not realized how tired she was. It was a delight, a new game, a holiday, to give up being a good sport. If her head ached or her arches throbbed, she complained piteously, babyishly. If her mood was quiet, she did not talk. If tears came to her eyes, she let them fall.

She fell readily into the habit of tears during the first year of her marriage. Even in her good sport days, she had been known to weep lavishly and disinterestedly on occasion. Her behavior at the theater was a standing joke. She could weep at anything in a play—tiny garments, love both unrequited and mutual, seduction, purity, faithful servitors, wedlock, the triangle.

"There goes Haze," her friends would say, watching her. "She's off again."

Wedded and relaxed, she poured her tears freely. To her who had laughed so much, crying was delicious. All sorrows became her sorrows; she was Tenderness. She would cry long and softly over newspaper accounts of kidnaped babies, deserted wives, unemployed men, strayed cats, heroic dogs. Even when the paper was no longer before her, her mind revolved upon these things and the drops slipped rhythmically over her plump cheeks.

"Honestly," she would say to Herbie, "all the sadness there is in the world when you stop to think about it!"

"Yeah," Herbie would say.

She missed nobody. The old crowd, the people who had brought her and Herbie together, dropped from their lives, lingeringly at first. When she thought of this at all, it was only to consider it fitting. This was marriage. This was peace.

But the thing was that Herbie was not amused.

For a time, he had enjoyed being alone with her. He found the voluntary isolation novel and sweet. Then it palled with a ferocious suddenness. It was as if one night, sitting with her in the steam-heated living-room, he would ask no more; and the next night he was through and done with the whole thing.

He became annoyed by her misty melancholies. At first, when he came home to find her softly tired and moody, he kissed her neck and patted her shoulder and begged her to tell her Herbie what was wrong. She loved that. But time slid by, and he found that there was never anything really, personally, the matter.

"Ah, for God's sake," he would say. "Crabbing again. All right, sit here and crab your head off. I'm going out."

And he would slam out of the flat and come back late and drunk.

She was completely bewildered by what happened to their marriage. First they were lovers; and then, it seemed without transition, they were enemies. She never understood it.

There were longer and longer intervals between his leaving his office and his arrival at the apartment. She went through agonies of picturing him run over and bleeding, dead and covered with a sheet. Then she lost her fears for his safety and grew sullen and wounded. When a person wanted to be with a person, he came as soon as possible. She desperately wanted him to want to be with her; her own hours only marked the time till he would come. It was often nearly nine o'clock before he came home to dinner. Always he had had many drinks, and their effect would die in him, leaving him loud and querulous and bristling for affronts.

He was too nervous, he said, to sit and do nothing for an evening. He boasted, probably not in all truth, that he had never read a book in his life.

"What am I expected to do—sit around this dump on my tail all night?" he would ask, rhetorically. And again he would slam out.

She did not know what to do. She could not manage him. She could not meet him.

She fought him furiously. A terrific domesticity had come upon her, and she would bite and scratch to guard it. She wanted what she called "a nice home." She wanted a sober, tender husband, prompt at dinner, punctual at work. She wanted sweet, comforting evenings. The idea of intimacy with other men was terrible to her; the thought that Herbie might be seeking entertainment in other women set her frantic.

It seemed to her that almost everything she read—novels from the drug-store lending library, magazine stories, women's pages in the papers—dealt with wives who lost their husbands' love. She could bear those, at that, better than accounts of neat, companionable marriage and living happily ever after.

She was frightened. Several times when Herbie came home in the evening, he found her determinedly dressed—she had had to alter those of her clothes that were not new, to make them fasten—and rouged.

"Let's go wild tonight, what do you say?" she would hail him. "A person's got lots of time to hang around and do nothing when they're dead."

So they would go out, to chop houses and the less expensive cabarets. But it turned out badly. She could no longer find amusement in watching Herbie drink. She could not laugh at his whimsicalities, she was so tensely counting his indulgences. And she was unable to keep back her remonstrances—"Ah, come on, Herb, you've had enough, haven't you? You'll feel something terrible in the morning."

He would be immediately enraged. All right, crab; crab, crab, crab, crab, that was all she ever did. What a lousy sport *she* was! There would be scenes, and one or the other of them would rise and stalk out in fury.

She could not recall the definite day that she started drinking, herself. There was nothing separate about her days. Like drops upon a window-pane, they ran together and trickled away. She had been married six months; then a year; then three years.

She had never needed to drink, formerly. She could sit for most of a night at a table where the others were imbibing earnestly and never droop in looks or spirits, nor be bored by the doings of those about her. If she took a cocktail, it was so unusual as to cause twenty minutes or so of jocular comment. But now anguish was in her. Frequently, after a quarrel, Herbie would stay out for the night, and she could not learn from him where the time had been spent. Her heart felt tight and sore in her breast, and her mind turned like an electric fan.

She hated the taste of liquor. Gin, plain or in mixtures, made her promptly sick. After experiment, she found that Scotch whisky was best for her. She took it without water, because that was the quickest way to its effect.

Herbie pressed it on her. He was glad to see her drink. They both felt it might restore her high spirits, and their good times together might again be possible.

" 'Atta girl," he would approve her. "Let's see you get boiled, baby."

But it brought them no nearer. When she drank with him, there would be a little while of gaiety and then, strangely without beginning, they would be in a wild quarrel. They would wake in the morning not sure what it had all been about, foggy as to what had been said and done, but each deeply injured and bitterly resentful. There would be days of vengeful silence.

There had been a time when they had made up their quarrels, usually in bed. There would be kisses and little names and assurances of fresh starts. . . . "Oh, it's going to be great now, Herb. We'll have swell times. I was a crab. I guess I must have been tired. But everything's going to be swell. You'll see."

Now there were no gentle reconciliations. They resumed friendly relations only in the brief magnanimity caused by liquor, before more liquor drew them into new battles. The scenes became more violent. There were shouted invectives and pushes, and sometimes sharp slaps. Once she had a black eye. Herbie was horrified next day at sight of it. He did not go to work; he followed her about, suggesting remedies and heaping dark blame on himself. But after they had had a few drinks—"to pull themselves together"—she made so many wistful references to her bruise that he shouted at her and rushed out and was gone for two days.

Each time he left the place in a rage, he threatened never to come back. She did not believe him, nor did she consider separation. Somewhere in her head or her heart was the lazy, nebulous hope that things would change and she and Herbie settle suddenly into soothing married life. Here were her home, her furniture, her husband, her station. She summoned no alternatives.

She could no longer bustle and potter. She had no more vicarious tears; the hot drops she shed were for herself. She walked ceaselessly about the rooms, her thoughts running mechanically round and round Herbie. In those days began the hatred of being alone that she was never to overcome. You could be by yourself when things were all right, but when you were blue you got the howling horrors.

She commenced drinking alone, little, short drinks all through the day. It was only with Herbie that alcohol made her nervous and quick in offense. Alone, it blurred sharp things for her. She lived in a haze of it. Her life took on a dream-like quality. Nothing was astonishing.

A Mrs. Martin moved into the flat across the hall. She was a great blonde woman of forty, a promise in looks of what Mrs. Morse was to be. They made acquaintance, quickly became inseparable. Mrs. Morse spent her days in the opposite apartment. They drank together, to brace themselves after the drinks of the nights before.

She never confided her troubles about Herbie to Mrs. Martin. The subject was too bewildering to her to find comfort in talk. She let it be assumed that her husband's business kept him much away. It was not regarded as important; husbands, as such, played but shadowy parts in Mrs. Martin's circle.

Mrs. Martin had no visible spouse; you were left to decide for yourself whether he was or was not dead. She had an admirer, Joe, who came to see her almost nightly. Often he brought several friends with him—"The Boys," they were called. The Boys were big, red, good-humored men, perhaps forty-five, perhaps fifty. Mrs. Morse was glad of invitations to join the parties—Herbie was scarcely ever at home at night now. If he did come home, she did not visit Mrs. Martin. An evening alone with Herbie meant inevitably a quarrel, yet she would stay with him. There was always her thin and wordless idea that, maybe, this night, things would begin to be all right.

The Boys brought plenty of liquor along with them whenever they came to Mrs. Martin's. Drinking with them, Mrs. Morse became lively and good-natured and audacious. She was quickly popular. When she had drunk enough to cloud her most recent battle with Herbie, she was excited by their approbation. Crab, was she? Rotten sport, was she? Well, there were some that thought different.

Ed was one of The Boys. He lived in Utica—had "his own business" there, was the awed report—but he came to New York almost every week. He was married. He showed Mrs. Morse the then current photographs of Junior and Sister, and she praised them abundantly and sincerely. Soon it was accepted by the others that Ed was her particular friend.

He staked her when they all played poker; sat next her and occasionally rubbed his knee against hers during the game. She was rather lucky. Frequently she went home with a twenty-dollar bill or a ten-dollar bill or a handful of crumpled dollars. She was glad of them. Herbie was getting, in her words, something awful about money. To ask him for it brought an instant row.

"What the hell do you do with it?" he would say. "Shoot it all on Scotch?"

"I try to run this house half-way decent," she would retort. "Never thought of that, did you? Oh, no, his lordship couldn't be bothered with that."

Again, she could not find a definite day, to fix the beginning of Ed's proprietorship. It became his custom to kiss her on the mouth when he came in, as well as for farewell, and he gave her little quick kisses of approval all through the evening. She liked this rather more than she disliked it. She never thought of his kisses when she was not with him.

He would run his hand lingeringly over her back and shoulders.

"Some dizzy blonde, eh?" he would say. "Some doll."

One afternoon she came home from Mrs. Martin's to find Herbie in the bedroom. He had been away for several nights, evidently on a prolonged drinking bout. His face was gray, his hands jerked as if they were on wires. On the bed were two old suitcases, packed high. Only her photograph remained on his bureau, and the wide doors of his closet disclosed nothing but coat-hangers.

"I'm blowing," he said. "I'm through with the whole works. I got a job in Detroit."

She sat down on the edge of the bed. She had drunk much the night before, and the four Scotches she had had with Mrs. Martin had only increased her fogginess.

"Good job?" she said.

"Oh, yeah," he said. "Looks all right."

He closed a suitcase with difficulty, swearing at it in whispers.

"There's some dough in the bank," he said. "The bank book's in your top drawer. You can have the furniture and stuff."

He looked at her, and his forehead twitched.

"God damn it, I'm through, I'm telling you," he cried. "I'm through."

"All right, all right," she said. "I heard you, didn't I?"

She saw him as if he were at one end of a cannon and she at the other. Her head was beginning to ache bumpingly, and her voice had a dreary, tiresome tone. She could not have raised it.

"Like a drink before you go?" she asked.

Again he looked at her, and a corner of his mouth jerked up.

"Cockeyed again for a change, aren't you?" he said. "That's nice. Sure, get a couple of shots, will you?"

She went to the pantry, mixed him a stiff highball, poured herself a couple of inches of whisky and drank it. Then she gave herself another portion and brought the glasses into the bedroom. He had strapped both suitcases and had put on his hat and overcoat.

He took his highball.

"Well," he said, and he gave a sudden, uncertain laugh. "Here's mud in your eye."

"Mud in your eye," she said.

They drank. He put down his glass and took up the heavy suitcases.

"Got to get a train around six," he said.

She followed him down the hall. There was a song, a song that Mrs. Martin played doggedly on the phonograph, running loudly through her mind. She had never liked the thing.

"Night and daytime,
Always playtime.
Ain't we got fun?"

At the door he put down the bags and faced her.

"Well," he said. "Well, take care of yourself. You'll be all right, will you?"

"Oh, sure," she said.

He opened the door, then came back to her, holding out his hand.

" 'By, Haze," he said. "Good luck to you."

She took his hand and shook it.

"Pardon my wet glove," she said.

When the door had closed behind him, she went back to the pantry.

She was flushed and lively when she went in to Mrs. Martin's that evening. The Boys were there, Ed among them. He was glad to be in town, frisky and loud and full of jokes. But she spoke quietly to him for a minute.

"Herbie blew today," she said. "Going to live out west."

"That so?" he said. He looked at her and played with the fountain pen clipped to his waistcoat pocket.

"Think he's gone for good, do you?" he asked.

"Yeah," she said. "I know he is. I know. Yeah."

"You going to live on across the hall just the same?" he said. "Know what you're going to do?"

"Gee, I don't know," she said. "I don't give much of a damn."

"Oh, come on, that's no way to talk," he told her. "What you need—you need a little snifter. How about it?"

"Yeah," she said. "Just straight."

She won forty-three dollars at poker. When the game broke up, Ed took her back to her apartment.

"Got a little kiss for me?" he asked.

He wrapped her in his big arms and kissed her violently. She was entirely passive. He held her away and looked at her.

"Little tight, honey?" he asked, anxiously. "Not going to be sick, are you?"

"Me?" she said. "I'm swell."

II

When Ed left in the morning, he took her photograph with him. He said he wanted her picture to look at, up in Utica. "You can have that one on the bureau," she said.

She put Herbie's picture in a drawer, out of her sight. When she could look at it, she meant to tear it up. She was fairly successful in keeping her mind from racing around him. Whisky slowed it for her. She was almost peaceful, in her mist.

She accepted her relationship with Ed without question or enthusiasm. When he was away, she seldom thought definitely of him. He was good to her; he gave her frequent presents and a regular allowance. She was even able to save. She did not plan ahead of any day, but her wants were few, and you might as well put money in the bank as have it lying around.

When the lease of her apartment neared its end, it was Ed who suggested moving. His friendship with Mrs. Martin and Joe had become strained over a dispute at poker; a feud was impending.

"Let's get the hell out of here," Ed said. "What I want you to have is a place near the Grand Central. Make it easier for me."

So she took a little flat in the Forties. A colored maid came in every day to clean and to make coffee for her—she was "through with that housekeeping stuff," she said, and Ed, twenty years married to a passionately domestic woman, admired this romantic uselessness and felt doubly a man of the world in abetting it.

The coffee was all she had until she went out to dinner, but alcohol kept her fat. Prohibition she regarded only as a basis for jokes. You could always get all you wanted. She was never noticeably drunk and seldom nearly sober. It required a larger daily allowance to keep her misty-minded. Too little, and she was achingly melancholy.

Ed brought her to Jimmy's. He was proud, with the pride of the transient who would be mistaken for a native, in his knowledge of small, recent restaurants occupying the lower floors of shabby brownstone houses; places where, upon mentioning the name of an habitué friend, might be obtained strange whisky and fresh gin in many of their ramifications. Jimmy's place was the favorite of his acquaintances.

There, through Ed, Mrs. Morse met many men and women, formed quick friendships. The men often took her out when Ed was in Utica. He was proud of her popularity.

She fell into the habit of going to Jimmy's alone when she had no engagement. She was certain to meet some people she knew, and join them. It was a club for her friends, both men and women.

The women at Jimmy's looked remarkably alike, and this was curious, for, through feuds, removals, and opportunities of more profitable contacts, the personnel of the group changed constantly. Yet always the newcomers resembled those whom they replaced. They were all big women and stout, broad of shoulder and abundantly breasted, with faces thickly clothed in soft, high-colored flesh. They laughed loud and often, showing opáque and lusterless teeth like squares of crockery. There was about them the health of the big, yet a slight, unwholesome suggestion of stubborn preservation. They might have been thirty-six or forty-five or anywhere between.

They composed their titles of their own first names with their husbands' surnames—Mrs. Florence Miller, Mrs. Vera Riley, Mrs. Lilian Block. This gave at the same time the solidity of marriage and the glamour of freedom. Yet only one or two were actually divorced. Most of them never referred to their dimmed spouses; some, a shorter time separated, described them in terms of great biological interest. Several were mothers, each of an only child—a boy at school somewhere, or a girl being cared for by a grandmother. Often, well on towards morning, there would be displays of kodak portraits and of tears.

They were comfortable women, cordial and friendly and irrepressibly matronly. Theirs was the quality of ease. Become fatalistic, especially about money matters, they were unworried. Whenever their funds dropped alarmingly, a new donor appeared; this had always happened. The aim of each was to have one man, permanently, to pay all her bills, in return for which she would have immediately given up other admirers and probably would have become exceedingly fond of him; for the affections of all of them were, by now, unexacting, tranquil, and easily arranged. This end, however, grew increasingly difficult yearly. Mrs. Morse was regarded as fortunate.

Ed had a good year, increased her allowance and gave her a sealskin coat. But she had to be careful of her moods with him. He insisted upon gaiety. He would not listen to admissions of aches or weariness.

"Hey, listen," he would say, "I got worries of my own, and plenty. Nobody wants to hear other people's troubles, sweetie. What you got to do, you got to be a sport and forget it. See? Well, slip us a little smile, then. That's my girl."

She never had enough interest to quarrel with him as she had with Herbie, but she wanted the privilege of occasional admitted sadness. It was strange. The other women she saw did not have to fight their moods. There was Mrs. Florence Miller who got regular crying jags, and the men sought only to cheer and comfort her. The others spent whole evenings in grieved recitals of worries and ills; their escorts paid them deep sympathy. But she was instantly undesirable when she was low in spirits. Once, at Jimmy's, when she could not make herself lively, Ed had walked out and left her.

"Why the hell don't you stay home and not go spoiling everybody's evening?" he had roared.

Even her slightest acquaintances seemed irritated if she were not conspicuously light-hearted.

"What's the matter with you, anyway?" they would say. "Be your age, why don't you? Have a little drink and snap out of it."

When her relationship with Ed had continued nearly three years, he moved to Florida to live. He hated leaving her; he gave her a large check and some shares of a sound stock, and his pale eyes were wet when he said good-by. She did not miss him. He came to New York infrequently, perhaps two or three times a year, and hurried directly from the train to see her.

She was always pleased to have him come and never sorry to see him go.

Charley, an acquaintance of Ed's that she had met at Jimmy's, had long admired her. He had always made opportunities of touching her and leaning close to talk to her. He asked repeatedly of all their friends if they had ever heard such a fine laugh as she had. After Ed left, Charley became the main figure in her life. She classified him and spoke of him as "not so bad." There was nearly a year of Charley; then she divided her time between him and Sydney, another frequenter of Jimmy's; then Charley slipped away altogether.

Sydney was a little, brightly dressed, clever Jew. She was perhaps nearest contentment with him. He amused her always; her laughter was not forced.

He admired her completely. Her softness and size delighted him. And he thought she was great, he often told her, because she kept gay and lively when she was drunk.

"Once I had a gal," he said, "used to try and throw herself out of the window every time she got a can on. Jee-*zuss*," he added, feelingly.

Then Sydney married a rich and watchful bride, and then there was Billy. No—after Sydney came Ferd, then Billy. In her haze, she never recalled how men entered her life and left it. There were no surprises. She had no thrill at their advent, nor woe at their departure. She seemed to be always able to attract men. There was never another as rich as Ed, but they were all generous to her, in their means.

Once she had news of Herbie. She met Mrs. Martin dining at Jimmy's, and the old friendship was vigorously renewed. The still admiring Joe, while on a business trip, had seen Herbie. He had settled in Chicago, he looked fine, he was living with some woman—seemed to be crazy about her. Mrs. Morse had been drinking vastly that day. She took the news with mild interest, as one hearing of the sex peccadilloes of somebody whose name is, after a moment's groping, familiar.

"Must be damn near seven years since I saw him," she commented. "Gee. Seven years."

More and more, her days lost their individuality. She never knew dates, nor was sure of the day of the week.

"My God, was that a year ago!" she would exclaim, when an event was recalled in conversation.

She was tired so much of the time. Tired and blue. Almost everything could give her the blues. Those old horses she saw on Sixth Avenue—struggling and slipping along the car-tracks, or standing at the curb, their heads dropped level with their worn knees. The tightly stored tears would squeeze from her eyes as she teetered past on her aching feet in the stubby, champagne-colored slippers.

The thought of death came and stayed with her and lent her a sort of drowsy cheer. It would be nice, nice and restful, to be dead.

There was no settled, shocked moment when she first thought of killing herself; it seemed to her as if the idea had always been with her. She pounced upon all the accounts of suicides in the newspapers. There was an epidemic of self-killings—or maybe it was just that she searched for the stories of them so eagerly that she found many. To read of them roused reassurance in her; she felt a cozy solidarity with the big company of the voluntary dead.

She slept, aided by whisky, till deep into the afternoons, then lay abed, a bottle and glass at her hand, until it was time to dress to go out for dinner. She was beginning to feel towards alcohol a little puzzled distrust, as toward an old friend who has refused a simple favor. Whisky could still soothe her for most of the time, but there were sudden, inexplicable moments when the cloud fell treacherously away from her, and she was sawed by the sorrow and bewilderment and nuisance of all living. She played voluptuously with the thought of cool, sleepy retreat. She had never been troubled by religious belief and no vision of an after-life intimidated her. She dreamed by day of never again putting on tight shoes, of never having to laugh and listen and admire, of never more being a good sport. Never.

But how would you do it? It made her sick to think of jumping from heights. She could not stand a gun. At the theater, if one of the actors drew a revolver, she crammed her fingers into her ears and could not even look at the stage until after the shot had been fired. There was no gas in her flat. She looked long at the bright blue veins in her slim wrists—a cut with a razor blade, and there you'd be. But it would hurt, hurt like hell, and there would be blood to see. Poison—something tasteless and quick and painless—was the thing. But they wouldn't sell it to you in drugstores, because of the law.

She had few other thoughts.

There was a new man now—Art. He was short and fat and exacting and hard on her patience when he was drunk. But there had been only occasionals for some time before him, and she was glad of a little stability. Too, Art must be away for weeks at a stretch, selling silks, and that was restful. She was convincingly gay with him, though the effort shook her.

"The best sport in the world," he would murmur, deep in her neck. "The best sport in the world."

One night, when he had taken her to Jimmy's, she went into the dressing-room with Mrs. Florence Miller. There, while designing curly mouths on their faces with lip-rouge, they compared experiences of insomnia.

"Honestly," Mrs. Morse said, "I wouldn't close an eye if I didn't go to bed full of Scotch. I lie there and toss and turn and toss and turn. Blue! Does a person get blue lying awake that way!"

"Say, listen Hazel," Mrs. Miller said, impressively, "I'm telling you I'd be awake for a year if I didn't take veronal. That stuff makes you sleep like a fool."

"Isn't it poison, or something?" Mrs. Morse asked.

"Oh, you take too much and you're out for the count," said Mrs. Miller. "I just take five grains—they come in tablets. I'd be scared to fool around with it. But five grains, and you cork off pretty."

"Can you get it anywhere?" Mrs. Morse felt superbly Machiavellian.

"Get all you want in Jersey," said Mrs. Miller. "They won't give it to you here without you have a doctor's prescription. Finished? We'd better go back and see what the boys are doing."

That night, Art left Mrs. Morse at the door of her apartment; his mother was in town. Mrs. Morse was still sober, and it happened that there was no whisky left in her cupboard. She lay in bed, looking up at the black ceiling.

She rose early, for her, and went to New Jersey. She had never taken the tube, and did not understand it. So she went to the Pennsylvania Station and bought a railroad ticket to Newark. She thought of nothing in particular on the trip out. She looked at the uninspired hats of the women about her and gazed through the smeared window at the flat, gritty scene.

In Newark, in the first drug-store she came to, she asked for a tin of talcum powder, a nailbrush, and a box of veronal tablets. The powder and the brush were to make the hypnotic seem also a casual need. The clerk was entirely unconcerned. "We only keep them in bottles," he said, and wrapped up for her a little glass vial containing ten white tablets, stacked one on another.

She went to another drug-store and bought a face-cloth, an orange-wood stick, and a bottle of veronal tablets. The clerk was also uninterested.

"Well, I guess I got enough to kill an ox," she thought, and went back to the station.

At home, she put the little vials in the drawer of her dressing-table and stood looking at them with a dreamy tenderness.

"There they are, God bless them," she said, and she kissed her finger-tip and touched each bottle.

The colored maid was busy in the living-room.

"Hey, Nettie," Mrs. Morse called. "Be an angel, will you? Run around to Jimmy's and get me a quart of Scotch."

She hummed while she awaited the girl's return.

During the next few days, whisky ministered to her as tenderly as it had done when she first turned to its aid. Alone, she was soothed and vague, at Jimmy's she was the gayest of the groups. Art was delighted with her.

Then, one night, she had an appointment to meet Art at Jimmy's for an early dinner. He was to leave afterward on a business excursion, to be away for a week. Mrs. Morse had been drinking all the afternoon; while she dressed to go out, she felt herself rising pleasurably from drowsiness to high spirits. But as she came out into the street the effects of the whisky deserted her completely, and she was filled with a slow, grinding wretchedness so horrible that she stood swaying on the pavement, unable for a moment to move forward. It was a gray night with spurts of mean, thin snow, and the streets shone with dark ice. As she slowly crossed Sixth Avenue, consciously dragging one foot past the other, a big, scarred horse pulling a rickety express-wagon crashed to his knees before her. The driver swore and screamed and lashed the beast insanely, bringing the whip back over his shoulder for every blow, while the horse struggled to get a footing on the slippery asphalt. A group gathered and watched with interest.

Art was waiting, when Mrs. Morse reached Jimmy's.

"What's the matter with you, for God's sake?" was his greeting to her.

"I saw a horse," she said. "Gee, I—a person feels sorry for horses. I—it isn't just horses. Everything's kind of terrible, isn't it? I can't help getting sunk."

"Ah, sunk, me eye," he said. "What's the idea of all the bellyaching? What have you got to be sunk about?"

"I can't help it," she said.

"Ah, help it, me eye," he said. "Pull yourself together, will you? Come on and sit down, and take that face off you."

She drank industriously and she tried hard, but she could not overcome her melancholy. Others joined them and commented on her gloom, and she could do no more for them than smile weakly. She made little dabs at her eyes with her handkerchief, trying to time her movements so they would be unnoticed, but several times Art caught her and scowled and shifted impatiently in his chair.

When it was time for him to go to his train, she said she would leave, too, and go home.

"And not a bad idea, either," he said. "See if you can't sleep yourself out of it. I'll see you Thursday. For God's sake, try and cheer up by then, will you?"

"Yeah," she said. "I will."

In her bedroom, she undressed with a tense speed wholly unlike her usual slow uncertainty. She put on her nightgown, took off her hair-net and passed the comb quickly through her dry, vari-colored hair. Then she took the two little vials from the drawer and carried them into the bathroom. The splintering misery had gone from her, and she felt the quick excitement of one who is about to receive an anticipated gift.

She uncorked the vials, filled a glass with water and stood before the mirror, a tablet between her fingers. Suddenly she bowed graciously to her reflection, and raised the glass to it.

"Well, here's mud in your eye," she said.

The tablets were unpleasant to take, dry and powdery and sticking obstinately half-way down her throat. It took her a long time to swallow all twenty of them. She stood watching her reflection with deep, impersonal interest, studying the movements of the gulping throat. Once more she spoke aloud.

"For God's sake, try and cheer up by Thursday, will you?" she said. "Well, you know what he can do. He and the whole lot of them."

She had no idea how quickly to expect effect from the veronal. When she had taken the last tablet, she stood uncertainly, wondering, still with a courteous, vicarious interest, if death would strike her down then and there. She felt in no way strange, save for a slight stirring of sickness from the effort of swallowing the tablets, nor did her reflected face look at all different. It would not be immediate, then; it might even take an hour or so.

She stretched her arms high and gave a vast yawn.

"Guess I'll go to bed," she said. "Gee, I'm nearly dead."

That struck her as comic, and she turned out the bathroom light and went in and laid herself down in her bed, chuckling softly all the time.

"Gee, I'm nearly dead," she quoted. "That's a hot one!"

III

Nettie, the colored maid, came in late the next afternoon to clean the apartment, and found Mrs. Morse in her bed. But then, that was not unusual. Usually, though, the sounds of cleaning waked her, and she did not like to wake up. Nettie, an agreeable girl, had learned to move softly about her work.

But when she had done the living-room and stolen in to tidy the little square bedroom, she could not avoid a tiny clatter as she arranged the objects on the dressing-table. Instinctively, she glanced over her shoulder at the sleeper, and without warning a sickly uneasiness crept over her. She came to the bed and stared down at the woman lying there.

Mrs. Morse lay on her back, one flabby, white arm flung up, the wrist against her forehead. Her stiff hair hung untenderly along her face. The bed covers were pushed down, exposing a deep square of soft neck and a pink nightgown, its fabric worn uneven by many launderings; her great breasts, freed from their tight confiner, sagged beneath her arm-pits. Now and then she made knotted, snoring sounds, and from the corner of her opened mouth to the blurred turn of her jaw ran a lane of crusted spittle.

"Mis' Morse," Nettie called. "Oh, Mis' Morse! It's terrible late."

Mrs. Morse made no move.

"Mis' Morse," said Nettie. "Look, Mis' Morse. How'm I goin' get this bed made?"

Panic sprang upon the girl. She shook the woman's hot shoulder.

"Ah, wake up, will yuh?" she whined. "Ah, please wake up."

Suddenly the girl turned and ran out in the hall to the elevator door, keeping her thumb firm on the black, shiny button until the elderly car and its Negro attendant stood before her. She poured a jumble of words over the boy, and led him back to the apartment. He tiptoed creakingly in to the bedside; first gingerly, then so lustily that he left marks in the soft flesh, he prodded the unconscious woman.

"Hey, there!" he cried, and listened intently, as for an echo.

"Jeez. Out like a light," he commented.

At his interest in the spectacle, Nettie's panic left her. Importance was big in both of them. They talked in quick, unfinished whispers, and it was the boy's suggestion that he fetch the young doctor who lived on the ground floor. Nettie hurried along with him. They looked forward to the limelit moment of breaking their news of something untoward, something pleasurably unpleasant. Mrs. Morse had become the medium of drama. With no ill wish to her, they hoped that her state was serious, that she would not let them down by being awake and normal on their return. A little fear of this determined them to make the most, to the doctor, of her present condition. "Matter of life and death," returned to Nettie from her thin store of reading. She considered startling the doctor with the phrase.

The doctor was in and none too pleased at interruption. He wore a yellow and blue striped dressing-gown, and he was lying on his sofa, laughing with a dark girl, her face scaly with inexpensive powder, who perched on the arm. Half-emptied highball glasses stood beside them, and her coat and hat were neatly hung up with the comfortable implication of a long stay.

Always something, the doctor grumbled. Couldn't let anybody alone after a hard day. But he put some bottles and instruments into a case, changed his dressing-gown for his coat and started out with the Negroes.

"Snap it up there, big boy," the girl called after him. "Don't be all night."

The doctor strode loudly into Mrs. Morse's flat and on to the bedroom, Nettie and the boy right behind him. Mrs. Morse had not moved; her sleep was as deep, but soundless, now. The doctor looked sharply at her, then plunged his thumbs into the lidded pits above her eyeballs and threw his weight upon them. A high, sickened cry broke from Nettie.

"Look like he tryin' to push her right on th'ough the bed," said the boy. He chuckled.

Mrs. Morse gave no sign under the pressure. Abruptly the doctor abandoned it, and with one quick movement swept the covers down to the foot of the bed. With another he flung her nightgown back and lifted the thick, white legs, cross-hatched with blocks of tiny, iris-colored veins. He pinched them repeatedly, with long, cruel nips, back of the knees. She did not awaken.

"What's she been drinking?" he asked Nettie, over his shoulder.

With the certain celerity of one who knows just where to lay hands on a thing, Nettie went into the bathroom, bound for the cupboard where Mrs. Morse kept her whisky. But she stopped at the sight of the two vials, with their red and white labels, lying before the mirror. She brought them to the doctor.

"Oh, for the Lord Almighty's sweet sake!" he said. He dropped Mrs. Morse's legs, and pushed them impatiently across the bed. "What did she want to go taking that tripe for? Rotten yellow trick, that's what a thing like that is. Now we'll have to pump her out, and all that stuff. Nuisance, a thing like that is; that's what it amounts to. Here, George, take me down in the elevator. You wait here, maid. She won't do anything."

"She won't die on me, will she?" cried Nettie.

"No," said the doctor. "God, no. You couldn't kill her with an ax."

IV

After two days, Mrs. Morse came back to consciousness, dazed at first, then with a comprehension that brought with it the slow, saturating wretchedness.

"Oh, Lord, oh, Lord," she moaned, and tears for herself and for life striped her cheeks.

Nettie came in at the sound. For two days she had done the ugly, incessant tasks in the nursing of the unconscious, for two nights she had caught broken bits of sleep on the living-room couch. She looked coldly at the big, blown woman in the bed.

"What you been tryin' to do, Mis' Morse?" she said. "What kine o' work is that, takin' all that stuff?"

"Oh, Lord," moaned Mrs. Morse, again, and she tried to cover her eyes with her arms. But the joints felt stiff and brittle, and she cried out at their ache.

"Tha's no way to ack, takin' them pills," said Nettie. "You can thank you' stars you heah at all. How you feel now?"

"Oh, I feel great," said Mrs. Morse. "Swell, I feel."

Her hot, painful tears fell as if they would never stop.

"Tha's no way to take on, cryin' like that," Nettie said. "After what you done. The doctor, he says he could have you arrested, doin' a thing like that. He was fit to be tied, here."

"Why couldn't he let me alone?" wailed Mrs. Morse. "Why the hell couldn't he have?"

"Tha's terr'ble, Mis' Morse, swearin' an' talkin' like that," said Nettie, "after what people done for you. Here I ain' had no sleep at all for two nights, an' had to give up goin' out to my other ladies!"

"Oh, I'm sorry, Nettie," she said. "You're a peach. I'm sorry I've given you so much trouble. I couldn't help it. I just got sunk. Didn't you ever feel like doing it? When everything looks just lousy to you?"

"I wouldn' think o' no such thing," declared Nettie. "You got to cheer up. Tha's what you got to do. Everybody's got their troubles."

"Yeah," said Mrs. Morse. "I know."

"Come a pretty picture card for you," Nettie said. "Maybe that will cheer you up."

She handed Mrs. Morse a post-card. Mrs. Morse had to cover one eye with her hand, in order to read the message; her eyes were not yet focusing correctly.

It was from Art. On the back of a view of the Detroit Athletic Club he had written: "Greeting and salutations. Hope you have lost that gloom. Cheer up and don't take any rubber nickles. See you on Thursday."

She dropped the card to the floor. Misery crushed her as if she were between great smooth stones. There passed before her a slow, slow pageant of days spent lying in her flat, of evenings at Jimmy's being a good sport, making herself laugh and coo at Art and other Arts; she saw a long parade of weary horses and shivering beggars and all beaten, driven, stumbling things. Her feet throbbed as if she had crammed them into the stubby champagne-colored slippers. Her heart seemed to swell and harden.

"Nettie," she cried, "for heaven's sake pour me a drink, will you?"

The maid looked doubtful.

"Now you know, Mis' Morse," she said, "you been near daid. I don' know if the doctor he let you drink nothin' yet."

"Oh, never mind him," she said. "You get me one, and bring in the bottle. Take one yourself."

"Well," said Nettie.

She poured them each a drink, deferentially leaving hers in the bathroom to be taken in solitude, and brought Mrs. Morse's glass in to her.

Mrs. Morse looked into the liquor and shuddered back from its odor. Maybe it would help. Maybe, when you had been knocked cold for a few days, your very first drink would give you a lift. maybe whisky would be her friend again. She prayed without addressing a God, without knowing a God. Oh, please, please, let her be able to get drunk, please keep her always drunk.

She lifted the glass.

"Thanks, Nettie," she said. "Here's mud in your eye."

The maid giggled. "Tha's the way, Mis' Morse," she said. "You cheer up, now."

"Yeah," said Mrs. Morse. "Sure."

FROM THE DIARY OF A NEW YORK LADY

During Days of Horror, Despair, and World Change

MONDAY. Breakfast tray about eleven; didn't want it. The champagne at the Amorys' last night was *too* revolting, but what *can* you do? You can't stay until five o'clock on just *nothing*. They had those *divine* Hungarian musicians in the green coats, and Stewie Hunter took off one of his shoes and led them with it, and it *couldn't* have been funnier. He is *the* wittiest number in the *entire* world; he *couldn't* be more perfect. Ollie Martin brought me home and we both fell asleep in the car—*too* screaming. Miss Rose came about noon to do my nails, simply *covered* with *the* most divine gossip. The Morrises are going to separate *any minute*, and Freddie Warren *definitely* has ulcers, and Gertie Leonard simply *won't* let Bill Crawford out of her sight even with Jack Leonard *right there in the room*, and it's all *true* about Sheila Phillips and Babs Deering. It *couldn't* have been more thrilling. Miss Rose is *too* marvelous; I really think that a lot of times people like that are a lot more intelligent than a lot of people. Didn't notice until after she had gone that the damn fool had put that *revolting* tangerine-colored polish on my nails; *couldn't* have been more furious. Started to read a book, but too nervous. Called up and found I could get two tickets for the opening of "Run like a Rabbit" tonight for forty-eight dollars. Told them they had *the* nerve of the world, but what *can* you do? Think Joe said he was dining out, so telephoned some *divine* numbers to get someone to go to the theater with me, but they were all tied up. Finally got Ollie Martin. He *couldn't* have more poise, and what do *I* care if he *is* one? *Can't* decide whether to wear the green crepe or the red wool. Every time I look at my finger nails, I could *spit*. *Damn* Miss Rose.

Tuesday. Joe came barging in my room this morning at *practically nine o'clock*. *Couldn't* have been more furious. Started to fight, but *too* dead. Know he said he wouldn't be home to dinner. Absolutely *cold* all day; couldn't *move*. Last night *couldn't* have been more perfect. Ollie and I dined at Thirty-Eight East, absolutely *poisonous* food, and not one *living* soul that you'd be seen *dead* with, and "Run like a Rabbit" was *the* world's worst. Took Ollie up to the Barlows' party and it *couldn't* have been more attractive—*couldn't* have been more people absolutely *stinking*. They had those Hungarians in the green coats, and Stewie Hunter was leading them with a fork—everybody simply *died*. He had *yards* of green toilet paper hung around his neck like a lei; he *couldn't* have been in better form. Met a *really new number*, very tall, *too* marvelous, and one of those people that you can *really* talk to them. I told him sometimes I get so *nauseated* I could *yip*, and I felt I absolutely *had* to do something like write or paint. He said why didn't I write or paint. Came home alone; Ollie passed out *stiff*. Called up the new number three times today to get him to come to dinner and go with me to the opening of "Never Say Good Morning," but first he was out and then he was all tied up with his mother. Finally got Ollie Martin. Tried to read a book, but couldn't sit still. *Can't* decide whether to wear the red lace or the pink with the feathers. Feel *too* exhausted, but what *can* you do?

Wednesday. The most terrible thing happened *just this minute*. Broke one of my finger nails *right off short*. Absolutely *the* most horrible thing I ever had happen to me in my life. Called up Miss Rose to come over and shape it for me, but she was out for the day. I do have *the* worst luck in the *entire* world. Now I'll have to go around like this all day and all night, but what *can* you do? *Damn* Miss Rose. Last night *too* hectic. "Never Say Good Morning" *too* foul, *never* saw more poisonous clothes on the stage. Took Ollie up to the Ballards' party; *couldn't* have been better. They had those Hungarians in the green coats and Stewie Hunter was leading them with a freesia—*too* perfect. He had on Peggy Cooper's ermine coat and Phyllis Minton's silver turban; *simply* unbelievable. Asked simply *sheaves* of *divine* people to come here Friday night; got the address of those Hungarians in the green coats from Betty Ballard. She says just engage them until four, and then whoever gives them another three hundred dollars, they'll stay till five. *Couldn't* be cheaper. Started home with Ollie, but had to drop him at his house; he *couldn't* have been sicker. Called up the new number today to get him to come to dinner and go to the opening of "Everybody Up" with me tonight, but he was tied up. Joe's going to be out; he didn't *condescend* to say *where, of course*. Started to read the papers, but nothing in them except that Mona Wheatley is in Reno charging *intolerable cruelty*. Called up Jim Wheatley to see if he had anything to do tonight, but he was tied up. Finally got Ollie Martin. *Can't* decide whether to wear the white satin or the black chiffon or the yellow pebble crepe. Simply *wrecked* to the *core* about my finger nail. Can't *bear* it. *Never* knew *anybody* to have such *unbelievable* things happen to them.

Thursday. Simply *collapsing* on my *feet*. Last night *too* marvelous. "Everybody Up" *too* divine, *couldn't* be filthier, and the new number was there, *too* celestial, only he didn't see me. He was with Florence Keeler in that *loathsome* gold Schiaparelli model of hers that every *shopgirl* has had since *God* knows. He must be out of his *mind*; she wouldn't *look* at a man. Took Ollie to the Watsons' party; *couldn't* have been more thrilling. Everybody simply *blind*. They had those Hungarians in the green coats and Stewie Hunter was leading them with a lamp, and, after the lamp got broken, he and Tommy Thomas did adagio dances—*too* wonderful. Somebody told me Tommy's doctor told him he had to absolutely get *right out of town*, he has *the* world's worst stomach, but you'd *never* know it. Came home alone, couldn't find Ollie *anywhere*. Miss Rose came at noon to shape my nail, *couldn't* have been more fascinating. Sylvia Eaton can't go *out the door* unless she's had a hypodermic, and Doris Mason *knows every single word* about Douggie Mason and that girl up in Harlem, and Evelyn North won't be *induced* to keep away from those three acrobats, and they don't *dare* tell Stuyvie Raymond *what* he's got the matter with him. *Never* knew anyone that had a more simply *fascinating* life than Miss Rose. Made her take that *vile* tangerine polish off my nails and put on dark red. Didn't notice until after she had gone that it's practically *black* in electric light; *couldn't* be in a worse state. *Damn* Miss Rose. Joe left a note saying he was going to dine out, so telephoned the new number to get him to come to dinner and go with me to that new movie tonight, but he didn't answer. Sent him three telegrams to *absolutely surely* come tomorrow night. Finally got Ollie Martin for tonight. Looked at the papers, but nothing in them except that the Harry Motts are throwing a tea with Hungarian music on Sunday. Think will ask the new number to go to it with me; they must have meant to invite me. Began to read a book, but too exhausted. *Can't* decide whether to wear the new blue with the white jacket or save it till tomorrow night and wear the ivory moire. Simply *heartsick* every time I think of my nails. *Couldn't* be wilder. Could *kill* Miss Rose, but what *can* you do?

Friday. Absolutely *sunk*; *couldn't* be worse. Last night *too* divine, movie *simply* deadly. Took Ollie to the Kingslands' party, *too* unbelievable, everybody absolutely *rolling*. They had those Hungarians in the green coats, but Stewie Hunter wasn't there. He's got a *complete* nervous breakdown. Worried *sick* for fear he won't be well by tonight; will absolutely *never* forgive him if he doesn't come. Started home with Ollie, but dropped him at his house because he *couldn't* stop crying. Joe left word with the butler he's going to the country this afternoon for the week-end; *of course* he wouldn't *stoop* to say *what* country. Called up *streams* of marvelous numbers to get someone to come dine and go with me to the opening of "White Man's Folly," and then go somewhere after to dance for a while; can't *bear* to be the first one there at your own party. Everybody was tied up. Finally got Ollie Martin. *Couldn't* feel more depressed; never should have gone *anywhere near* champagne and Scotch together. Started to read a book, but too restless. Called up Anne Lyman to ask about the new baby and *couldn't* remember if it was a boy or girl—*must* get a secretary *next week*. Anne *couldn't* have been more of a help; she said she didn't know whether to name it Patricia or Gloria, so then of course I knew it was a girl *right away*. Suggested calling it Barbara; forgot she already had one. Absolutely *walking the floor* like a *panther* all day. Could *spit* about Stewie Hunter. Can't *face* deciding whether to wear the blue with the white jacket or the purple with the beige roses. Every time I look at those *revolting* black nails, I want to absolutely *yip*. I really have *the* most horrible things happen to me of anybody in the *entire* world. *Damn* Miss Rose.

SOLDIERS OF THE REPUBLIC

THAT Sunday afternoon we sat with the Swedish girl in the big café in Valencia. We had vermouth in thick goblets, each with a cube of honeycombed gray ice in it. The waiter was so proud of that ice he could hardly bear to leave the glasses on the table, and thus part from it forever. He went to his duty—all over the room they were clapping their hands and hissing to draw his attention—but he looked back over his shoulder.

It was dark outside, the quick, new dark that leaps down without dusk on the day; but, because there were no lights in the streets, it seemed as set and as old as midnight. So you wondered that all the babies were still up. There were babies everywhere in the café, babies serious without solemnity and interested in a tolerant way in their surroundings.

At the table next ours, there was a notably small one; maybe six months old. Its father, a little man in a big uniform that dragged his shoulders down, held it carefully on his knee. It was doing nothing whatever, yet he and his thin young wife, whose belly was already big again under her sleazy dress, sat watching it in a sort of ecstasy of admiration, while their coffee cooled in front of them. The baby was in Sunday white; its dress was patched so delicately that you would have thought the fabric whole had not the patches varied in their shades of whiteness. In its hair was a bow of new blue ribbon, tied with absolute balance of loops and ends. The ribbon was of no use; there was not enough hair to require restraint. The bow was sheerly an adornment, a calculated bit of dash.

"Oh, for God's sake, stop that!" I said to myself. "All right, so it's got a piece of blue ribbon on its hair. All right, so its mother went without eating so it could look pretty when its father came home on leave. All right, so it's her business, and none of yours. All right, so what have you got to cry about?"

The big, dim room was crowded and lively. That morning there had been a bombing from the air, the more horrible for broad daylight. But nobody in the café sat tense and strained, nobody desperately forced forgetfulness. They drank coffee or bottled lemonade, in the pleasant, earned ease of Sunday afternoon, chatting of small, gay matters, all talking at once, all hearing and answering.

There were many soldiers in the room, in what appeared to be the uniforms of twenty different armies until you saw that the variety lay in the differing ways the cloth had worn or faded. Only a few of them had been wounded; here and there you saw one stepping gingerly, leaning on a crutch or two canes, but so far on toward recovery that his face had color. There were many men, too, in civilian clothes—some of them soldiers home on leave, some of them governmental workers, some of them anybody's guess. There were plump, comfortable wives, active with paper fans, and old women as quiet as their grandchildren. There were many pretty girls and some beauties, of whom you did not remark, "There's a charming Spanish type," but said, "What a beautiful girl!" The women's clothes were not new, and their material was too humble ever to have warranted skillful cutting.

"It's funny," I said to the Swedish girl, "how when nobody in a place is best-dressed, you don't notice that everybody isn't."

"Please?" the Swedish girl said.

No one, save an occasional soldier, wore a hat. When we had first come to Valencia, I lived in a state of puzzled pain as to why everybody on the streets laughed at me. It was not because "West End Avenue" was writ across my face as if left there by a customs officer's chalked scrawl. They like Americans in Valencia, where they have seen good ones—the doctors who left their practices and came to help, the calm young nurses, the men of the International

Brigade. But when I walked forth, men and women courteously laid their hands across their splitting faces and little children, too innocent for dissembling, doubled with glee and pointed and cried, "*Ole!*" Then, pretty late, I made my discovery, and left my hat off; and there was laughter no longer. It was not one of those comic hats, either; it was just a hat.

The café filled to overflow, and I left our table to speak to a friend across the room. When I came back to the table, six soldiers were sitting there. They were crowded in, and I scraped past them to my chair. They looked tired and dusty and little, the way that the newly dead look little, and the first things you saw about them were the tendons in their necks. I felt like a prize sow.

They were all in conversation with the Swedish girl. She has Spanish, French, German, anything in Scandinavian, Italian, and English. When she has a moment for regret, she sighs that her Dutch is so rusty she can no longer speak it, only read it, and the same is true of her Rumanian.

They had told her, she told us, that they were at the end of forty-eight hours' leave from the trenches, and, for their holiday, they had all pooled their money for cigarettes, and something had gone wrong, and the cigarettes had never come through to them. I had a pack of American cigarettes–in Spain rubies are as nothing to them–and I brought it out, and by nods and smiles and a sort of breast stroke, made it understood that I was offering it to those six men yearning for tobacco. When they saw what I meant, each one of them rose and shook my hand. Darling of me to share my cigarettes with the men on their way back to the trenches. Little Lady Bountiful. The prize sow.

Each one lit his cigarette with a contrivance of yellow rope that stank when afire and was also used, the Swedish girl translated, for igniting grenades. Each one received what he had ordered, a glass of coffee, and each one murmured appreciatively over the tiny cornucopia of coarse sugar that accompanied it. Then they talked.

They talked through the Swedish girl, but they did to us that thing we all do when we speak our own language to one who has no knowledge of it. They looked us square in the face, and spoke slowly, and pronounced their words with elaborate movements of their lips. Then, as their stories came, they poured them at us so vehemently, so emphatically that they were sure we must understand. They were so convinced we would understand that we were ashamed for not understanding.

But the Swedish girl told us. They were all farmers and farmers' sons, from a district so poor that you try not to remember there is that kind of poverty. Their village was next that one where the old men and the sick men and the women and children had gone, on a holiday, to the bullring; and the planes had come over and dropped bombs on the bullring, and the old men and the sick men and the women and the children were more than two hundred.

They had all, the six of the, been in the war for over a year, and most of that time they had been in the trenches. Four of them were married. One had one child, two had three children, one had five. They had not had word from their families since they had left for the front. There had been no communication; two of them had learned to write from men fighting next them in the trench, but they had not dared to write home. They belonged to a union, and union men, of course, are put to death if taken. The village where their families lived had been captured, and if your wife gets a letter from a union man, who knows but they'll shoot her for the connection?

They told about how they had not heard from their families for more than a year. They did not tell it gallantly or whimsically or stoically. They told it as if—Well, look. You have been in the trenches, fighting, for a year. You have heard nothing of your wife and your children. They do not know if you are dead or alive or blinded. You do not know where they are, of if they are. You must talk to somebody. That is the way they told about it.

One of them, some six months before, had heard of his wife and his three children—they had such beautiful eyes, he said—from a brother-in-law in France. They were all alive then, he was told, and had a bowl of beans a day. But his wife had not complained of the food, he heard. What had troubled her was that she had no thread to mend the children's ragged clothes. So that troubled him, too.

"She has no thread," he kept telling us. "My wife has no thread to mend with. No thread."

We sat there, and listened to what the Swedish girl told us they were saying. Suddenly one of them looked at the clock, and then there was excitement. They jumped up, as a man, and there were calls for the waiter and rapid talk with him, and each of them shook the hand of each of us. We went through more swimming motions to explain to them that they were to take the rest of the cigarettes—fourteen cigarettes for six soldiers to take to war—and then they shook our hands again. Then all of us said "*Salud!*" as many times as could be for six of them and three of us, and then they filed out of the café, the six of them, tired and dusty and little, as men of a mighty horde are little.

Only the Swedish girl talked, after they had gone. The Swedish girl has been in Spain since the start of the war. She has nursed splintered men, and she has carried stretchers into the trenches and, heavier laden, back to the hospital. She has seen and heard too much to be knocked into silence.

Presently it was time to go, and the Swedish girl raised her hands above her head and clapped them twice together to summon the waiter. He came, but he only shook his head and his hand, and moved away.

The soldiers had paid for our drinks.

DUSK BEFORE FIREWORKS

He was a very good-looking young man indeed, shaped to be annoyed. His voice was intimate as the rustle of sheets, and he kissed easily. There was no tallying the gifts of Charvet handkerchiefs, *art moderne* ash-trays, monogrammed dressing-gowns, gold keychains, and cigarette-cases of thin wood, inlaid with views of Parisian comfort stations, that were sent him by ladies too quickly confident, and were paid for with the money of unwitting husbands, which is acceptable any place in the world. Every woman who visited his small, square apartment promptly flamed with the desire to assume charge of its redecoration. During his tenancy, three separate ladies had achieved this ambition. Each had left behind her, for her brief monument, much too much glazed chintz.

The glare of the latest upholstery was dulled, now, in an April dusk. There was a soft blur of mauve and gray over chairs and curtains, instead of the daytime pattern of heroic-sized double poppies and small, sad elephants. (The most recent of the volunteer decorators was a lady who added interest to her ways by collecting all varieties of elephants save those alive or stuffed; her selection of the chintz had been made less for the cause of contemporary design than in the hope of keeping ever present the wistful souvenirs of her hobby and, hence, of herself. Unhappily, the poppies, those flowers for forgetfulness, turned out to be predominant in the pattern.)

The very good-looking young man was stretched in a chair that was legless and short in back. It was a strain to see in that chair any virtue save the speeding one of modernity. Certainly it was a peril to all who dealt with it; they were far from their best within its arms, and they could never have wished to be remembered as they appeared while easing into its depths or struggling out again. All, that is, save the young man. He was a long young man, broad at the shoulders and chest and narrow everywhere else, and his muscles obeyed him at the exact instant of command. He rose and lay, he moved and was still, always in beauty. Several men disliked him, but only one woman really hated him. She was his sister. She was stump-shaped, and she had straight hair.

On the sofa opposite the difficult chair there sat a young woman, slight and softly dressed. There was no more to her frock than some dull, dark silk and a little chiffon, but the recurrent bill for it demanded, in bitter black and white, a sum well on toward the second hundred. Once the very good-looking young man had said that he liked women in quiet and conservative clothes, carefully made. The young woman was of those unfortunates who remember every word. This made living peculiarly trying for her when it was later demonstrated that the young man was also partial to ladies given to garments of slap-dash cut, and color like the sound of big brass instruments.

The young woman was temperately pretty in the eyes of most beholders; but there were a few, mainly hand-to-mouth people, artists and such, who could not look enough at her. Half a year before, she had been sweeter to see. Now there was tension about her mouth and unease along her brow, and her eyes looked wearied and troubled. The gentle dusk became her. The young man who shared it with her could not see these things.

She stretched her arms and laced her fingers high above her head.

"Oh, this is nice," she said. "It's nice being here."

"It's nice and peaceful," he said. "Oh, Lord. Why can't people just be peaceful? That's little enough to ask, isn't it? Why does there have to be so much hell, all the time?"

She dropped her hands to her lap.

"There doesn't have to be at all," she said. She had a quiet voice, and she said her words with every courtesy to each of them, as if she respected language. "There's never any need for hell."

"There's an awful lot of it around, sweet," he said.

"There certainly is," she said. "There's just as much hell as there are hundreds of little shrill, unnecessary people. It's the second-raters that stir up hell; first-rate people wouldn't. You need never have another bit of it in your beautiful life if—if you'll pardon my pointing—you could just manage to steel yourself against that band of spitting hell-cats that is included in your somewhat overcrowded acquaintance, my lamb. Ah, but I mean it, Hobie, dear. I've been wanting to tell you for so long. But it's so rotten hard to say. If I say it, it makes me sound just like one of them—makes me seem inexpensive and jealous. Surely, you know, after all this time, I'm not like that. It's just that I worry so about you. You're so fine, you're so lovely, it nearly kills me to see you just eaten up by a lot of things like Margot Wadsworth and Mrs. Holt and Evie Maynard and those. You're so much better than that. You know that's why I'm saying it. You know I haven't got a stitch of jealousy in me. Jealous! Good heavens, if I were going to be jealous, I'd be it about someone worth while, and not about any silly, stupid, idle, worthless, selfish, hysterical, vulgar, promiscuous, sex-ridden——"

"Darling!" he said.

"Well, I'm sorry," she said. "I guess I'm sorry. I didn't really mean to go into the subject of certain of your friends. Maybe the way they behave isn't their fault, said she, lying in her teeth. After all, you can't expect them to know what it's about. Poor things, they'll never know how sweet it can be, how lovely it always is when we're alone together. It is, isn't it? Ah, Hobie, isn't it?"

The young man raised his slow lids and looked at her. He smiled with one end of his beautiful curly mouth.

"Uh-huh," he said.

He took his eyes from hers and became busy with an ash-tray and a spent cigarette. But he still smiled.

"Ah, don't," she said. "You promised you'd forget about—about last Wednesday. You said you'd never remember it again. Oh, whatever made me do it! Making scenes. Having tantrums. Rushing out into the night. And then coming crawling back. Me, that wanted to show you how different a woman could be! Oh, please, please don't let's think about it. Only tell me I wasn't as terrible as I know I was."

"Darling," he said, for he was often a young man of simple statements, "you were the worst I ever saw."

"And doesn't that come straight from Sir Hubert!" she said. "Oh, dear. Oh, dear, oh, dear. What can I say? 'Sorry' isn't nearly enough. I'm broken. I'm in little bits. Would you mind doing something about putting me together again?"

She held out her arms to him.

The young man rose, came over to the sofa, and kissed her. He had intended a quick, good-humored kiss, a moment's stop on a projected trip out to his little pantry to mix cocktails. But her arms clasped him so close and so gladly that he dismissed the plan. He lifted her to her feet, and did not leave her.

Presently she moved her head and hid her face above his heart.

"Listen," she said, against cloth. "I want to say it all now, and then never say it any more. I want to tell you that there'll never, never be anything like last Wednesday again. What we have is so much too lovely ever to cheapen. I promise, oh, I promise you, I won't ever be like—like anybody else."

"You couldn't be, Kit," he said.

"Ah, think that always," she said, "and say it sometimes. It's so sweet to hear. Will you, Hobie?"

"For your size," he said, "You talk an awful lot." His fingers slid to her chin and he held her face for his greater convenience.

After a while she moved again.

"Guess who I'd rather be, right this minute, than anybody in the whole world," she said.

"Who?" he said.

"Me," she said.

The telephone rang.

The telephone was in the young man's bedroom, standing in frequent silence on the little table by his bed. There was no door to the bed-chamber; a plan which had disadvantages, too. Only a curtained archway sequestered its intimacies from those of the living-room. Another archway, also streaming chintz, gave from the bedroom upon a tiny passage, along which were ranged the bathroom and the pantry. It was only by entering either of these, closing the door behind, and turning the faucets on to the full that any second person in the apartment could avoid hearing what was being said over the telephone. The young man sometimes thought of removing to a flat of more sympathetic design.

"There's that damn telephone," the young man said.

"Isn't it?" the young woman said. "And wouldn't it be?"

"Let's not answer it," he said. "Let's let it ring."

"No, you mustn't," she said. "I must be big and strong. Anyway, maybe it's only somebody that just died and left you twenty million dollars. Maybe it isn't some other woman at all. And if it is, what difference does it make? See how sweet and reasonable I am? Look at me being generous."

"You can afford to be, sweetheart," he said.

"I know I can," she said. "After all, whoever she is, she's way off on an end of a wire, and I'm right here."

She smiled up at him. So it was nearly half a minute before he went away to the telephone.

Still smiling, the young woman stretched her head back, closed her eyes and flung her arms wide. A long sigh raised her breast. Thus she stood, then she went and settled back on the sofa. She essayed whistling softly, but the issuing sounds would not resemble the intended tune and she felt, though interested, vaguely betrayed. Then she looked about the dusk-filled room. Then she pondered her finger nails, bringing each bent hand close to her eyes, and could find no fault. Then she smoothed her skirt along her legs and shook out the chiffon frills at her wrists. Then she spread her little handkerchief on her knee and with exquisite care traced the "Katherine" embroidered in script across one of its corners. Then she gave it all up and did nothing but listen.

"Yes?" the young man was saying. "Hello? Hello. I *told* you this is Mr. Ogden. Well, I *am* holding the wire. I've *been* holding the wire. *You're* the one that went away. Hello? Ah, now listen–Hello? Hey. Oh, what the hell *is* this? Come back, will you? Operator! Hello, *Yes,* this is Mr. Ogden. Who? Oh, hello, Connie. How are you, dear? What? You're what? Oh, that's too bad. What's the matter? Why can't you? Where are you, in Greenwich? Oh, I see. When, now? Why, Connie, the only thing is I've got to go right out. So if you came in to town now, it really wouldn't do much– Well, I couldn't very well do that, dear. I'm keeping these people waiting as it is. I say I'm late now, I was just going out the door when you called. Why, I'd better not say that, Connie, because there's no telling when I'll be able to break away. Look, why don't you wait and come in to town tomorrow some time? What? Can't you tell me now? Oh– Well– Oh, Connie, there's no reason to talk like that. Why, of course I'd do anything in the world I could, but I tell you I can't tonight. No, no, no, no, no, it isn't that at all. No, it's nothing like that, I tell you. These people are friends of my sister's, and it's just one of those things you've got to do. Why don't you be a good girl and go to bed early, and then you'll feel better tomorrow? Hm? Will you do that? What? Of course I do, Connie. I'll try to later on if I can, dear. Well, all right, if you want to, but I don't know what time I'll be home. Of course I do. Of course I do. Yes, *do*, Connie. You be a good girl, won't you? 'By, dear."

The young man returned, through the chintz. He had a rather worn look. It was, of course, becoming to him.

"God," he said, simply.

The young woman on the sofa looked at him as if through clear ice.

"And how *is* dear Mrs. Holt?" she said.

"Great," he said. "Corking. Way up at the top of her form." He dropped wearily into the low chair. "She says she has something she wants to tell me."

"It can't be her age," she said.

He smiled without joy. "She says it's too hard to say over the wire," he said.

"Then it may be her age," she said. "She's afraid it might sound like her telephone number."

"About twice a week," he said, "Connie has something she must tell you right away, that she couldn't possibly say over the telephone. Usually it turns out she's caught the butler drinking again."

"I see," she said.

"Well," he said. "Poor little Connie."

"Poor little Connie," she said. "Oh, my God. That saber-toothed tigress. Poor little Connie."

"Darling, why do we have to waste time talking about Connie Holt?" he said. "Can't we just be peaceful?"

"Not while that she-beast prowls the streets," she said. "Is she coming in to town tonight?"

"Well, she was," he said, "but then she more or less said she wouldn't."

"Oh, she will," she said. "You get right down out of that fool's paradise you're in. She'll shoot out of Greenwich like a bat out of hell, if she thinks there's a chance of seeing you. Ah, Hobie, you don't really want to see that old thing, do you? Do you? Because if you do–Well, I suppose maybe you do. Naturally, if she has something she must tell you right away, you want to see her. Look, Hobie, you know you can see me any time. It isn't a bit important, seeing me tonight. Why don't you call up Mrs. Holt and tell her to take the next train in? She'd get here quicker by train than by motor, wouldn't she? Please go ahead and do it. It's quite all right about me. Really."

"You know," he said, "I knew that was coming. I could tell it by the way you were when I came back from the telephone. Oh, Kit, what makes you want to talk like that? You know damned well the last thing I want to do is see Connie Holt. You know how I want to be with you. Why do you want to work up all this? I watched you just sit there and deliberately talk yourself into it, starting right out of nothing. Now what's the idea of that? Oh, good Lord, what's the matter with women, anyway?"

"Please don't call me 'women' " she said.

"I'm sorry, darling," he said. "I didn't mean to use bad words." He smiled at her. She felt her heart go liquid, but she did her best to be harder won.

"Doubtless," she said, and her words fell like snow when there is no wind, "I spoke ill-advisedly. If I said, as I must have, something to distress you, I can only beg you to believe that that was my misfortune, and not my intention. It seemed to me as if I were doing only a courteous thing in suggesting that you need feel no obligation about spending the evening with me, when you would naturally wish to be with Mrs. Holt. I simply felt that—Oh, the hell with it! I'm no good at this. Of course I didn't mean it, dearest. If you had said, 'All right,' and had gone and told her to come in, I should have died. I just said it because I wanted to hear you say it was me you wanted to be with. Oh, I need to hear you say that, Hobie. It's—it's what I live on, darling."

"Kit," he said, "you ought to know, without my saying it. You know. It's this feeling you *have* to say things—that's what spoils everything."

"I suppose so," she said. "I suppose I know so. Only—the thing is, I get so mixed up, I just—I just can't go on. I've got to be reassured, dearest. I didn't need to be at first, when everything was gay and sure, but things aren't—well, they aren't the same now. There seem to be so many others that— So I need so terribly to have you tell me that it's me and not anybody else. Oh, I *had* to have you say that, a few minutes ago. Look, Hobie. How do you think it makes me feel to sit here and hear you lie to Connie Holt—to hear you say you have to go out with friends of your sister's? Now why couldn't you say you had a date with me? Are you ashamed of me, Hobie? Is that it?"

"Oh, Kit," he said, "for heaven's sake! I don't know why I did it. I did it before I even thought. I did it—well, sort of instinctively, I guess, because it seemed to be the easiest thing to do. I suppose I'm just weak."

"No!" she said. "You weak? Well! And is there any other news tonight?"

"I know I am," he said. "I know it's weak to do anything in the world to avoid a scene."

"Exactly what," she said, "is Mrs. Holt to you and you to her that she may make a scene if she learns that you have an engagement with another woman?"

"Oh, God!" he said. "I told you I don't give a damn about Connie Holt. She's nothing to me. Now will you for Gods's sake let it drop?"

"Oh, she's nothing to you," she said. "I see. Naturally, that would be why you called her 'dear' every other word."

"If I did," he said, "I never knew I was saying it. Good Lord, that doesn't mean anything. It's simply a—a form of nervousness, I suppose. I say it when I can't think what to call people. Why, I call telephone operators 'dear.' "

"I'm sure you do!" she said.

They glared. It was the young man who gave first. He went and sat close to her on the sofa, and for a while there were only murmurs. Then he said, "Will you stop? Will you stop it? Will you always be just like this—just sweet and the way you're meant to be and no fighting?"

"I will," she said. "Honest, I mean to. Let's not let anything come between us again ever. Mrs. Holt, indeed! Hell with her."

"Hell with her," he said. There was another silence, during which the young man did several things that he did extraordinarily well.

Suddenly the young woman stiffened her arms and pushed him away from her.

"And how do I know," she said, "that the way you talk to me about Connie Holt isn't just the way you talk to her about me when I'm not here? How do I know that?"

"Oh, my Lord," he said. "Oh, my dear, sweet Lord. Just when everything was all right. Ah, stop it, will you, baby? Let's just be quiet. Like this. See?"

A little later he said. "Look, sweet, how about a cocktail? Mightn't that be an idea? I'll go make them. And would you like the lights lighted?"

"Oh, no," she said. "I like it better in the dusk, like this. It's sweet. Dusk is so personal, somehow. And this way you can't see those lampshades. Hobie, if you knew how I hate your lampshades!"

"Honestly?" he said, with less injury than bewilderment in his voice. He looked at the shades as if he saw them for the first time. They were of vellum, or some substance near it, and upon each was painted a panorama of the right bank of the Seine, with the minute windows of the buildings cut out, under the direction of a superior mind, so that light might come through. "What's the matter with them, Kit?"

"Dearest, if you don't know, I can't ever explain it to you," she said. "Among other things, they're banal, inappropriate, and unbeautiful. They're exactly what Evie Maynard *would* have chosen. She thinks, just because they show views of Paris, that they're pretty darned sophisticated. She is that not uncommon type of woman that thinks any reference to la belle France is an invitation to the waltz. 'Not uncommon.' If that isn't the mildest word-picture that ever was painted of that——"

"Don't you like the way she decorated the apartment?" he said.

"Sweetheart," she said. "I think it's poisonous. You know that."

"Would you like to do it over?" he said.

"I should say not," she said. "Look, Hobie, don't you remember me? I'm the one that doesn't want to decorate your flat. Now do you place me? But if I ever *did*, the first thing I should do would be to paint these walls putty color—no, I guess first I'd tear off all this chintz and fling it to the winds, and then I'd——"

The telephone rang.

The young man threw one stricken glance at the young woman and then sat motionless. The jangles of the bell cut the dusk like little scissors.

"I think," said the young woman, exquisitely, "that your telephone is ringing. Don't let me keep you from answering it. As a matter of fact, I really must go powder my nose."

She sprang up, dashed through the bedroom, and into the bathroom. There was the sound of a closed door, the grind of a firmly turned key, and then immediately the noise of rushing waters.

When she returned, eventually, to the living-room, the young man was pouring a pale, cold liquid into small glasses. He gave one to her, and smiled at her over it. It was his wistful smile. It was of his best.

"Hobie," she said, "is there a livery stable anywhere around here where they rent wild horses?"

"What?" he said.

"Because if there is," she said, "I wish you'd call up and ask them to send over a couple of teams. I want to show you they couldn't drag me into asking who that was on the telephone."

"Oh," he said, and tried his cocktail. "Is this dry enough, sweet? Because you like them dry, don't you? Sure it's all right? Really? Ah, wait a second, darling. Let *me* light your cigarette. There. Sure you're all right?"

"I can't stand it," she said. "I just lost all my strength of purpose—maybe the maid will find it on the floor in the morning. Hobart Ogden, who was that on the telephone?"

"Oh, that?" he said. "Well, that was a certain lady who shall be nameless."

"I'm sure she should be," she said. "She doubtless has all the other qualities of a—Well. I didn't quite say it, I'm keeping my head. Ah, dearest, was that Connie Holt again?"

"No, that was the funniest thing," he said. "That was Evie Maynard. Just when we were talking about her."

"Well, well, well," she said. "Isn't it a small world? And what's on her mind, if I may so flatter her? Is *her* butler tight, too?"

"Evie hasn't got a butler," he said. He tried smiling again, but found it better to abandon the idea and concentrate on refilling the young woman's glass. "No, she's just dizzy, the same as usual. She's got a cocktail party at her apartment, and they all want to go out on the town, that's all."

"Luckily," she said, "you had to go out with these friends of your sister's. You were just going out the door when she called."

"I never told her any such thing!" he said. "I said I had a date I'd been looking forward to all week."

"Oh, you didn't mention any names?" she said.

"There's no reason why I should, to Evie Maynard," he said. "It's none of her affair, any more than what she's doing and who she's doing it with is any concern of mine. She's nothing in my life. You know that. I've hardly seen her since she did the apartment. I don't care if I never see her again. I'd *rather* I never saw her again."

"I should think that might be managed, if you've really set your heart on it," she said.

"Well, I do what I can," he said. "She wanted to come in now for a cocktail, she and some of those interior decorator boys she has with her, and I told her absolutely no."

"And you think that will keep her away?" she said. "Oh, no. She'll be here. She and her feathered friends. Let's see—they ought to arrive just about the time that Mrs. Holt has thought it over and come in to town. Well. It's shaping up into a lovely evening, isn't it?"

"Great," he said. "And if I may say so, you're doing everything you can to make it harder, you little sweet." He poured more cocktails. "Oh, Kit, why are you being so nasty? Don't do it, darling. It's not like you. It's so unbecoming to you."

"I know it's horrible," she said. "It's—well, I do it in defense, I suppose, Hobie. If I didn't say nasty things, I'd cry. I'm afraid to cry; it would take me so long to stop. I—oh, I'm so hurt, dear. I don't know what to think. All these women. All these awful women. If they were fine, if they were sweet and gentle and intelligent, I shouldn't mind. Or maybe I should. I don't know. I don't know much of anything, any more. My mind goes round and round. I thought what we had was so different. Well—it wasn't. Sometimes I think it would be better never to see you any more. But then I know I couldn't stand that. I'm too far gone now. I'd do anything to be with you! And so I'm just another of those women to you. And I used to come first, Hobie—oh, I did! I did!"

"You did!" he said. "And you do!"

"And I always will?" she said.

"And you always will," he said, "as long as you'll only be your own self. Please be sweet again, Kit. Like this, darling. Like this, child."

Again they were close, and again there was no sound.

The telephone rang.

They started as if the same arrow had pierced them. Then the young woman moved slowly back.

"You know," she said, musingly, "this is my fault. I did this. It was me. I was the one that said let's meet here, and not at my house. I said it would be quieter, and I had so much I wanted to talk to you about. I said we could be quiet and alone here. Yes, I said that."

"I give you my word," he said, "that damn thing hasn't rung in a week."

"It was lucky for me, wasn't it?" she said, "that I happened to be here the last time it did. I am known as Little Miss Horseshoes. Well. Oh, please do answer it, Hobie. It drives me even crazier to have it ring like this."

"I hope to God," the young man said, "that it's a wrong number." He held her to him, hard. "Darling," he said. Then he went to the telephone.

"Hello," he said into the receiver. "Yes? Oh, hello there. How are you, dear—how are you? Oh, did you? Ah, that's too bad. Why, you see I was out with these friends on my—I was out till quite late. Oh, you did? Oh, that's too bad, dear, you waited up all that time. No, I did *not* say that, Margot, I said I'd come if I possibly could. That's exactly what I said. I did so. Well, then you misunderstood me. Well, you must have. Now, there's no need to be unreasonable about it. Listen, what I said, I said I'd come if it was possible, but I didn't think there was a chance. If you think hard, you'll remember, dear. Well, I'm terribly sorry, but I don't see what you're making so much fuss about. It was just a misunderstanding, that's all. Why don't you calm down and be a good little girl? Won't you? Why, I can't tonight, dear. Because I *can't*. Well, I have a date I've had for a long time. Yes. Oh, no, it isn't anything like that! Oh, now, please, Margot! Margot, please don't! Now don't do that! I tell you I won't be here. All right, come ahead, but I won't be in. Listen, I can't talk to you when you're like this. I'll call you tomorrow, dear. I tell you I won't be *in,* dear! Please be good. Certainly I do. Look. I have to run now. I'll call you, dear. 'By."

The young man came back to the living-room, and sent his somewhat shaken voice ahead of him.

"How about another cocktail, sweet?" he said. "Don't you think we really ought—" Through the thickening dark, he saw the young woman. She stood straight and tense. Her fur scarf was knotted about her shoulders, and she was drawing on her second glove.

"What's this about?" the young man said.

"I'm so sorry," the young woman said, "but I truly must go home."

"Oh, really?" he said. "May I ask why?"

"It's sweet of you," she said, "to be interested enough to want to know. Thank you so much. Well, it just happens, I can't stand any more of this. There is somewhere, I think, some proverb about a worm's eventually turning. It is doubtless from the Arabic. They so often are. Well, good night, Hobie, and thank you so much for those delicious cocktails. They've cheered me up wonderfully."

She held out her hand. He caught it tight in both of his.

"Ah, now listen," he said. "Please don't do this, Kit. Please, don't, darling. Please. This is just the way you were last Wednesday."

"Yes," she said. "And for exactly the same reason. Please give me back my hand. Thank you. Well, good night, Hobie, and good luck, always."

"All right," he said. "If this is what you want to do."

"Want to do!" she said. "It's nothing *I* want. I simply felt it would be rather easier for you if you could be alone, to receive your telephone calls. Surely you cannot blame me for feeling a bit *de trop*."

"My Lord, do you think I want to talk to those fools?" he said. "What can I do? Take the telephone receiver off? Is that what you want me to do?"

"It's a good trick of yours," she said. "I gather that was what you did last Wednesday night, when I kept trying to call you after I'd gone home, when I was in holy agony there."

"I did not!" he said. "They must have been calling the wrong number. I tell you I was alone here all the time you were gone."

"So you said," she said.

"I don't lie to you, Kit," he said.

"That," she said, "is the most outrageous lie you have ever told me. Good night, Hobie."

Only from the young man's eyes and voice could his anger be judged. The beautiful scroll of his mouth never straightened. He took her hand and bowed over it.

"Good night, Kit," he said.

"Good night," she said. "Well, good night. I'm sorry it must end like this. But if you want other things—well, they're what you want. You can't have both them and me. Good night, Hobie."

"Good night, Kit," he said.

"I'm sorry," she said. "It does seem too bad. Doesn't it?"

"It's what you want," he said.

"I?" she said. "It's what *you* do."

"Oh, Kit, can't you understand?" he said. "You always used to. Don't you know how I am? I just say things and do things that don't mean anything, just for the sake of peace, just for the sake of not having a feud. That's what gets me in trouble. You don't have to do it, I know. You're luckier than I am."

"Luckier?" she said. "Curious word."

"Well, stronger, then," he said. "Finer. Honester. Decenter. All those. Ah, don't do this, Kit. Please. Please take those things off, and come sit down."

"Sit down?" she said. "And wait for the ladies to gather?"

"They're not coming," he said.

"How do you know?" she said. "They've come here before, haven't they? How do you know they won't come tonight?"

"I don't know!" he said. "I don't know what the hell they'll do. I don't know what the hell you'll do, any more. And I thought you were different!"

"I was different," she said, "just so long as you thought I was different."

"Ah, Kit," he said, "Kit. Darling. Come and be the way we were. Come and be sweet and peaceful. Look. Let's have a cocktail, just to each other, and then let's go out to some quiet place for dinner, where we can talk. Will you?"

"Well–" she said. "If you think––"

"I think," he said.

The telephone rang.

"Oh, my *God*!" shrieked the young woman. "Go answer it, you damned–you damned *stallion*!"

She rushed for the door, opened it, and was gone. She was, after all, different. She neither slammed the door nor left it stark open.

The young man stood, and he shook his remarkable head slowly. Slowly, too, he turned and went into the bedroom.

He spoke into the telephone receiver drearily at first, then he seemed to enjoy both hearing and speaking. He used a woman's name in address. It was not Connie; it was not Evie; it was not

Margot. Glowingly he besought the unseen one to meet him; tepidly he agreed to await her coming where he was. He besought her, then, to ring his bell first three times and then twice, for admission. No, no, no, he said, this was not for any reason that might have occurred to her; it was simply that some business friend of his had said something about dropping in, and he wanted to make sure there would be no such intruders. He spoke of his hopes, indeed his assurances, of an evening of sweetness and peace. He said "good-by," and he said "dear."

The very good-looking young man hung up the receiver, and looked long at the dial of his wrist-watch, now delicately luminous. He seemed to be calculating. So long for a young woman to reach her home, and fling herself upon her couch, so long for tears, so long for exhaustion, so long for remorse, so long for rising tenderness. Thoughtfully he lifted the receiver from its hook and set it on end upon the little table.

Then he went into the living-room, and sped the dark before the tiny beams that sifted through the little open windows in the panoramas of Paris.

NEW YORK TO DETROIT

"ALL ready with Detroit," said the telephone operator.

"Hello," said the girl in New York.

"Hello?" said the young man in Detroit.

"Oh, Jack!" she said. "Oh, darling, it's so wonderful to hear you. You don't know how much I——"

"Hello?" he said.

"Ah, can't you hear me?" she said. "Why, I can hear you just as if you were right beside me. Is this any better, dear? Can you hear me now?"

"Who did you want to speak to?" he said.

"You, Jack!" she said. "You, you. This is Jean, darling. Oh, please try to hear me. This is Jean."

"Who?" he said.

"Jean," she said. "Ah, don't you know my voice? It's Jean, dear. Jean."

"Oh, hello there," he said. "Well. Well, for heaven's sake. How are you?"

"I'm all right," she said. "Oh, I'm not, either, darling. I–oh, it's just terrible. I can't stand it any more. Aren't you coming back? Please, when are you coming back? You don't know how awful it is, without you. It's been such a long time, dear–you said it would be just four or five days, and it's nearly three weeks. It's like years and years. Oh, it's been so awful, sweetheart–it's just——"

"Hey, I'm terribly sorry," he said, "but I can't hear one damn thing you're saying. Can't you talk louder, or something?"

"I'll try, I'll try," she said. "Is this better? Now can you hear?"

"Yeah, now I can, a little," he said. "Don't talk so fast, will you? What did you say, before?"

"I said it's just awful without you," she said. "It's such a long time, dear. And I haven't had a word from you. I—oh, I've just been nearly crazy, Jack. Never even a post-card, dearest, or a——"

"Honestly, I haven't had a second," he said. "I've been working like a fool. God, I've been rushed."

"Ah, have you?" she said. "I'm sorry, dear. I've been silly. But it was just—oh, it was just hell, never hearing a word. I thought maybe you'd telephone to say good-night, sometimes, —you know, the way you used to, when you were away."

"Why, I was going to, a lot of times," he said, "but I thought you'd probably be out, or something."

"I haven't been out," she said. "I've been staying here, all by myself. It's—it's sort of better, that way. I don't want to see people. Everybody says, 'When's Jack coming back?' and 'What do you hear from Jack?' and I'm afraid I'll cry in front of them. Darling, it hurts so terribly when they ask me about you, and I have to say I don't——"

"This is the damndest, lousiest connection I ever saw in my life," he said. "What hurts? What's the matter?"

"I said, it hurts so terribly when people ask me about you," she said, "and I have to say—Oh, never mind. Never mind. How are you, dear? Tell me how you are."

"Oh, pretty good," he said. "Tired as the devil. You all right?"

"Jack, I—that's what I wanted to tell you," she said. "I'm terribly worried. I'm nearly out of my mind. Oh, what will I do, dear, what are we going to do? Oh, Jack, Jack, darling!"

"Hey, how can I hear you when you mumble like that?" he said. "Can't you talk louder? Talk right into the what-you-call-it."

"I can't scream it over the telephone!" she said. "Haven't you any sense? Don't you know what I'm telling you? Don't you know? Don't you know?"

"I give up," he said. "First you mumble, and then you yell. Look, this doesn't make sense. I can't hear anything, with this rotten connection. Why don't you write me a letter, in the morning? Do that, why don't you? And I'll write you one. See?"

"Jack, listen, listen!" she said. "You listen to me! I've got to talk to you. I tell you I'm nearly crazy. Please, dearest, hear what I'm saying. Jack, I—"

"Just a minute," he said. "Someone's knocking at the door. *Come in. Well, for cryin' out loud! Come on in, bums. Hang your coats up on the floor, and sit down. The Scotch is in the closet, and there's ice in that pitcher. Make yourselves at home—act like you were in a regular bar. Be with you right away.* Hey, listen, there's a lot of crazy Indians just come in here, and I can't hear myself think. You go ahead and write me a letter tomorrow. Will you?"

"Write you a letter!" she said. "Oh, God, don't you think I'd have written you before, if I'd known where to reach you? I didn't even know that, till they told me at your office today. I got so—"

"Oh, yeah, did they?" he said. "I thought I—*Ah, pipe down, will you? Give a guy a chance. This is an expensive talk going on here*. Say, look, this must be costing you a million dollars. You oughtn't to do this."

"What do you think I care about that?" she said. "I'll die if I don't talk to you. I tell you I'll die, Jack. Sweetheart, what is it? Don't you want to talk to me? Tell me what makes you this way. Is it—don't you really like me any more? Is that it? Don't you, Jack?"

"Hell, I can't hear," he said. "Don't what?"

"Please," she said. "Please, please. Please, Jack, listen. When are you coming back, darling? I need you so. I need you so terribly. When are you coming back?"

"Why, that's the thing," he said. "That's what I was going to write you about tomorrow. *Come on, now, how about shutting up just for a minute? A joke's a joke*. Hello. Hear me all right? Why, you see, the way things came out today, it looks a little bit like I'd have to go on to Chicago for a while. Looks like a pretty big thing, and it won't mean a very long time, I don't believe. Looks as if I'd be going out there next week, I guess."

"Jack, no!" she said. "Oh, don't do that! You can't do that. You can't leave me alone like this. I've got to see you, dearest. I've got to. You've got to come back, or I've got to come there to you. I can't go through this. Jack, I can't, I—"

"Look, we better say good-night now," he said. "No use trying to make out what you say, when you talk all over yourself like that. And there's so much racket here—*Hey, can the harmony, will you? God, it's terrible. Want me to be thrown out of here?* You go get a good night's sleep, and I'll write you all about it tomorrow."

"Listen!" she said. "Jack, don't go 'way! Help me, darling. Say something to help me through tonight. Say you love me, for God's sake say you still love me. Say it. Say it."

"Ah, I can't talk," he said. "This is fierce. I'll write you first thing in the morning. 'By. Thanks for calling up."

"Jack!" she said. "Jack, don't go. Jack, wait a minute. I've got to talk to you. I'll talk quietly. I won't cry. I'll talk so you can hear me. Please, dear, please—"

"All through with Detroit?" said the operator.

"No!" she said. "No, no, no! Get him, get him back again right away! Get him back. No, never mind. Never mind it now. Never—"

GLORY IN THE DAYTIME

Mr. Murdock was one who carried no enthusiasm whatever for plays and their players, and that was too bad, for they meant so much to little Mrs. Murdock. Always she had been in a state of devout excitement over the luminous, free, passionate elect who serve the theater. And always she had done her wistful worshiping, along with the multitudes, at the great public altars. It is true that once, when she was a particularly little girl, love had impelled her to write Miss Maude Adams a letter beginning "Dearest Peter," and she had received from Miss Adams a miniature thimble inscribed "A kiss from Peter Pan." (That was a day!) And once, when her mother had taken her holiday shopping, a limousine door was held open and there had passed her, as close as *that*, a wonder of sable and violets and round red curls that seemed to tinkle on the air; so, forever after, she was as good as certain that she had been not a foot away from Miss Billie Burke. But until some three years after her marriage, these had remained her only personal experiences with the people of the lights and the glory.

Then it turned out that Miss Noyes, new come to little Mrs. Murdock's own bridge club, knew an actress. She actually knew an actress; the way you and I know collectors of recipes and members of garden clubs and amateurs of needlepoint.

The name of the actress was Lily Wynton, and it was famous. She was tall and slow and silvery; often she appeared in the role of a duchess, or of a Lady Pam or an Honorable Moira. Critics recurrently referred to her as "that great lady of our stage." Mrs. Murdock had attended, over years, matinee performances of the Wynton successes. And she had no more thought that she would one day have opportunity to meet Lily Wynton face to face than she had thought—well, than she had thought of flying!

Yet it was not astounding that Miss Noyes should walk at ease among the glamorous. Miss Noyes was full of depths and mystery, and she could talk with a cigarette still between her lips. She was always doing something difficult, like designing her own pajamas, or reading Proust, or modeling torsos in plasticine. She played excellent bridge. She liked little Mrs. Murdock. "Tiny one," she called her.

"How's for coming to tea tomorrow, tiny one? Lily Wynton's going to drop up," she said, at a therefore memorable meeting of the bridge club. "You might like to meet her."

The words fell so easily that she could not have realized their weight. Lily Wynton was coming to tea. Mrs. Murdock might like to meet her. Little Mrs. Murdock walked home through the early dark, and stars sang in the sky above her.

Mr. Murdock was already at home when she arrived. It required but a glance to tell that for him there had been no singing stars that evening in the heavens. He sat with his newspaper opened at the financial page, and bitterness had its way with his soul. It was not the time to cry happily to him of the impending hospitalities of Miss Noyes; not the time, that is, if one anticipated exclamatory sympathy. Mr. Murdock did not like Miss Noyes. When pressed for a reason, he replied that he just plain didn't like her. Occasionally he added, with a sweep that might have commanded a certain admiration, that all those women made him sick. Usually, when she told him of the temperate activities of the bridge club meetings, Mrs. Murdock kept any mention of Miss Noyes's name from the accounts. She had found that this omission made for a more agreeable evening. But now she was caught in such a sparkling swirl of excitement that she had scarcely kissed him before she was off on her story.

"Oh, Jim," she cried. "Oh, what do you think! Hallie Noyes asked me to tea tomorrow to meet Lily Wynton!"

"Who's Lily Wynton?" he said.

"Ah, Jim," she said. "Ah, really, Jim. Who's Lily Wynton! Who's Greta Garbo, I suppose!"

"She some actress or something?" he said.

Mrs. Murdock's shoulders sagged. "Yes, Jim," she said. "Yes. Lily Wynton's an actress."

She picked up her purse and started slowly toward the door. But before she had taken three steps, she was again caught up in her sparkling swirl. She turned to him, and her eyes were shining.

"Honestly," she said, "it was the funniest thing you ever heard in your life. We'd just finished the last rubber—oh, I forgot to tell you, I won three dollars, isn't that pretty good for me?—and Hallie Noyes said to me, 'Come on in to tea tomorrow. Lily Wynton's going to drop up,' she said. Just like that, she said it. Just as if it was anybody."

"Drop up?" he said. "How can you drop *up*?"

"Honestly, I don't know what I said when she asked me," Mrs. Murdock said. "I suppose I said I'd love to—I guess I must have. But I was so simply— Well, you know how I've always felt about Lily Wynton. Why, when I was a little girl, I used to collect her pictures. And I've seen her in, oh, everything she's ever been in, I should think, and I've read every word about her, and interviews and all. Really and truly, when I think of *meeting* her— Oh, I'll simply die. What on earth shall I say to her?"

"You might ask her how she'd like to try dropping down, for a change," Mr. Murdock said.

"All right, Jim," Mrs. Murdock said. "If that's the way you want to be."

Wearily she went toward the door, and this time she reached it before she turned to him. There were no lights in her eyes.

"It—it isn't so awfully nice," she said, "to spoil somebody's pleasure in something. I was so thrilled about this. You don't see what it is to me, to meet Lily Wynton. To meet somebody like that, and see what they're like, and hear what they say, and maybe get to know them. People like that mean—well, they mean something different to me. They're not like this. They're not like me. Who do I ever see? What do I ever hear? All my whole life, I've wanted to know—I've almost prayed that someday I could meet— Well. All right, Jim."

She went out, and on to her bedroom.

Mr. Murdock was left with only his newspaper and his bitterness for company. But he spoke aloud.

" 'Drop up!' " he said. " 'Drop *up*,' for God's sake!"

The Murdocks dined, not in silence, but in pronounced quiet. There was something straitened about Mr. Murdock's stillness; but little Mrs. Murdock's was the sweet, far quiet of one given over to dreams. She had forgotten her weary words to her husband, she had passed through her excitement and her disappointment. Luxuriously she floated on innocent visions of days after the morrow. She heard her own voice in future conversations. . . .

I saw Lily Wynton at Hallie's the other day, and she was telling me all about her new play—no, I'm, terribly sorry, but it's a secret, I promised her I wouldn't tell anyone the name of it . . . Lily Wynton dropped up to tea yesterday, and we just got to talking, and she told me the most interesting things about her life; she said she'd never dreamed of telling them to anyone else. . . . Why, I'd love to come, but I promised to have lunch with Lily Wynton. . . . I had a long, long letter from Lily Wynton. . . . Lily Wynton called me up this morning. . . . Whenever I feel blue, I just go and have a talk with Lily Wynton, and then I'm all right again. . . . Lily Wynton told me . . . Lily Wynton and I . . . "Lily," I said to her . . .

The next morning, Mr. Murdock had left for his office before Mrs. Murdock rose. This had happened several times before, but not often. Mrs. Murdock felt a little queer about it. Then she told herself that it was probably just as well. Then she forgot all about it, and gave her mind to the selection of a costume suitable to the afternoon's event. Deeply she felt that her small wardrobe included no dress adequate to the occasion; for , of course, such an occasion had never before arisen. She finally decided upon a frock of dark blue serge with fluted white muslin about the neck and wrists. It was her style, that was the most she could say for it. And that was all she could say for herself. Blue serge and little white ruffles—that was she.

The very becomingness of the dress lowered her spirits. A nobody's frock, worn by a nobody. She blushed and went hot when she recalled the dreams she had woven the night before, the mad visions of intimacy, of equality with Lily Wynton. Timidity turned her heart liquid, and she thought of telephoning Miss Noyes and saying she had a bad cold and could not come. She steadied, when she planned a course of conduct to pursue at teatime. She would not try to say anything; if she stayed silent, she could not sound foolish. She would listen and watch and worship and then come home, stronger, braver, better for an hour she would remember proudly all her life.

Miss Noyes's living-room was done in the early modern period. There were a great many oblique lines and acute angles, zigzags of aluminum and horizontal stretches of mirror. The color scheme was sawdust and steel. No seat was more than twelve inches above the floor, no table was made of wood. It was, as has been said of larger places, all right for a visit.

Little Mrs. Murdock was the first arrival. She was glad of that; no, maybe it would have been better to have come after Lily Wynton; no, maybe this was right. The maid motioned her toward the living-room, and Miss Noyes greeted her in the cool voice and the warm words that were her special combination. She wore black velvet trousers, a red cummerbund, and a white silk shirt, opened at the throat. A cigarette clung to her lower lip, and her eyes, as was her habit, were held narrow against its near smoke.

"Come in, come in, tiny one," she said. "Bless its little heart. Take off its little coat. Good Lord, you look easily eleven years old in that dress. Sit ye doon, here beside of me. There'll be a spot of tea in a jiff."

Mrs. Murdock sat down on the vast, perilously low divan, and, because she was never good at reclining among cushions, held her back straight. There was room for six like her, between herself and her hostess. Miss Noyes lay back with one ankle flung upon the other knee, and looked at her.

"I'm a wreck," Miss Noyes announced. "I was modeling like a mad thing, all night long. It's taken everything out of me. I was like a thing bewitched."

"Oh, what were you making?" cried Mrs. Murdock.

"Oh, Eve," Miss Noyes said. "I always do Eve. What else is there to do? You must come pose for me some time, tiny one. You'd be nice to do. Ye-es, you'd be very nice to do. My tiny one."

"Why, I—" Mrs. Murdock said, and stopped. "Thank you very much, though," she said.

"I wonder where Lily is," Miss Noyes said. "She said she'd be here early—well, she always says that. You'll adore her, tiny one. She's really rare. She's a real person. And she's been through perfect hell. God, what a time she's had!"

"Ah, what's been the matter?" said Mrs. Murdock.

"Men," Miss Noyes said. "Men. She never had a man that wasn't a louse." Gloomily she stared at the toe of her flat-heeled patent leather pump. "A pack of lice, always. All of them. Leave her for the first little floozie that comes along."

"But—" Mrs. Murdock began. No, she couldn't have heard right. How could it be right? Lily Wynton was a great actress. A great actress meant romance. Romance meant Grand Dukes and Crown Princes and diplomats touched with gray at the temples and lean, bronzed, reckless Younger Sons. It meant pearls and emeralds and chinchilla and rubies red as the blood that was shed for them. It meant a grim-faced boy sitting in the fearful Indian midnight, beneath the dreary whirring of the *punkahs*, writing a letter to the lady he had seen but once; writing his poor heart out, before he turned to the service revolver that lay beside him on the table. It meant a golden-locked poet, floating face downward in the sea, and in his pocket his last great sonnet to the lady of ivory. It meant brave, beautiful men, living and dying for the lady who was the pale bride of art, whose eyes and heart were soft with only compassion for them.

A pack of lice. Crawling after little floozies; whom Mrs. Murdock swiftly and hazily pictured as rather like ants.

"But—" said little Mrs. Murdock.

"She gave them all her money," Miss Noyes said. "She always did. Or if she didn't, they took it anyway. Took every cent she had, and then spat in her face. Well, maybe I'm teaching her a little bit of sense now. Oh, there's the bell—that'll be Lily. No, sit ye doon, tiny one. You belong there."

Miss Noyes rose and made for the archway that separated the living-room from the hall. As she passed Mrs. Murdock, she stooped suddenly, cupped her guest's round chin, and quickly, lightly kissed her mouth.

"Don't tell Lily," she murmured, very low.

Mrs. Murdock puzzled. Don't tell Lily what? Could Hallie Noyes think that she might babble to the Lily Wynton of these strange confidences about the actress's life? Or did she mean— But she had no more time for puzzling. Lily Wynton stood in the archway. There she stood, one hand resting on the wooden molding and her body swayed toward it, exactly as she stood for her third-act entrance of her latest play, and for a like half-minute.

You would have known her anywhere, Mrs. Murdock thought. Oh, yes, anywhere. Or at least you would have exclaimed, "That woman looks something like Lily Wynton." For she was somehow different in the daylight. Her figure looked heavier, thicker, and her face—there was so much of her face that the surplus sagged from the strong, fine bones. And her eyes, those famous dark, liquid eyes. They were dark, yes, and certainly liquid, but they were set in little hammocks of folded flesh, and seemed to be set but loosely, so readily did they roll. Their whites, that were visible all around the irises, were threaded with tiny scarlet veins.

"I suppose footlights are an awful strain on their eyes," thought little Mrs. Murdock.

Lily Wynton wore, just as she should have, black satin and sables, and long white gloves were wrinkled luxuriously about her wrists. But there were delicate streaks of grime in the folds of her gloves, and down the shining length of her gown there were small, irregularly shaped dull patches; bits of food or drops of drink, or perhaps both, sometime must have slipped their carriers and found brief sanctuary there. Her hat—oh, her hat. It was romance, it was mystery, it was strange, sweet sorrow; it was Lily Wynton's hat, of all the world, and no other could dare it. Black it was, and tilted, and a great, soft plume drooped from it to follow her cheek and curl across her throat. Beneath it, her hair had the various hues of neglected brass. But, oh, her hat.

"Darling!" cried Miss Noyes.

"Angel," said Lily Wynton. "My sweet."

It was that voice. It was that deep, soft, glowing voice. "Like purple velvet," someone had written. Mrs. Murdock's heart beat visibly.

Lily Wynton cast herself upon the steep bosom of her hostess, and murmured there. Across Miss Noyes's shoulder she caught sight of little Mrs. Murdock.

"And who is this?" she said. She disengaged herself.

"That's my tiny one," Miss Noyes said. "Mrs. Murdock."

"What a clever little face," said Lily Wynton. "Clever, clever little face. What does she do, sweet Hallie? I'm sure she writes, doesn't she? Yes, I can feel it. She writes beautiful, beautiful words. Don't you, child?"

"Oh, no, really I—" Mrs. Murdock said.

"And you must write me a play," said Lily Wynton. "A beautiful, beautiful play. And I will play in it, over and over the world, until I am a very, very old lady. And then I will die. But I will never be forgotten, because of the years I played in your beautiful, beautiful play."

She moved across the room. There was a slight hesitancy, a seeming insecurity, in her step, and when she would have sunk into a chair, she began to sink two inches, perhaps, to its right. But she swayed just in time in her descent, and was safe.

"To write," she said, smiling sadly at Mrs. Murdock, "to write. And such a little thing, for such a big gift. Oh, the privilege of it. But the anguish of it, too. The agony."

"But, you see, I—" said little Mrs. Murdock.

"Tiny one doesn't write, Lily," Miss Noyes said. She threw herself back upon the divan. "She's a museum piece. She's a devoted wife."

"A wife!" Lily Wynton said. "A wife. Your first marriage, child?"

"Oh, yes," said Mrs. Murdock.

"How sweet," Lily Wynton said. "How sweet, sweet, sweet. Tell me, child, do you love him very, very much?"

"Why, I—" said little Mrs. Murdock, and blushed. "I've been married for ages," she said.

"You love him," Lily Wynton said. "You love him. And is it sweet to go to bed with him?"

"Oh—" said Mrs. Murdock, and blushed till it hurt.

"The first marriage," Lily Wynton said. "Youth, youth. Yes, when I was your age I used to marry, too. Oh, treasure your love, child, guard it, live in it. Laugh and dance in the love of your man. Until you find out what he's really like."

There came a sudden visitation upon her. Her shoulders jerked upward, her cheeks puffed, her eyes sought to start from their hammocks. For a moment she sat thus, then slowly all subsided into place. She lay back in her chair, tenderly patting her chest. She shook her head sadly, and there was grieved wonder in the look with which she held Mrs. Murdock.

"Gas," said Lily Wynton, in the famous voice. "Gas. Nobody knows what I suffer from it."

"Oh, I'm so sorry," Mrs. Murdock said. "Is there anything——"

"Nothing," Lily Wynton said. "There is nothing. There is nothing that can be done for it. I've been everywhere."

"How's for a spot of tea, perhaps?" Miss Noyes said. "It might help." She turned her face toward the archway and lifted up her voice. "Mary! Where the hell's the tea?"

"You don't know," Lily Wynton said, with her grieved eyes fixed on Mrs. Murdock, "you don't know what stomach distress is. You can never, never know, unless you're a stomach sufferer yourself. I've been one for years. Years and years and years."

"I'm terribly sorry," Mrs. Murdock said.

"Nobody knows the anguish," Lily Wynton said. "The agony."

The maid appeared, bearing a triangular tray upon which was set an heroic-sized tea service of bright white china, each piece a hectagon. She set it down on a table within the long reach of Miss Noyes and retired, as she had come, bashfully.

"Sweet Hallie," Lily Wynton said, "my sweet. Tea—I adore it. I worship it. But my distress turns it to gall and wormwood in me. Gall and wormwood. For hours, I should have no peace. Let me have a little, tiny bit of your beautiful, beautiful brandy, instead."

"You really think you should, darling?" Miss Noyes said. "You know——"

"My angel," said Lily Wynton, "it's the only thing for acidity."

"Well," Miss Noyes said. "But do remember you've got a performance tonight." Again she hurled her voice at the archway. "Mary! Bring the brandy and a lot of soda and ice and things."

"Oh, no, my saint," Lily Wynton said. "No, no, sweet Hallie. Soda and ice are rank poison to me. Do you want to freeze my poor, weak stomach? Do you want to kill poor, poor Lily?"

"Mary!" roared Miss Noyes. "Just bring the brandy and a glass." She turned to little Mrs. Murdock. "How's for your tea, tiny one? Cream? Lemon?"

"Cream, if I may, please," Mrs. Murdock said. "And two lumps of sugar, please, if I may."

"Oh, youth, youth," Lily Wynton said. "Youth and love."

The maid returned with an octagonal tray supporting a decanter of brandy and a wide, squat, heavy glass. Her head twisted on her neck in a spasm of diffidence.

"Just pour it for me, will you, my dear?" said Lily Wynton. "Thank you. And leave the pretty, pretty decanter here, on this enchanting little table. Thank you. You're so good to me."

The maid vanished, fluttering. Lily Wynton lay back in her chair, holding in her gloved hand the wide, squat glass, colored brown to the brim. Little Mrs. Murdock lowered her eyes to her teacup, carefully carried it to her lips, sipped, and replaced it on its saucer. When she raised her eyes, Lily Wynton lay back in her chair, holding in her gloved hand the wide, squat, colorless glass.

"My life," Lily Wynton said, slowly, "is a mess. A stinking mess. It always has been, and it always will be. Until I am a very, very old lady. Ah, little Clever-Face, you writers don't know what struggle is."

"But really I'm not—" said Mrs. Murdock.

"To write," Lily Wynton said. "To write. To set one word beautifully beside another word. The privilege of it. The blessed, blessed peace of it. Oh, for quiet, for rest. But do you think those cheap bastards would close that play while it's doing a nickel's worth of business? Oh, no. Tired as I am, sick as I am, I must drag along. Oh, child, child, guard your precious gift. Give thanks for it. It is the greatest thing of all. It is the only thing. To write."

"Darling, I told you tiny one doesn't write," said Miss Noyes. "How's for making more sense? She's a wife."

"Ah, yes, she told me. She told me she had perfect, passionate love," Lily Wynton said. "Young love. It is the greatest thing. It is the only thing." She grasped the decanter; and again the squat glass was brown to the brim.

"What time did you start today, darling?" said Miss Noyes.

"Oh, don't scold me, sweet love," Lily Wynton said. "Lily hasn't been naughty. Her wuzzunt naughty dirl 't all. I didn't get up until late, late, late. And though I parched, though I burned, I didn't have a drink until after my breakfast. 'It is for Hallie,' I said." She raised the glass to her mouth, tilted it, and brought it away, colorless.

"Good Lord, Lily," Miss Noyes said. "Watch yourself. You've got to walk on that stage tonight, my girl."

"All the world's a stage," said Lily Wynton. "And all the men and women merely players. They have their entrance and their exitses, and each man in his time plays many parts, his act being seven ages. At first, the infant, mewling and puking——"

"How's the play doing?" Miss Noyes said.

"Oh, lousily," Lily Wynton said. "Lousily, lousily, lousily. But what isn't? What isn't, in this terrible, terrible world? Answer me that." She reached for the decanter.

"Lily, listen," said Miss Noyes. "Stop that. Do you hear?"

"Please, sweet Hallie," Lily Wynton said. "Pretty please. Poor, poor Lily."

"Do you want me to do what I had to do last time?" Miss Noyes said. "Do you want me to strike you, in front of tiny one, here?"

Lily Wynton drew herself high. "You do not realize," she said, icily, "what acidity is." She filled the glass and held it, regarding it as though through a lorgnon. Suddenly her manner changed, and she looked up and smiled at little Mrs. Murdock.

"You must let me read it," she said. "You mustn't be so modest."

"Read—?" said little Mrs. Murdock.

"Your play," Lily Wynton said. "Your beautiful, beautiful play. Don't think I am too busy. I always have time. I have time for everything. Oh, my God, I have to go to the dentist tomorrow. Oh, the suffering I have gone through with my teeth. Look!" She set down her glass, inserted a gloved forefinger in the corner of her mouth, and dragged it to the side. "Oogh!" she insisted. "Oogh!"

Mrs. Murdock craned her neck shyly, and caught a glimpse of shining gold.

"Oh, I'm so sorry," she said.

"As wah ee id a me ass ime," Lily Wynton said. She took away her forefinger and let her mouth resume its shape. "That's what he did to me last time," she repeated. "The anguish of it. The agony. Do you suffer with your teeth, little Clever-Face?"

"Why, I'm afraid I've been awfully lucky," Mrs. Murdock said. "I——"

"You don't know," Lily Wynton said. "Nobody knows what it is. You writers—you don't know." She took up her glass, sighed over it, and drained it.

"Well," Miss Noyes said. "Go ahead and pass out, then, darling. You'll have time for a sleep before the theater."

"To sleep," Lily Wynton said. "To sleep, perchance to dream. The privilege of it. Oh, Hallie, sweet, sweet Hallie, poor Lily feels so terrible. Rub my head for me, angel. Help me."

"I'll go get the Eau de Cologne," Miss Noyes said. She left the room, lightly patting Mrs. Murdock's knee as she passed her. Lily Wynton sat in her chair and closed her famous eyes.

"To sleep," she said. "To sleep, perchance to dream."

"I'm afraid," little Mrs. Murdock began. "I'm afraid," she said, "I really must be going home. I'm afraid I didn't realize how awfully late it was."

"Yes, go, child," Lily Wynton said. She did not open her eyes. "Go to him. Go to him, live in him, love him. Stay with him always. But when he starts bringing them into the house—get out."

"I'm afraid—I'm afraid I didn't quite understand," Mrs. Murdock said.

"When he starts bringing his fancy women into the house," Lily Wynton said. "You must have pride, then. You must go. I always did. But it was always too late then. They'd got all my money. That's all they want, marry them or not. They say it's love, but it isn't. Love is the only thing. Treasure your love, child. Go back to him. Go to bed with him. It's the only thing. And your beautiful, beautiful play."

"Oh, dear," said little Mrs. Murdock. "I—I'm afraid it's really terribly late."

There was only the sound of rhythmic breathing from the chair where Lily Wynton lay. The purple voice rolled along the air no longer.

Little Mrs. Murdock stole to the chair upon which she had left her coat. Carefully she smoothed her white muslin frills, so that they would be fresh beneath the jacket. She felt a tenderness for her frock; she wanted to protect it. Blue serge and little ruffles—they were her own.

When she reached the outer door of Miss Noyes's apartment, she stopped a moment and her manners conquered her. Bravely she called in the direction of Miss Noyes's bedroom.

"Good-by, Miss Noyes," she said. "I've simply got to run. I didn't realize it was so late. I had a lovely time—thank you ever so much."

"Oh, good-by, tiny one," Miss Noyes called. "Sorry Lily went by-by. Don't mind her—she's really a real person. I'll call you up, tiny one. I want to see you. Now where's that damned Cologne?"

"Thank you ever so much," Mrs. Murdock said. She let herself out of the apartment.

Little Mrs. Murdock walked homeward, through the clustering dark. Her mind was busy, but not with memories of Lily Wynton. She thought of Jim; Jim, who had left for his office before she had arisen that morning, Jim, whom she had not kissed good-by. Darling Jim. There were no others born like him. Funny Jim, stiff and cross and silent; but only because he knew so much. Only because he knew the silliness of seeking afar for the glamour and beauty and romance of living. When they were right at home all the time, she thought. Like the Blue Bird, thought little Mrs. Murdock.

Darling Jim. Mrs. Murdock turned in her course, and entered an enormous shop where the most delicate and esoteric of foods were sold for heavy sums. Jim liked red caviar. Mrs. Murdock bought a jar of the shiny, glutinous eggs. They would have cocktails that night, though they had no guests, and the red caviar would be served with them for a surprise, and it would be a little, secret party to celebrate her return to contentment with her Jim, a party to mark her happy renunciation of all the glory of the world. She bought, too, a large, foreign cheese. It would give a needed touch to dinner. Mrs. Murdock had not given much attention to ordering dinner, that morning. "Oh, anything you want, Signe," she had said to the maid. She did not want to think of that. She went on home with her packages.

Mr. Murdock was already there when she arrived. He was sitting with his newspaper opened to the financial page. Little Mrs. Murdock ran in to him with her eyes a-light. It is too bad that the light in a person's eyes is only the light in a person's eyes, and you cannot tell at a look what causes it. You do not know if it is excitement about you, or about something else. The evening before, Mrs. Murdock had run in to Mr. Murdock with her eyes a-light.

"Oh, hello," he said to her. He looked back at this paper, and kept his eyes there. "What did you do? Did you drop up to Hank Noyes's?"

Little Mrs. Murdock stopped right where she was.

"You know perfectly well, Jim," she said, "that Hallie Noyes's first name is Hallie."

"It's Hank to me," he said. "Hank or Bill. Did what's-her-name show up? I mean drop up. Pardon me."

"To whom are you referring?" said Mrs. Murdock, perfectly.

"What's-her-name," Mr. Murdock said. "The movie star."

"If you mean Lily Wynton," Mrs. Murdock said, "she is not a movie star. She is an actress. She is a great actress."

"Well, did she drop up?" he said.

Mrs. Murdock's shoulders sagged. "Yes," she said. "Yes, she was there, Jim."

"I suppose you're going on the stage now," he said.

"Ah, Jim," Mrs. Murdock said. "Ah, Jim, please. I'm not sorry at all I went to Hallie Noyes's today. It was—it was a real experience to meet Lily Wynton. Something I'll remember all my life."

"What did she do?" Mr. Murdock said. "Hang by her feet?"

"She did no such thing!" Mrs. Murdock said. "She recited Shakespeare, if you want to know."

"Oh, my God," Mr. Murdock said. "That must have been great."

"All right, Jim," Mrs. Murdock said. "If that's the way you want to be."

Wearily she left the room and went down the hall. She stopped at the pantry door, pushed it open, and spoke to the pleasant little maid.

"Oh, Signe," she said. "Oh, good evening, Signe. Put these things somewhere, will you? I got them on the way home. I thought we might have them some time."

Wearily little Mrs. Murdock went on down the hall to her bedroom.

THE LAST TEA

THE young man in the chocolate-brown suit sat down at the table, where the girl with the artificial camellia had been sitting for forty minutes.

"Guess I must be late," he said. "Sorry you been waiting."

"Oh, goodness!" she said. "I just got here myself, just about a second ago. I simply went ahead and ordered because I was dying for a cup of tea. I was late, myself. I haven't been here more than a minute."

"That's good," he said. "Hey, hey, easy on the sugar—one lump is fair enough. And take away those cakes. Terrible! Do I feel terrible!"

"Ah," she said, "you do? Ah. Whadda matter?"

"Oh, I'm ruined," he said. "I'm in terrible shape."

"Ah, the poor boy," she said. "Was it feelin' mizzable? Ah, and it came way up here to meet me! You shouldn't have done that—I'd have understood. Ah, just think of it coming all the way up here when it's so sick!"

"Oh, that's all right," he said. "I might as well be here as any place else. Any place is like any other place, the way I feel today. Oh, I'm all shot."

"Why, that's just awful," she said. "Why, you poor sick thing. Goodness, I hope it isn't influenza. They say there's a lot of it around."

"Influenza!" he said. "I wish that was all I had. Oh, I'm poisoned. I'm through. I'm off the stuff for life. Know what time I got to bed? Twenty minutes past five, A.M., this morning. What a night! What an evening!"

"I thought," she said, "that you were going to stay at the office and work late. You said you'd be working every night this week."

"Yeah, I know," he said. "But it gave me the jumps, thinking about going down there and sitting at that desk. I went up to May's—she was throwing a party. Say, there was somebody there said they knew you."

"Honestly?" she said. "Man or woman?"

"Dame," he said. "Name's Carol McCall. Say, why haven't I been told about her before? That's what I call a girl. What a looker she is!"

"Oh, really?" she said. "That's funny—I never heard of anyone that thought that. I've heard people say she was sort of nice-looking, if she wouldn't make up so much. But I never heard of anyone that thought she was pretty."

"Pretty is right," he said. "What a couple of eyes she's got on her!"

"Really?" she said. "I never noticed them particularly. But I haven't seen her for a long time—sometimes people change, or something."

"She says she used to go to school with you," he said.

"Well, we went to the same school," she said. "I simply happened to go to public school because it happened to be right near us, and Mother hated to have me crossing streets. But she was three or four classes ahead of me. She's ages older than I am."

"She's three or four classes ahead of them all," he said. "Dance! Can she step! 'Burn your clothes, baby,' I kept telling her. I must have been fried pretty."

"I was out dancing myself, last night," she said. "Wally Dillon and I. He's just been pestering me to go out with him. He's the most wonderful dancer. Goodness! I didn't get home till I don't know what time. I must look just simply a wreck. Don't I?"

"You look all right," he said.

"Wally's crazy," she said. "The things he says! For some crazy reason or other, he's got it into his head that I've got beautiful eyes, and, well, he just kept talking about them till I didn't know where to look, I was so embarrassed. I got so red, I thought everybody in the place would be looking at me. I got just as red as a brick. Beautiful eyes! Isn't he crazy?"

"He's all right," he said. "Say, this little McCall girl, she's had all kinds of offers to go into moving pictures. 'Why don't you go ahead and go?' I told her. But she says she doesn't feel like it."

"There was a man up at the lake, two summers ago," she said. "He was a director or something with one of the big moving-picture people—oh, he had all kinds of influence!—and he used to keep insisting and insisting that I ought to be in the movies. Said I ought to be doing sort of Garbo parts. I used to just laugh at him. Imagine!"

"She's had about a million offers," he said. "I told her to go ahead and go. She keeps getting these offers all the time."

"Oh, really?" she said. "Oh, listen, I knew I had something to ask you. Did you call me up last night, by any chance?"

"Me?" he said. "No, I didn't call you."

"While I was out, Mother said this man's voice kept calling up," she said. "I thought maybe it might be you, by some chance. I wonder who it could have been. Oh—I guess I know who it was. Yes, that's who it was!"

"No, I didn't call you," he said. "I couldn't have seen a telephone, last night. What a head I had on me, this morning! I called Carol up, around ten, and she said she was feeling great. Can that girl hold her liquor!"

"It's a funny thing about me," she said. "It just makes me feel sort of sick to see a girl drink. It's just something in me, I guess. I don't mind a man so much, but it makes me feel perfectly terrible to see a girl get intoxicated. It's just the way I am, I suppose."

"Does she carry it!" he said. "And then feels great the next day. There's a girl! Hey, what are you doing there? I don't want any more tea, thanks. I'm not one of these tea boys. And these tea rooms give me the jumps. Look at all those old dames, will you? Enough to give you the jumps."

"Of course, if you'd rather be some place, drinking, with I don't know what kinds of people," she said, "I'm sure I don't see how I can help that. Goodness, there are enough people that are glad enough to take me to tea. I don't know how many people keep calling me up and pestering me to take me to tea. Plenty of people!"

"All right, all right, I'm here, aren't I?" he said. "Keep your hair on."

"I could name them all day," she said.

"All right," he said. "What's there to crab about?"

"Goodness, it isn't any of my business what you do," she said. "But I hate to see you wasting your time with people that aren't nearly good enough for you. That's all."

"No need worrying over me," he said. "I'll be all right. Listen. You don't have to worry."

"It's just I don't like to see you wasting your time," she said, "staying up all night and then feeling terribly the next day. Ah, I was forgetting he was so sick. Ah, I was mean, wasn't I, scolding him when he was so mizzable. Poor boy. How's he feel now?"

"Oh, I'm all right," he said. "I feel fine. You want anything else? How about getting a check? I got to make a telephone call before six."

"Oh, really?" she said. "Calling up Carol?"

"She said she might be in around now," he said.

"Seeing her tonight?" she said.

"She's going to let me know when I call up," he said. "She's probably got about a million dates. Why?"

"I was just wondering," she said. "Goodness, I've got to fly! I'm having dinner with Wally, and he's so crazy, he's probably there now. He's called me up about a hundred times today."

"Wait till I pay the check," he said, "and I'll put you on a bus."

"Oh, don't bother," she said. "It's right at the corner. I've got to fly. I suppose you want to stay and call up your friend from here?"

"It's an idea," he said. "Sure you'll be all right?"

"Oh, sure," she said. Busily she gathered her gloves and purse, and left her chair. He rose, not quite fully, as she stopped beside him.

"When'll I see you again?" she said.

"I'll call you up," he said. "I'm all tied up, down at the office and everything. Tell you what I'll do. I'll give you a ring."

"Honestly, I have more dates!" she said. "It's terrible. I don't know when I'll have a minute. But you call up, will you?"

"I'll do that," he said. "Take care of yourself."

"You take care of yourself," she said. "Hope you'll feel all right."

"Oh, I'm fine," he said. "Just beginning to come back to life."

"Be sure and let me know how you feel," she said. "Will you? Sure, now? Well, good-by. Oh, have a good time tonight!"

"Thanks," he said. "Hope you have a good time, too."

"Oh, I will," she said. "I expect to. I've got to rush! Oh, I nearly forgot! Thanks ever so much for the tea. It was lovely."

"Be yourself, will you?" he said.

"It was," she said. "Well. Now don't forget to call me up, will you? Sure? Well, good-by."

"Solong," he said.

She walked on down the little lane between the blue-painted tables.

SENTIMENT

OH, ANYWHERE, *driver, anywhere—it doesn't matter. Just keep driving.*

It's better here in this taxi than it was walking. It's no good my trying to walk. There is always a glimpse through the crowd of someone who looks like him—someone with his swing of the shoulders, his slant of the hat. And I think it's he, I think he's come back. And my heart goes to scalding water and the buildings sway and bend above me. No, it's better to be here. But I wish the driver would go fast, so fast that people walking by would be a long gray blur, and I could see no swinging shoulders, no slanted hat. It's bad stopping still in the traffic like this. People pass too slowly, too clearly, and always the next one might be— No, of course it couldn't be. I know that. Of course I know it. But it might be, it might.

And people can look in and see me, here. They can see if I cry. Oh, let them—it doesn't matter. Let them look and be damned to them.

Yes, you look at me. Look and look and look, you poor, queer tired woman. It's a pretty hat, isn't it? It's meant to be looked at. That's why it's so big and red and new, that's why it has these great soft poppies on it. Your poor hat is all weary and done with. It looks like a dead cat, a cat that was run over and pushed out of the way against the curbstone. Don't you wish you were I and could have a new hat whenever you pleased? You could walk fast, couldn't you, and hold your head high and raise your feet from the pavement if you were on your way to a new hat, a beautiful hat, a hat that cost more than ever you had? Only I hope you wouldn't choose one like mine. For red is mourning, you know. Scarlet red for a love that's dead. Didn't you know that?

She's gone now. The taxi is moving and she's left behind forever. I wonder what she thought when our eyes and our lives met. I wonder did she envy me, so sleek and safe and young. Or did she realize how quick I'd be to fling away all I have if I could bear in my breast the still, dead heart that she carries in hers. She doesn't feel. She doesn't even wish. She is done with hoping and burning, if ever she burned and she hoped. Oh, that's quite nice, it has a real lilt. She is done with hoping and burning, if ever she— Yes, it's pretty. Well—I wonder if she's gone her slow way a little happier, or, perhaps, a little sadder for knowing that there is one worse off than herself.

This is the sort of thing he hated so in me. I know what he would say. "Oh, for heaven's sake!" he would say. "Can't you stop that fool sentimentalizing? Why do you have to do it? Why do you *want* to do it? Just because you see an old charwoman on the street, there's no need to get sobbing about her. She's all right. She's fine. 'When your eyes and your lives met'—oh, come on now. Why, she never even saw you. And her 'still, dead heart,' nothing! She's probably on her way to get a bottle of bad gin and have a roaring time. You don't have to dramatize *everything*. You don't have to insist that *everybody's* sad. Why are you always so sentimental? Don't *do* it, Rosalie." That's what he would say. I know.

But he won't say that or anything else to me, any more. Never anything else, sweet or bitter. He's gone away and he isn't coming back. "Oh, of course I'm coming back!" he said. "No, I don't know just when—I told you that. Ah, Rosalie, don't go making a national tragedy of it. It'll be a few months, maybe—and if ever two people needed a holiday from each other! It's nothing to cry about. I'll be back. I'm not going to stay away from New York forever."

But I knew. I knew. I knew because he had been far away from me long before he went. He's gone away and he won't come back. He's gone away and he won't come back, he's gone away and he'll never come back. Listen to the wheels saying it, on and on and on. That's sentimental, I suppose. Wheels don't say anything. Wheels can't speak. But I *hear* them.

I wonder why it's wrong to be sentimental. People are so contemptuous of feeling. "You wouldn't catch *me* sitting alone and mooning," they say. "Moon" is what they say when they mean remember, and they are so proud of not remembering. It's strange, how they pride themselves upon their lacks. "I never take anything seriously," they say. "I simply couldn't imagine," they say, "letting myself care so much that I could be hurt." They say, "No one person could be that important to *me*." And why, why do they think they're right?

Oh, who's right and who's wrong and who decides? Perhaps it was I who was right about that charwoman. Perhaps she *was* weary and still-hearted, and perhaps, for just that moment, she knew all about me. She needn't have been all right and fine and on her way for gin, just because he said so. Oh. Oh, I forgot. He didn't say so. He wasn't here; he isn't here. It was I, imagining what he would say. And I thought I heard him. He's always with me, he and all his beauty and his cruelty. But he mustn't be any more. I mustn't think of him. That's it, don't think of him. Yes. Don't breathe, either. Don't hear. Don't see. Stop the blood in your veins.

I can't go on like this. I can't, I can't. I cannot stand this frantic misery. If I knew it would be over in a day or a year or two months, I could endure it. Even if it grew duller sometimes and wilder sometimes, it could be borne. But it is always the same and there is no end.

"Sorrow like a ceaseless rain
Beats upon my heart.
People twist and scream in pain—
Dawn will find them still again;
This has neither wax nor wane,
Neither stop nor start."

Oh, let's see—how does the next verse go? Something, something, something, something, something to rhyme with "wear." Anyway, it ends:

"All my thoughts are slow and brown:
Standing up or sitting down
Little matters, or what gown
Or what shoes I wear."

Yes, that's the way it goes. And it's right, it's so right. What is it to me what I wear? Go and buy yourself a big red hat with poppies on it—that ought to cheer you up. Yes—go buy it and loathe it. How am I to go on, sitting and staring and buying big red hats and hating them, and then sitting and staring again—day upon day upon day upon day? Tomorrow and tomorrow and tomorrow. How am I to drag through them like this?

But what else is there for me? "Go out and see your friends and have a good time," they say. "Don't sit alone and dramatize yourself." Dramatize yourself! If it be drama to feel a steady—no, a *ceaseless* rain beating upon my heart, then I do dramatize myself. The shallow people, the little people, how can they know what suffering is, how could their thick hearts be torn? Don't they know, the empty fools, that I could not see again the friends we saw together, could not go back to the places where he and I have been? For he's gone, and it's ended. It's ended, it's ended. And when it ends, only those places where you have known sorrow are kindly to you. If you revisit the scenes of your happiness, your heart must burst of its agony.

And that's sentimental, I suppose. It's sentimental to know that you cannot bear to see the places where once all was well with you, that you cannot bear reminders of a dead loveliness. Sorrow is tranquillity remembered in emotion. It—oh, I think that's quite good. "Remembered in emotion"—that's a really nice reversal. I wish I could say it to him. But I won't say anything to him, ever again, ever, ever again. He's gone, and it's over, and I dare not think of the dead days. All my thoughts must be slow and brown, and I must——

Oh, no, no, no! Oh, the driver shouldn't go through this street! This was our street, this is the place of our love and our laughter. I can't do this, I can't, I can't. I will crouch down here, and hold my hands tight, tight over my eyes, so that I cannot look. I must keep my poor heart still, and I must be like the little, mean, dry-souled people who are proud not to remember.

But, oh, I see it, I see it, even though my eyes are blinded. Though I had no eyes, my heart would tell me this street, out of all streets. I know it as I know my hands, as I know his face. Oh, why can't I be let to die as we pass through?

We must be at the florist's shop on the corner now. That's where he used to stop to buy me primroses, little yellow primroses massed tight together with a circle of their silver-backed leaves about them, clean and cool and gentle. He always said that orchids and camellias were none of my affair. So when there were no spring and no primroses, he would give me lilies-of-the-valley and little, gay rosebuds and mignonette and bright blue cornflowers. He said he couldn't stand the thought of me without flowers—it would be all wrong; I cannot bear flowers near me, now. And the little gray florist was so interested and so glad—and there was the day he called me "madam"! Ah, I can't, I can't.

And now we must be at the big apartment house with the big gold doorman. And the evening the doorman was holding the darling puppy on a big, long leash, and we stopped to talk to it, and he took it up in his arms and cuddled it, and that was the only time we ever saw the doorman smile! And next is the house with the baby, and he always would take off his hat and bow very solemnly to her, and sometimes she would give him her little starfish of a hand. And then is the tree with the rusty iron bars around it, where he would stop to turn and wave to me, as I leaned out the window to watch him. And people would look at him, because people always had to look at him, but he never noticed. It was our tree, he said; it wouldn't dream of belonging to anybody else. And very few city people had their own personal tree, he said. Did I realize that, he said.

And then there's the doctor's house, and the three thin gray houses and then—oh, God, we must be at our house now! Our house, though we had only the top floor. And I loved the long, dark stairs, because he climbed them every evening. And our little prim pink curtains at the windows, and the boxes of pink geraniums that always grew for me. And the little stiff entry and the funny mail-box, and his ring at the bell. And I waiting for him in the dusk, thinking he would never come; and yet the waiting was lovely, too. And then when I opened the door to him— Oh, no, no, no! Oh, no one could bear this. No one, no one.

Ah, why, why, why must I be driven through here? What torture could there be so terrible as this? It will be better if I uncover my eyes and look. I will see our tree and our house again, and then my heart will burst and I will be dead. I will look, I will look.

But where's the tree? Can they have cut down our tree—*our* tree? And where's the apartment house? And where's the florist's shop? And where—oh, where's our house, where's——

Driver, what street is this? Sixty-Fifth? Oh. No, nothing, thank you. I—I thought it was Sixty-Third . . .

YOU WERE PERFECTLY FINE

The pale young man eased himself carefully into the low chair, and rolled his head to the side, so that the cool chintz comforted his cheek and temple.

"Oh, dear," he said. "Oh, dear, oh, dear, oh, dear. Oh."

The clear-eyed girl, sitting light and erect on the couch, smiled brightly at him.

"Not feeling so well today?" she said.

"Oh, I'm great," he said. "Corking, I am. Know what time I got up? Four o'clock this afternoon, sharp. I kept trying to make it, and every time I took my head off the pillow, it would roll under the bed. This isn't my head I've got on now. I think this is something that used to belong to Walt Whitman. Oh, dear, oh, dear, oh, dear."

"Do you think maybe a drink would make you feel better?" she said.

"The hair of the mastiff that bit me?" he said. "Oh, no, thank you. Please never speak of anything like that again. I'm through. I'm all, all through. Look at that hand; steady as a humming-bird. Tell me, was I very terrible last night?"

"Oh, goodness," she said, "everybody was feeling pretty high. You were all right."

"Yeah," he said. "I must have been dandy. Is everybody sore at me?"

"Good heavens, no," she said. "Everyone thought you were terribly funny. Of course, Jim Pierson was a little stuffy, there for a minute at dinner. But people sort of held him back in his chair, and got him calmed down. I don't think anybody at the other tables noticed it at all. Hardly anybody."

"He was going to sock me?" he said. "Oh, Lord. What did I do to him?"

"Why, you didn't do a thing," she said. "You were perfectly fine. But you know how silly Jim gets, when he thinks anybody is making too much fuss over Elinor."

"Was I making a pass at Elinor?" he said. "Did I do that?"

"Of course you didn't," she said. "You were only fooling, that's all. She thought you were awfully amusing. She was having a marvelous time. She only got a little tiny bit annoyed just once, when you poured the clam-juice down her back."

"My God," he said. "Clam-juice down that back. And every vertebra a little Cabot. Dear God. What'll I ever do?"

"Oh, she'll be all right," she said. "Just send her some flowers, or something. Don't worry about it. It isn't anything."

"No, I won't worry," he said. "I haven't got a care in the world. I'm sitting pretty. Oh, dear, oh, dear. Did I do any other fascinating tricks at dinner?"

"You were fine," she said. "Don't be so foolish about it. Everybody was crazy about you. The maître d'hôtel was a little worried because you wouldn't stop singing, but he really didn't mind. All he said was, he was afraid they'd close the place again, if there was so much noise. But he didn't care a bit, himself. I think he loved seeing you have such a good time. Oh, you were just singing away, there, for about an hour. It wasn't so terribly loud, at all."

"So I sang," he said. "That must have been a treat. I sang."

"Don't you remember?" she said. "You just sang one song after another. Everybody in the place was listening. They loved it. Only you kept insisting that you wanted to sing some song about some kind of fusiliers or other, and everybody kept shushing you, and you'd keep trying to start it again. You were wonderful. We were all trying to make you stop singing for a minute, and eat something, but you wouldn't hear of it. My, you were funny."

"Didn't I eat any dinner?" he said.

"Oh, not a thing," she said. "Every time the waiter would offer you something, you'd give it right back to him, because you said that he was your long-lost brother, changed in the cradle by a gypsy band, and that anything you had was his. You had him simply roaring at you."

"I bet I did," he said. "I bet I was comical. Society's Pet, I must have been. And what happened then, after my overwhelming success with the waiter?"

"Why, nothing much," she said. "You took a sort of dislike to some old man with white hair, sitting across the room, because you didn't like his necktie and you wanted to tell him about it. But we got you out, before he got really mad."

"Oh, we got out," he said. "Did I walk?"

"Walk! Of course you did," she said. "You were absolutely all right. There was that nasty stretch of ice on the sidewalk, and you did sit down awfully hard, you poor dear. But good heavens, that might have happened to anybody."

"Oh, sure," he said. "Louisa Alcott or anybody. So I fell down on the sidewalk. That would explain what's the matter with my– Yes. I see. And then what, if you don't mind?"

"Ah, now, Peter!" she said. "You can't sit there and say you don't remember what happened after that! I did think that maybe you were just a little tight at dinner–oh, you were perfectly all right, and all that, but I did know you were feeling pretty gay. But you were so serious, from the time you fell down–I never knew you to be that way. Don't you know, how you told me I had never seen your real self before? Oh, Peter, I just couldn't bear it, if you didn't remember that lovely long ride we took together in the taxi! Please, you do remember that, don't you? I think it would simply kill me, if you didn't."

"Oh, yes," he said. "Riding in the taxi. Oh, yes, sure. Pretty long ride, hmm?"

"Round and round and round the park," she said. "Oh, and the trees were shining so in the moonlight. And you said you never knew before that you really had a soul."

"Yes," he said. "I said that. That was me."

"You said such lovely, lovely things," she said. "And I'd never known, all this time, how you had been feeling about me, and I'd never dared to let you see how I felt about you. And then last night—oh, Peter dear, I think that taxi ride was the most important thing that ever happened to us in our lives."

"Yes," he said. "I guess it must have been."

"And we're going to be so happy," she said. "Oh, I just want to tell everybody! But I don't know—I think maybe it would be sweeter to keep it all to ourselves."

"I think it would be," he said.

"Isn't it lovely?" she said.

"Yes," he said. "Great."

"Lovely!" she said.

"Look here," he said, "do you mind if I have a drink? I mean, just medicinally, you know. I'm off the stuff for life, so help me. But I think I feel a collapse coming on."

"Oh, I think it would do you good," she said. "You poor boy, it's a shame you feel so awful. I'll go make you a whisky and soda."

"Honestly," he said, "I don't see how you could ever want to speak to me again, after I made such a fool of myself, last night. I think I'd better go join a monastery in Tibet."

"You crazy idiot!" she said. "As if I could ever let you go away now! Stop talking like that. You were perfectly fine."

She jumped up from the couch, kissed him quickly on the forehead, and ran out of the room.

The pale young man looked after her and shook his head long and slowly, then dropped it in his damp and trembling hands.

"Oh, dear," he said. "Oh, dear, oh, dear, oh, dear."

THE CUSTARD HEART

No living eye, of human being or caged wild beast or dear, domestic animal, had beheld Mrs. Lanier when she was not being wistful. She was dedicated to wistfulness, as lesser artists to words and paint and marble. Mrs. Lanier was not of the lesser; she was of the true. Surely the eternal example of the true artist is Dickens's actor who blacked himself all over to play Othello. It is safe to assume that Mrs. Lanier was wistful in her bathroom, and slumbered soft in wistfulness through the dark and secret night.

If nothing should happen to the portrait of her by Sir James Weir, there she will stand, wistful for the ages. He has shown her at her full length, all in yellows, the delicately heaped curls, the slender, arched feet like elegant bananas, the shining stretch of the evening gown; Mrs. Lanier habitually wore white in the evening but white is the devil's own hue to paint, and could a man be expected to spend his entire six weeks in the States on the execution of a single commission? Wistfulness rests, immortal, in the eyes dark with sad hope, in the pleading mouth, the droop of the little head on the sweet long neck, bowed as if in submission to the three ropes of Lanier pearls. It is true that, when the portrait was exhibited, one critic expressed in print his puzzlement as to what a woman who owned such pearls had to be wistful about; but that was doubtless because he had sold his saffron-colored soul for a few pennies to the proprietor of a rival gallery. Certainly, no man could touch Sir James on pearls. Each one is as distinct, as individual as is each little soldier's face in a Meissonier battle scene.

For a time, with the sitter's obligation to resemble the portrait, Mrs. Lanier wore yellow of evenings. She had gowns of velvet like poured country cream and satin with the lacquer of buttercups and chiffon that spiraled about her like golden smoke. She wore them, and listened in shy surprise to the resulting comparisons to daffodils, and butterflies in the sunshine, and such; but she knew.

"It just isn't me," she sighed at last, and returned to her lily draperies. Picasso had his blue period, and Mrs. Lanier her yellow one. They both knew when to stop.

In the afternoons, Mrs. Lanier wore black, thin and fragrant, with the great pearls weeping on her breast. What her attire was by morning, only Gwennie, the maid who brought her breakfast tray, could know; but it must, of course, have been exquisite. Mr. Lanier—certainly there was a Mr. Lanier; he had even been seen—stole past her door on his way out to his office, and the servants glided and murmured, so that Mrs. Lanier might be spared as long as possible from the bright new cruelty of the day. Only when the littler, kinder hours had succeeded noon could she bring herself to come forth and face the recurrent sorrows of living.

There was duty to be done, almost daily, and Mrs. Lanier made herself brave for it. She must go in her town car to select new clothes and to have fitted to her perfection those she had ordered before. Such garments as hers did not just occur; like great poetry, they required labor. But she shrank from leaving the shelter of her house, for everywhere without were the unlovely and the sad, to assail her eyes and her heart. Often she stood shrinking for several minutes by the baroque mirror in her hall before she could manage to hold her head high and brave, and go on.

There is no safety for the tender, no matter how straight their route, how innocent their destination. Sometimes, even in front of Mrs. Lanier's dressmaker's or her furrier's or her lingère's or her milliner's, there would be a file of thin girls and small, shabby men, who held placards in their cold hands and paced up and down and up and down with slow, measured steps. Their faces would be blue and rough from the wind, and blank with the monotony of their treadmill. They looked so little and poor and strained that Mrs. Lanier's hands would fly to her heart in pity. Her eyes would be luminous with sympathy and her sweet lips would part as if on a whisper of cheer, as she passed through the draggled line into the shop.

Often there would be pencil-sellers in her path, a half of a creature set upon a sort of roller-skate thrusting himself along the pavement by his hands, or a blind man shuffling after his wavering cane. Mrs. Lanier must stop and sway, her eyes closed, one hand about her throat to support her lovely, stricken head. Then you could actually see her force herself, could see the effort ripple her body, as she opened her eyes and gave these miserable ones, the blind and the seeing alike, a smile of such tenderness, such sorrowful understanding, that it was like the exquisite sad odor of hyacinths on the air. Sometimes, if the man was not too horrible, she could even reach in her purse for a coin and, holding it as lightly as if she had plucked it from a silvery stem, extend her slim arm and drop it in his cup. If he was young and new at his life, he would offer her pencils for the worth of her money; but Mrs. Lanier wanted no returns. In gentlest delicacy she would slip away, leaving him with mean wares intact, not a worker for his livelihood like a million others, but signal and set apart, rare in the fragrance of charity.

So it was, when Mrs. Lanier went out. Everywhere she saw them, the ragged, the wretched, the desperate, and to each she gave her look that spoke with no words.

"Courage," it said. "And you—oh, wish me courage, too!"

Frequently, by the time she returned to her house, Mrs. Lanier would be limp as a freesia. Her maid Gwennie would have to beseech her to lie down, to gain the strength to change her gown for a filmier one and descend to her drawing-room, her eyes darkly mournful, but her exquisite breasts pointed high.

In her drawing-room, there was sanctuary. Here her heart might heal from the blows of the world, and be whole for its own sorrow. It was a room suspended above life, a place of tender fabrics and pale flowers, with never a paper or a book to report the harrowing or describe it. Below the great sheet of its window swung the river, and the stately scows went by laden with strange stuff in rich tapestry colors; there was no necessity to belong to the sort who must explain that it was garbage. An island with a happy name lay opposite, and on it stood a row of prim, tight buildings, naïve as a painting by Rousseau. Sometimes there could be seen on the island the brisk figures of nurses and internes, sporting in the lanes. Possibly there were figures considerably less brisk beyond the barred windows of the buildings, but that was not to be wondered about in the presence of Mrs. Lanier. All those who came to her drawing-room came in one cause: to shield her heart from hurt.

Here in her drawing-room, in the lovely blue of the late day, Mrs. Lanier sat upon opalescent taffeta and was wistful. And here to her drawing-room, the young men came and tried to help her bear her life.

There was a pattern to the visits of the young men. They would come in groups of three or four or six, for a while; and then there would be one of them who would stay a little after the rest had gone, who presently would come a little earlier than the others. Then there would be days when Mrs. Lanier would cease to be at home to the other young men, and that one young man would be alone with her in the lovely blue. And then Mrs. Lanier would no longer be at home to that one young man, and Gwennie would have to tell him and tell him, over the telephone, that Mrs. Lanier was out, that Mrs. Lanier was ill, that Mrs. Lanier could not be disturbed. The groups of young men would come again; that one young man would not be with them. But there would be, among them, a new young man, who presently would stay a little later and come a little earlier, who eventually would plead with Gwennie over the telephone.

Gwennie—her widowed mother had named her Gwendola, and then, as if realizing that no other dream would ever come true, had died—was little and compact and unnoticeable. She had been raised on an upstate farm by an uncle and aunt hard as the soil they fought for their lives. After their deaths, she had no relatives anywhere. She came to New York, because she had heard stories of jobs; her arrival was at the time when Mrs. Lanier's cook needed a kitchen-maid. So in her own house, Mrs. Lanier had found her treasure.

Gwennie's hard little farm-girl's fingers could set invisible stitches, could employ a flatiron as if it were a wand, could be as summer breezes in the robing of Mrs. Lanier and the tending of her hair. She was as busy as the day was long; and her days frequently extended from daybreak to daybreak. She was never tired, she had no grievance, she was cheerful without being expressive about it. There was nothing in her presence or the sight of her to touch the heart and thus cause discomfort.

Mrs. Lanier would often say that she didn't know what she would do without her little Gwennie; if her little Gwennie should ever leave her, she said, she just couldn't go on. She looked so lorn and fragile as she said it that one scowled upon Gwennie for the potentialities of death or marriage that the girl carried within her. Yet there was no pressing cause for worry, for Gwennie was strong as a pony and had no beau. She had made no friends at all, and seemed not to observe the omission. Her life was for Mrs. Lanier; like all others who were permitted close, Gwennie sought to do what she could to save Mrs. Lanier from pain.

They could all assist in shutting out reminders of the sadness abroad in the world, but Mrs. Lanier's private sorrow was a more difficult matter. There dwelt a yearning so deep, so secret in her heart that it would often be days before she could speak of it, in the twilight, to a new young man.

"If I only had a little baby," she would sigh, "a little, little baby, I think I could be almost happy." And she would fold her delicate arms, and lightly, slowly rock them, as if they cradled that little, little one of her dear dreams. Then, the denied madonna, she was at her most wistful, and the young man would have lived or died for her, as she bade him.

Mrs. Lanier never mentioned why her wish was unfulfilled; the young man would know her to be too sweet to place blame, too proud to tell. But, so close to her in the pale light, he would understand, and his blood would swirl with fury that such clods as Mr. Lanier remained unkilled. He would beseech Mrs. Lanier, first in halting murmurs, then in rushes of hot words, to let him take her away from the hell of her life and try to make her almost happy. It would be after this that Mrs. Lanier would be out to the young man, would be ill, would be incapable of being disturbed.

Gwennie did not enter the drawing-room when there was only one young man there; but when the groups returned she served unobtrusively, drawing a curtain or fetching a fresh glass. All the Lanier servants were unobtrusive, light of step and correctly indistinct of feature. When there must be changes made in the staff, Gwennie and the housekeeper arranged the replacements and did not speak of the matter to Mrs. Lanier, lest she should be stricken by desertions or saddened by tales of woe. Always the new servants resembled the old, alike in that they were unnoticeable. That is, until Kane, the new chauffeur, came.

The old chauffeur had been replaced because he had been the old chauffeur too long. It weighs cruelly heavy on the tender heart when a familiar face grows lined and dry, when familiar shoulders seem daily to droop lower, a familiar nape is hollow between cords. The old chauffeur saw and heard and functioned with no difference; but it was too much for Mrs. Lanier to see what was befalling him. With pain in her voice, she had told Gwennie that she could stand the sight of him no longer. So the old chauffeur had gone, and Kane had come.

Kane was young, and there was nothing depressing about his straight shoulders and his firm, full neck to one sitting behind them in the town car. He stood, a fine triangle in his fitted uniform, holding the door of the car open for Mrs. Lanier and bowed his head as she passed. But when he was not at work, his head was held high and slightly cocked, and there was a little cocked smile on his red mouth.

Often, in the cold weather when Kane waited for her in the car, Mrs. Lanier would humanely bid Gwennie to tell him to come in and wait in the servants' sitting-room. Gwennie brought him coffee and looked at him. Twice she did not hear Mrs. Lanier's enameled electric bell.

Gwennie began to observe her evenings off; before, she had disregarded them and stayed to minister to Mrs. Lanier. There was one night when Mrs. Lanier had floated late to her room, after a theater and a long conversation, done in murmurs, in the drawing-room. And Gwennie had not been waiting, to take off the white gown, and put away the pearls, and brush the bright hair that curled like the petals of forsythia. Gwennie had not yet returned to the house from her holiday. Mrs. Lanier had had to arouse a parlor-maid and obtain unsatisfactory aid from her.

Gwennie had wept, next morning, at the pathos of Mrs. Lanier's eyes; but tears were too distressing for Mrs. Lanier to see, and the girl stopped them. Mrs. Lanier delicately patted her arm, and there had been nothing more of the matter, save that Mrs. Lanier's eyes were darker and wider for this new hurt.

Kane became a positive comfort to Mrs. Lanier. After the sorry sights of the streets, it was good to see Kane standing by the car, solid and straight and young, with nothing in the world the trouble with him. Mrs. Lanier came to smile upon him almost gratefully, yet wistfully, too, as if she would seek of him the secret of not being sad.

And then, one day, Kane did not appear at his appointed time. The car, which should have been waiting to convey Mrs. Lanier to her dressmaker's, was still in the garage, and Kane had not appeared there all day. Mrs. Lanier told Gwennie immediately to telephone the place where he roomed and find out what this meant. The girl had cried out at her, cried out that she had called and called and called, and he was not there and no one there knew where he was. The crying out must have been due to Gwennie's loss of head in her distress at this disruption of Mrs. Lanier's day; or perhaps it was the effect on her voice of an appalling cold she seemed to have contracted, for her eyes were heavy and red and her face pale and swollen.

There was no more of Kane. He had had his wages paid him on the day before he disappeared, and that was the last of him. There was never a word and not another sight of him. At first, Mrs. Lanier could scarcely bring herself to believe that such betrayal could exist. Her heart, soft and sweet as a perfectly made crème renversée, quivered in her breast, and in her eyes lay the far light of suffering.

"Oh, how could he do this to me?" she asked piteously of Gwennie. "How could he do this to poor me?"

There was no discussion of the defection of Kane; it was too painful a subject. If a caller heedlessly asked whatever had become of that nice-looking chauffeur, Mrs. Lanier would lay her hand over her closed lids and slowly wince. The caller would be suicidal that he had thus unconsciously added to her sorrows, and would strive his consecrated best to comfort her.

Gwennie's cold lasted for an extraordinarily long time. The weeks went by, and still, every morning, her eyes were red and her face white and puffed. Mrs. Lanier often had to look away from her when she brought the breakfast tray.

She tended Mrs. Lanier as carefully as ever; she gave no attention to her holidays, but stayed to do further service. She had always been quiet, and she became all but silent, and that was additionally soothing. She worked without stopping and seemed to thrive, for, save for the effects of the curious cold, she looked round and healthy.

"See," Mrs. Lanier said in tender raillery, as the girl attended the group in the drawing-room, "see how fat my little Gwennie's getting! Isn't that cute?"

The weeks went on, and the pattern of the young men shifted again. There came the day when Mrs. Lanier was not at home to a group; when a new young man was to come and be alone with her, for his first time, in the drawing-room. Mrs. Lanier sat before her mirror and lightly touched her throat with perfume, while Gwennie heaped the golden curls.

The exquisite face Mrs. Lanier saw in the mirror drew her closer attention, and she put down the perfume and leaned toward it. She drooped her head a little to the side and watched it closely; she saw the wistful eyes grow yet more wistful, the lips curve to a pleading smile. She folded her arms close to her sweet breast and slowly rocked them, as if they cradled a dream-child. She watched the mirrored arms sway gently, caused them to sway a little slower.

"If I only had a little baby," she sighed. She shook her head. Delicately she cleared her throat, and sighed again on a slightly lower note. "If I only had a little, little baby, I think I could be almost happy."

There was a clatter from behind her, and she turned, amazed. Gwennie had dropped the hair-brush to the floor and stood swaying, with her face in her hands.

"Gwennie!" said Mrs. Lanier. "Gwennie!"

The girl took her hands from her face, and it was as if she stood under a green light.

"I'm sorry," she panted. "Sorry. Please excuse me. I'm—oh, I'm going to be sick!"

She ran from the room so violently that the floor shook.

Mrs. Lanier sat looking after Gwennie, her hands at her wounded heart. Slowly she turned back to her mirror, and what she saw there arrested her; the artist knows the masterpiece. Here was the perfection of her career, the sublimation of wistfulness; it was that look of grieved bewilderment that did it. Carefully she kept it upon her face as she rose from the mirror and, with her lovely hands still shielding her heart, went down to the new young man.

A Note on the Type

The principal text of this Modern Library edition
was composed in a digitized version of
Horley Old Style, a typeface issued by
the English type foundry Monotype in 1925.
It has such distinctive features
as lightly cupped serifs and an oblique horizontal bar
on the lowercase "e."